HEALING ADULT CHILDREN OF DIVORCE

Healing Adult Children of Divorce

*Taking Care of Unfinished Business
So You Can Be Whole Again*

Dr. Archibald D. Hart

VINE
BOOKS

Servant Publications
Ann Arbor, Michigan

Vine Books is an imprint of Servant Publications especially
designed to serve Evangelical Christians.

Published by Servant Publications
P.O. Box 8617
Ann Arbor, Michigan 48107

Cover design by Michael Andaloro

91 92 93 94 95 96 10 9 8 7 6 5 4 3 2 1

Printed in the United States of America
ISBN 0-89283-727-6

Library of Congress Cataloging-in-Publication Data
Hart, Archibald D.
    Healing adult children of divorce : taking care of unfinished
business so you can be whole again / Archibald D. Hart.
        p.   c.m.
    Includes bibliographical references.
    ISBN 0-89283-727-6
    1. Adult children of divorced parents—Rehabilitation.
I. Title.
    RC569.5.A3H37 1991
    158.9'24—dc20   91-20957

To my wife, Kathleen,
without whose love and endless patience
I would not have been able to recover
from my own childhood experience
of divorce.

Contents

Introduction: The ACOD Syndrome / 17

> *Adult children of divorce should be afforded the same recognition for their pain and need for growth that adult children of alcoholics have gradually won.*

PART ONE
Understanding Your Need for Recovery / 23

1. Growing Up in a Divorced Family / 25

   > *Adult consequences of childhood divorce can affect your emotions, important relationships, health, and career choices.*

2. Assessing the Divorce Damage in Your Life / 41

   > *The evidence is clear: Divorce leaves scars, and facing those scars must be the starting point of healing.*

3. The "Blended Family" Blues / 59

   > *Remarriage after divorce tends to add stress and confusion to an already tense and confused situation. Many children carry into adulthood the scars of being "blended" against their wills.*

PART TWO
Beginning Your Recovery / 75

4. Facing Your Unfinished Business / 77

   > *The unfinished business of your parents' divorce is no doubt lurking in the shadows of your life, waiting for your attention. Only when you attend to this business will you be complete and healthy again.*

Personal Inventories

Preface

THIS BOOK WAS PAINFUL FOR ME TO WRITE because so much of it is about myself. As an adult child of divorce, I personally experienced most of what I describe. It is now forty-six years since my parents divorced. The process of adjustment to the consequence of divorce has lasted for all those forty-six years and is likely to continue for the rest of my life.

Am I unusual in this respect? I don't think so. Although I periodically encounter adults who honestly believe their parents' divorce did not damage them in any way (and I am thankful this is true) I believe their experience is the exception and not the rule. The great majority of children whose parents divorce carry the scars of the divorce with them every day—and into adulthood. They feel the impact of early parental conflict deep within their psyches. Many hurt in so many places of the heart that they have become numb to it.

Not a few are also into denial. "Oh, I doubt if my parents' divorce affected me. I was a tough kid—I knew how to stand up for myself. I just laughed it off; it didn't bother me at all."

But their unhappiness tells a different story. What does it mean to be an adult child of divorce? It means that your life has been struck by a major traumatic event (or, rather, a series of events) that has shaken your security, disrupted your social and psychological development, and left you with challenges and demands for adjustment that other children have not had to face. It probably also means that your faith and belief in God was constantly challenged. If you are an adult child of divorce, you are clearly part of an "at risk" population.

As I will show in this book, the impact of divorce on children is no less serious than that of alcoholism—and much has been written about what it means to be an adult child of an alcoholic. Divorce is

11

often preceded by many years of intense hostility that creates conflict in the hearts and minds of children, just as alcohol or drug abuse does. And this conflict often continues just as intensely after a divorce, with battles over custody rights and financial support. Every study I have reviewed about the damaging effects of divorce has shown that the years *following* divorce can be just as destructive as those that preceded it. And with millions of people having to grow up in divorced families, this represents a lot of pain and emotional suffering over a long period of time.

All children whose parents divorce eventually grow up and take their place in society as adults. They face the tasks everyone faces: establishing and maintaining relationships, making a living, learning to be responsible, becoming healthy human beings, growing spiritually. But they've had a bad start—most of them. Depending on when the divorce occurred and the seriousness of the marital conflict, they will have been affected in some way or other—just as I have.

This book is about and for these *adult children of divorce*. I will refer to you simply as ACODs.

In the book, I will try to answer many important questions:

- *How* does being an adult child of divorce affect you as an adult?
- *What* tasks now remain for you to accomplish?
- *What* hidden forces now work in you, and *how* can you get them in the open?
- *How* can you understand yourself better?
- *How* does being an ACOD affect your present relationships, your marriage, and your own children?

And, most important:

- *How* can you take care of the "unfinished business" stemming from your parents' divorce and move on from there to live a full and meaningful life?

You need to know ahead of time that this book pays attention to spiritual needs and spiritual solutions as well as psychological ones. The longer I work as a therapist and a student of human need, the more convinced I become that real healing must involve us at the deepest level of our lives—the spiritual dimension. I want to speak with spiritual wisdom, not just psychological insight. I long for your total healing, not just relief of some superficial pain. I want to point you to a new, more satisfying life as an adult child of divorce.

As you face the detrimental effects of divorce on your childhood and become aware of its residual impact, I hope you will be spurred to give priority to personal and spiritual growth. And let me assure you that growth is possible! Most of us are resilient enough that just a little well-directed help can set us on the "right track" to health and wholeness again.

As you journey through this book, please remember that it has been *my* journey also. I write as much from personal experience as from the reports of others. However, much of what I went through in the past and feel today has been repeatedly validated by my work with many ACOD clients and by my reading and research. I have been especially concerned to consult many resources to ensure that I am not overstating my case or exaggerating my concern about the lifelong damage caused by childhood divorce.

Ours is a society of divorce, and the already high divorce rate threatens to skyrocket further in years to come. As a nation, we throw away marriages like paper towels. But divorce is not just a statistic. It translates to emotional trauma and distress for those least able to fend for themselves—the children. We need all the help we can get to stop the divorce cycle and undo its devastating consequences.

I trust this book will make a contribution to the healing of adult children of divorce. And, speaking more personally, I hope it helps you in your struggle to move beyond your childhood pain and to grow toward health in your own life and relationships.

Acknowledgments

I WOULD LIKE TO EXPRESS the deepest appreciation to the many who have helped me bring this book to print:

- To Ann Spangler and Beth Feia at Servant Publications for their confidence, creative brainstorming, and encouragement to undertake this project.
- To Anne Christian Buchanan for her great skill as an editor and her helpful suggestions and comments.
- To my secretary, Nova Hutchins, for so patiently deciphering my handwriting and transforming it into word-processed splendor.
- To my office administrator, Bertha Jacklitch, and other members of my academic staff—Kathy Smith, Maryan Hinkel, Freda Carver, and Lynelle Bush—for being so helpful and relieving me of many chores so that I can find the time to write.
- To those friends and clients who have, over many years, trusted me with their intimate secrets and helped me to unravel the complex syndrome which is the topic of this book.

To all of you I say a deeply felt "Thanks."

The ACOD Syndrome

Do CHILDREN OF DIVORCING families carry a significant risk of developmental damage that lingers into adulthood? If so, is there any substantial evidence to support this? If childhood divorce does influence the adult life of a victim, what aspects of adult life are most affected? More to the point, is your own experience of childhood divorce keeping you from a full and happy life?

These questions will be addressed more fully in the chapters that follow. But they are so important that I want to make a case for the "ACOD (Adult Children of Divorce) syndrome" right at the outset.

According to the National Center for Health Statistics, one million children under eighteen years of age are affected by divorce in the United States every year.[1] I doubt that anyone would deny that divorce affects these children negatively. The literature of the field is crowded with reports, studies, anecdotes, and opinions to show that children are vulnerable and at great risk when a household breaks up. Many factors influence how children are damaged, as we will see. But empirically and clinically, divorce can be shown to be a disruptive experience that has significant impact on children.[2]

Judith Wallerstein's impressive studies, for instance, show clearly that there are many losers and few winners in divorce. (See her book, *Second Chances*, coauthored with Sandra Blakeslee.[3]) So does the work of Diane Medved, a clinical psychologist who started out a few years ago to write a neutral book on divorce. In the middle of her research, Dr. Medved finally gave up her neutral stance and concluded that no one ever emerges from a divorce unscathed. Her book, *The Case against Divorce*,[4] clearly portrays the lack of stability, economic degradation, long-term emotional trauma, and insecurity that plague divorced families. My book, *Children and Divorce*,[5] makes a similar case about the impact of divorce on children.

I cannot help but conclude from research and experience—both personal and clinical—that divorce is a disaster for everyone involved, especially children. But the key question facing us here is: Does divorce alter the lives of its most helpless victims, the children, *to such an extent that they will feel the impact of the divorce in adulthood?* Will they need to engage in some form of "recovery" later in life? Is there really such a problem as an Adult Child of Divorce (ACOD) syndrome?

I cannot help but conclude from my research and my experience that divorce is a disaster for everyone involved, especially children.

If children are seriously affected by divorce, sustaining much pain and anguish before, during, and after the separation of the parents, wouldn't such pain have lasting consequences? Would a "divorced" child's disillusionment, anger, and fear shape such crucial adult behaviors as choosing a mate or raising children?

My own experience seems to answer all these questions in the affirmative. And I am not alone in this opinion. Joanne Pedro-Carroll, addressing the 1990 Convention of the American Psychological Association, estimated that about one-third of children whose parents divorce suffer long-term emotional side effects from the divorce.[6] In addition, a recent double edition of the *Journal of Divorce* was given over to research reports on developmental and clinical issues affecting the children of divorce.[7] Again and again, reports published in this journal allude to the developmental impact of divorce on children, an impact which continues into adulthood.

Survey research, conducted by the Loneliness Research Project at

New York University, provides strong evidence that Adult Children of Divorce tend to be lonelier as adults than those from intact families.[8] ACODs report lower self-esteem, more crying spells, constant worry, more insomnia, guilt, feelings of worthlessness and despair. When alone, ACODs felt afraid, anxious, and angry.

Nevertheless, some researchers have challenged these ideas, arguing that children are "naturally resilient" and eventually bounce back from their divorce experience without any long-term damage. Kulka and Weingarten of the Survey Research Center at the University of Michigan, for instance, claim that they could find no differences between people from intact and nonintact families in major mental-health adjustment areas.[9]

My critique of Kulka and Weingarten's research, as well as other research in a similar vein, is that they tend to use rather gross measures of pathology when making comparisons. In other words, such research is designed to determine whether adult children of divorce suffer more from *severe* psychological disturbance than do other adults.

But that's not the point. I know of no clinician who would claim that divorce in childhood predisposes anyone to psychosis or other severe psychiatric disorders. Adult children of divorce are basically normal people who have been robbed of some significant steps in the growing-up process. The impact of divorce on their lives has more to do with their general level of happiness than it does with the incidence of severe mental or emotional illness.

MEASURING THE LONG-TERM COSTS

If we are going to research how divorce affects children as adults, I believe we need much finer and more sophisticated measures of adult adjustment, happiness, and styles of relating than can be shown by most studies. In other words, we need to know how the lives of "divorced" children have been changed deep down in their psyches—at the core of their being.

We lack such measures at the present time. But the ACOD's misery shows up very clearly in psychotherapy, which is why anecdotal or nar-

rative approaches to understanding this impact have been more powerful than other methods. They tell a much more detailed story of the
ACOD's distress than any series of tests.

There can be little question that children in divorcing families usually sustain the greatest pain and turmoil during and after the divorce
itself.[10] Many children, unfortunately, never grow past that crisis emotionally. These children, when they become adults, are filled with fear,

---

*Adult children of divorce are basically normal people
who have been robbed of some significant steps in the
growing-up process.*

---

anxiety, anger, and disillusionment. Their experience of divorce and its
consequences shapes the agenda for the rest of their lives. It may have
a major influence on whom they select as a mate, what work they do,
how well they perform as a parent, and how they interact with life in
general. Their offspring, in turn, can also be shaped by this divorce
background.

Maria and Thomas Lasswell, in their book *Marriage and the Family,*
summarize the long-term psychological costs of divorce to children by
saying that while most children recuperate from the effects of divorce
within a couple of years, two basic differences can be found in later life
between children raised in intact homes and those who have experienced divorce before age sixteen.[11]

- Children from divorced homes have a greater tendency to identify
  childhood or adolescence (or both) as the unhappiest period of
  their lives. The experience of divorce becomes the yardstick by
  which they measure future misery.
- Children of divorce tend to experience a greater measure of high
  anxiety in later life. This is especially true for males.

To those two indicators I would add a third. According to my experience, adult children of divorce tend to suffer a propensity to depres-

sion—not necessarily major depression, but a chronic, low-grade depression that results from a poor adjustment to losses in life. Even little losses or disappointments seem to create a rather exaggerated reaction in those who have suffered many childhood losses.

EVERYONE'S EXPERIENCE IS DIFFERENT

I should also stress at this point that *many* factors will determine whether or not, and to what extent, divorce will damage a child. As we will see, the child's age, sex, and position in the family will affect the impact of divorce, as will dysfunctional patterns within the family, coexisting problems such as alcoholism and mental illness, and the overall changes the divorce brings to a child's life.

Divorce almost always places children in a single-parent household, at least for a while. Divorce may eventually bring stepmothers and stepfathers into the picture. For many, divorce means poverty—or at least a dramatic drop in standard of living, while for many others, divorce means diminished parenting, dashed hopes, disillusioned dreams, and perpetual conflict. All these experiences—and more—combine to shape the child of divorce. But the divorce itself is still a central variable in this complex interplay of traumatizing life events.

It is true that some children seem to emerge from divorce relatively intact. Some are helped by loving parents who have worked hard to make healthy adjustments themselves, by grandparents who make an effort to ease the trauma, by well-adjusted stepparents who work to provide a stable environment. Some separated parents do manage to stay involved in the lives of their children; some do allow their children to have a say in custody and visitation rights—and all these efforts help give their children an edge when it comes to healthy adjustment. Other children just seem to be natural survivors; somehow they work out principles of healthy adjustment by themselves.

My experience and my research, however, lead me to believe that such "good news" stories are the exception rather than the rule for adult children of divorce. It is difficult to find hard evidence to back up that belief; no systematic, well-controlled studies have probed into the underlying pain of otherwise-normal ACODs. And the picture is further complicated by the powerful psychological defense mechanism of denial. Many ACODs, like people in other painful circumstances, stoutly resist acknowledging the source of their hurt.

Clearly, we need more research into the long-term effects of divorce on children. But that doesn't mean that healing has to wait for further research. For the purposes of this book, I will try to describe the ACOD syndrome as I have experienced it both personally and clinically and leave it to you to decide whether "the shoe fits" in your particular situation.

Part One

Understanding Your Need for Recovery

IF YOU ARE AN ADULT CHILD OF DIVORCE, you have a lot of company. As the divorce rate soars, so does the number of adults whose childhoods—like yours—were shaped by the dissolution of a home.

What does it mean to be an adult child of divorce? It means you have probably been subjected to extraordinary conflict and forced to adapt to huge changes in your life before your capacity for adjustment was fully developed. Perhaps you spent a significant portion of your childhood with one parent missing. You may never have known the joy of a secure home environment nor enjoyed a warm, accepting, and understanding parent-child relationship. Marital conflict and disruption brought you stress, anxiety, and depression at a time when learning, adventure, and relative security should have been your experience.

"But that's all in the past now," you may argue.

But is it? I believe not, and in this opening section I attempt to show why. I also want to show how divorce in childhood typically affects adult feelings and behavior.

More important, I hope this section will help you identify some of the scars divorce has left in your own life. Understanding the source of your particular pain and allowing yourself the freedom to grieve your losses is the important first step you must take on the long but fulfilling road to freedom.

CHAPTER 1

Growing Up in a Divorced Family

PETER JUST CELEBRATED his forty-sixth birthday. Handsome, virile, intelligent, and friendly, he seems to have everything going for him—a good marriage, two beautiful and well-adjusted teenage children, a satisfying job, and many wonderful friends.

Nevertheless, Peter is an unhappy man. Depression has been his dominant mood for more than thirty years. In addition, he periodically engages in self-destructive behaviors. Sometimes, when things are bothering him, he will pinch himself so hard that he leaves bruises. On the verge of an important accomplishment in his job, he will do something inexplicable to sabotage his success. And he does the same sort of thing in his marriage. When things are going well and everyone is happy, he overreacts or does something stupid to cause the family to react against him.

"In some strange way I almost enjoy having them angry at me," he explains. "Their hurt becomes my hurt, and it seems that I have this need to hurt both others and myself."

And then Peter adds, "I'm sure it's related to my parents' divorce, because I started doing it then."

I believe Peter is right. Like you—and like millions of other Americans—he grew up in a divorced family. And as an adult, Peter is paying a high price for his parents' divorce. His story eloquently illustrates the purpose of this book: to take a hard and honest look at how divorce in childhood might be affecting your adult behavior... and to point toward a path of health and healing.

A LEGACY OF PAIN

Peter's parents had everything going for them when they started their life together—similar beliefs, similar values, the support of family and friends. And yet, things went wrong almost from the week after the honeymoon. Peter's father was jealous and insecure, so he kept a close watch on his new wife—often accusing her of flirting with other men. She was naturally friendly and outgoing, while he was reserved and a little shy, and this difference in their personalities caused many tensions.

The marital friction didn't end when Peter and his little sister were born. Instead, over the years, the conflict intensified. And while the fighting always took place behind closed doors, Peter and his younger sister always knew something was wrong. Although their parents' squabbling was a fact of life for the children, they never got used to it. Somehow they sensed that a time-bomb was ticking away in their home.

Still, they weren't prepared when the bomb finally went off. Peter was just a few days past his eleventh birthday when his mother called him aside and told him that his father had left home. The announcement came out of the blue. No warning. No preparation. Not even an apology. No one told Peter what had caused the breakup or asked him what he thought about the situation. His feelings didn't seem to count at all. He was left bewildered, frightened, and deeply angry. He even remembered times when he had provoked his parents and he wondered if the divorce was his fault.

The months and years that followed were painful and confusing for Peter. Several times his parents tried to reconcile their differences. Grandparents gave advice, friends took sides, and several pastors and counselors did their best to slow down the impending breakup, but to no avail.

THE HURT DOESN'T STOP!

Shortly after Peter's twelfth birthday, Peter's parents filed for divorce. And by now Peter was feeling so numb he didn't care. Surely, he thought, the pain would be over soon.

But he was wrong. Divorce is never a single event that a child "gets over," like going to the dentist. It is a series of apparent catastrophes. One crisis gives way to the next. Every stage demands change. Every phase brings its own pain.

Peter cried often as he told me his story many years later. Usually his tears were full of anger or remorse. When he first started in therapy, he would stop and brush them away quickly. But after awhile, he simply let them flow. Grief had finally begun to do its healing work, and I did nothing to prevent him from feeling the deep pain as he described the years that followed his parents' divorce.

Divorce is never a single event that a child "gets over,"
like going to the dentist.

The hostility between his parents did not stop after the divorce was final; if anything, the conflict grew worse—and it no longer took place behind closed doors. Because Peter's father now lived in his own apartment and only periodically visited their home, shouting matches took place in the hallway or on the front steps. Peter's father continued to be intensely jealous of his ex-wife, and his verbal abuse of her chilled and humiliated his terrified children.

Because both parents were preoccupied with their private war over settlement and custody, they paid little attention to the emotional needs of their children. Grandparents provided some emotional support, but Peter still felt isolated and lonely. He couldn't express his grief to anyone, nor could he ask for comfort. He knew his mother couldn't help; she was hurting enough herself. His little sister couldn't help—who ever heard of a big brother crying on a little sister's shoulder? His pain had nowhere to go but inside.

Peter began the habit of feeling sorry for himself. He learned to wallow in his misery—falling deeper and deeper into sadness. Hours were spent in melancholy brooding. And he developed a fascination for a penknife he had received as a birthday present. It was still new and very sharp. He opened and closed it over and over.

Once he accidentally cut himself on the arm and was surprised at how little pain he felt as he watched the thin trickle of blood ooze down his skin. He discovered that when emotional pain is very intense, physical pain is hardly noticeable. In fact, making yourself hurt on the outside almost feels good because it seems to relieve the inner hurt. Soon he developed a habit that would stick with him into his adult life.

Now, at forty-six, Peter continues to hurt himself in many ways to relieve his inward pain, although he's only beginning to understand why. "Maybe I have blamed myself all these years for their breakup and have a need to punish myself."

And then he adds, "It's strange how something that happened so long ago can still have such a hold on me."

THE COMMON DENOMINATOR OF DIVORCE

Is Peter correct in thinking that many of his present problems can be traced to his parents' divorce? Or is he exaggerating the effect of his childhood experience? To answer this question and to understand how divorce affects children in later life, we need to ask how it differs from other childhood traumas—such as death in the family, physical or sexual abuse, alcoholism, drug addiction, mental illness, or chronic conflict. Often such family dysfunctions are the cause of the divorce—either the major defect in the marriage or just the straw that breaks the camel's back.

Often, of course, it is difficult to distinguish the effects of a childhood divorce from the effects of other childhood traumas. Say, for example, that you are a child of divorce and that one or both of your parents were also alcoholics. Which factor—divorce or alcoholism—takes precedence in defining your adult problems? Basically, it's a futile debate. It's like swimming in the rain and then trying to determine whether the pool or the rain is making you wet!

Both divorce and other traumas, such as alcoholism in the family, can cause problems in later life for children who experience them. One problem may have been around longer than the other, or one may cause more conscious conflict than the other. But both have an impact. And the two also interact with each other, so that the *interaction* causes a third set of effects.

In this book, I will attempt to isolate the common denominator of divorce—to distinguish the negative impact of the divorce itself from the combined impact of other childhood traumas. Keep in mind, however, that such additional problems in the family will almost certainly increase the negative impact of divorce.

SINS OF THE FATHERS—
LEARNING FROM THE ACOA MOVEMENT

Divorce is one of those situations in which the sins of fathers (and mothers) most certainly visit themselves upon the heads of their children. I don't say this to make moms and dads feel guilty—most feel guilty enough as it is. Being a parent has to be the hardest job in the world, and being a perfect parent is impossible! But the facts are that parents do things that leave an indelible and negative imprint on children.

We readily admit this fundamental law when we examine what it means to grow up with an alcoholic parent. Adult children of alcoholics have long known that their parents' sins have affected them, but it is only recently that the extent of this damage has been fully recognized and the so-called "ACOA syndrome" examined. Until a decade ago, the focus of recovery was almost entirely on the alcoholic or addict and his or her treatment. Now we realize that alcoholism's effect on other family members, especially children, was devastating and affected how the children behaved as adults.

Many ACOAs, for example, feel different from other adults. They feel that something is wrong with them, but they can't always articulate what that "something" is. They constantly seek approval or affirmation from others, but then they tend to sabotage their relationships. They tend to go to extremes in their attitudes and behavior—becoming either overly responsible or totally irresponsible, taking themselves too seriously or not seriously enough, judging themselves without mercy or living as if "anything goes," scrupulously telling the truth or lying without compunction.

The key word for many ACOAs is *over*—they overachieve, overeat, overwork, overexercise, overcommit, or overspend. This makes them strong candidates for "hidden" addictions—those addictions that are not directly related to alcohol or drugs. Their addictions tend to be to work, sex, pain, gambling, TV, eating, power, religion, shopping, and a host of risk-taking behaviors. I discuss these problems in detail in *Healing Life's Hidden Addictions*.[1] With minor variations, these are also the problems of ACODs.

My point here is that "the sins of your parents" tend to visit you in certain identifiable forms. Just as there is a clearly identifiable pattern of behavior associated with being an adult child of an alcoholic, there is also a pattern—a syndrome—associated with being a child of divorce. *Both* are damaging to a child's development. Granted, there are degrees of damage for both ACOAs and ACODs. The impact varies—but each invariably makes a negative impact.

Just as there is a clearly identifiable pattern of behavior associated with being an adult child of an alcoholic, there is also a pattern—a syndrome—associated with being a child of divorce.

It is probably pointless to argue which of the two factors, divorce or alcoholism, does more long-term damage to children. If pressed, part of me would argue for divorce, simply because it affects more people and is socially more acceptable. But that would seem to minimize the pain of ACOAs. Many of these people have struggled valiantly to overcome deep emotional scars, and ACODs can learn much from their experience. All I would ask is that ACODS be afforded the same recognition for their pain and their growth that ACOAs have gradually won.

The ACOA movement has provided us with a much greater understanding of the vulnerability of children, but it has also provoked criticism that potentially could be applied to ACODs. The dramatic increase in ACOA support groups has caused some critics to react with impatience. "What good is all this navel gazing?" they ask. "Why don't you stop blaming your parents, get out of yourself, and get on with your life?"

These reactions usually come from those who grew up in functional homes who just don't understand. (Or they come from people living in denial about their own pain.) I've learned that a person must spend some time talking with and walking in the shoes of those who have grown up in an alcoholic home in order to understand the indignities they have experienced, the extent to which their parents' sin has scarred them, and the courage and support they need to overcome their past. And the same is true of those who have grown up in broken homes.

It is true that we can do nothing to undo the past. Nevertheless, the pain of the ACOA—and the ACOD—is real, and the consequences cannot just be shrugged off. Liberal doses of understanding and forgiveness are required. Old habits of handling emotion must be broken and new, healthier habits relearned. Healing is a process; it rarely results from a simple act of the will.

But healing *can* happen—and it can happen for you. As we will see, you need not pass the "sins of your parents" on to the next generation. You need not be prisoner to forces in your childhood over which you had no control; you can break free. With some understanding of how you've been affected—and with spiritual help—you can begin to write a new script for your life. I hope this book will help you do so.

HOW IS YOUR PARENTS' DIVORCE AFFECTING YOU NOW?

While I will later discuss in some depth many of the adult consequences of childhood divorce, it may be helpful to begin with a brief overview of some typical long-term consequences of childhood divorce—problems you may be experiencing in your life right now.

In general, the adult consequences of childhood divorce fall into four general categories:

- Emotional consequences,
- Relationship and social consequences,
- Physical consequences, and
- Academic and vocational consequences.

I will discuss each category briefly at this point—just enough to help you understand the ways in which you may have been affected by your parents' divorce. As you read through the list, please remember that many other childhood conflicts—not just divorce—can cause adult symptoms like these. As I proceed, I will try to distinguish the more specific effects of divorce.

EMOTIONAL CONSEQUENCES OF DIVORCE

Divorce makes a major impact on psychological development because it strikes at the core of every child's most fundamental need: the need for a stable, secure, and abuse-free environment in which to grow emotionally.

Divorce makes a major impact on psychological development because it strikes at the core of every child's most fundamental need: the need for a stable, secure, and abuse-free environment in which to grow emotionally.

How do emotional consequences show themselves in adulthood? Here are some characteristics you may note in yourself:

- *You have diminished self-esteem.* ACODs tend to feel inferior to others, even though they may be high achievers.
- *You are depression-prone.* ACODs tend to overreact or exaggerate losses, and this often leads to depression problems.
- *You experience an underlying, pervasive anxiety.* ACODs tend to be haunted by persistent, vague feelings of anxiety and insecurity.
- *Your resentment is easily triggered.* In a conflict-ridden family, a person easily becomes "triangled"—that is, gets caught between the conflicts of others. In such a no-win situation, resentment easily becomes a way of life—a habitual attitude that persists into adulthood. Residual anger toward parents remains unresolved and easily triggers resentment toward other people as well.
- *You crave entertainment—especially TV, movies, and other fantasy media.* ACODS often tend to avoid boredom at all costs, having learned at an early age how to use distraction to escape emotional pain. And they are particularly attracted to those specific forms of entertainment that feed a rich fantasy life—including television, movies, and romance or adventure novels.

- *You love to daydream and fantasize.* Imagination provides hurting people with a way to achieve anything they want and to restore all that is broken in their lives. Hours spent ruminating over one's hurts can thus be turned over to fantasy experiences that provide comfort and hope. You may have no heroes in real life—but you are the hero in your own reverie.
- *You avoid risk, pain, and rapid change.* Often the changes brought about by divorce are too rapid to allow children to adjust. One day everything seemed okay; the next day, disaster struck. As a result, ACODs come to fear rapid change and to avoid taking risks. Failures only add more pain, so ACODs try to keep them to an absolute minimum. They tend to "play it safe" in work, relationships, or recreation.
- *You feel paralyzed emotionally when you face a personal problem.* ACODS often feel overwhelmed and incapable of coping. When problems come quickly, the feeling can reach panic proportions.
- *You often feel helpless to bring about change.* This feeling usually underlies your emotional paralysis, and it connects directly with your divorce experience. Children typically feel helpless to prevent the marriage breakup and helpless in other areas as well. They are too small, too weak, too immature, too hurt, too frightened, too anxious, and too angry to be of much help. So a feeling of helplessness may persist into adulthood.
- *You have difficulty controlling anger.* Divorcing parents tend to provide models for acting out anger. And children feel their own intense anger at the family conflict so deeply that later in life they may project this anger onto others, lashing out at anyone that gets in their way. This tendency is aggravated by the fact that discipline is often neglected during a divorce, so children don't learn the appropriate boundaries for aggressive behavior.

RELATIONAL AND SOCIAL CONSEQUENCES

The emotional disruptions resulting from a divorce in your childhood may also have an influence on the relational and social aspects of your life:

- *You often feel rejection.* ACODs have a tendency to feel that others don't like them, that they are "outcasts." This causes them to avoid intimacy except when it is very "safe."
- *You volunteer for blame.* Many children feel responsible for their parents' marital breakup. At an early age you learn to blame yourself for their conflict, and this sense of guilt continues into adulthood. You feel responsible every time someone around you gets upset.
- *You can't handle conflict.* Children who are "caught in the middle" of parental conflict develop a tendency to retreat. Thereafter they try to avoid all conflict—so many conflicts remain unresolved.
- *You have difficulty communicating.* Many children of divorce come to feel that communication inevitably creates conflict and invites rejection. Because silence seems to prevent trouble (at least superficially), many ACODs prefer not to share deeply or speak honestly.
- *You find it hard to form lasting relationships.* ACODs tend to fear commitment. They were betrayed by a parent or parents, so whom can they trust now? In addition, those who lacked a model for lifelong commitment in marriage find it difficult to work one out for themselves.
- *You frequently experience loneliness.* ACODs often find relationships difficult to build and hold on to. Sometimes by choice, but often just because of circumstances, they tend to feel lonely and abandoned.
- *You are often moody or sulky.* Because sadness and depression are a major part of every divorced child's experience, moodiness or sulkiness becomes a common outlet for self-pity. Many ACODs want to be with people, but quickly retreat into silence. They tend to be variable in their responsiveness, pensive, peevish, testy, and sullen. When others try to talk them out of their glumness, they play hard to get—putting up an "I don't care" front but longing for others to break it down.
- *Not getting hurt is a big priority for you.* Children of divorce have usually had enough hurt for one lifetime, so they go out of their way to avoid further pain. When dating, for example, they may gravitate toward "safe" channels such as "video dating" or personal ads rather than face the risk of simply asking someone out.

PHYSICAL CONSEQUENCES

Because emotional difficulties often find expression in physical symptoms, you may find yourself experiencing the following:

- *You often feel vaguely "out of touch."* Some adult children of divorce feel as if they were walking around in a kind of "fog." This could, in fact, be a symptom of low-grade depression. The body is "switched off," adrenaline levels are low, there is little energy. Physically, many ACODs live in a chronic "grieving" mode.
- *You experience significant gastrointestinal disturbances, frequent headaches, and other physical symptoms of stress.* Anxiety and stress always affect the stomach and digestive system. Stomach discomfort, ulcers, excessive gas, and colitis are quite common for adult children of divorce. Similarly, headaches and other stress-related symptoms such as muscle aches, insomnia, and lower back pain are common among ACODs, especially when they are under stress.
- *You tend to overeat or undereat.* Food is a natural tranquilizer. For this reason, many ACODs overeat as a way of dulling their emotional pain. To others, however, food represents a comfort that must be denied. They feel a strong need to punish themselves— to prevent pleasure at all costs—so they either deny themselves food or they "purge" after they have eaten. Either way, this pain seems better than the intolerable hurt of abandonment or neglect.

ACADEMIC AND VOCATIONAL CONSEQUENCES

Finally, the effects of divorce may play themselves out in your academic or vocational life:

- *You have trouble making decisions.* This is true in minor matters ("What shall I wear?") as well as in major ("What shall I do with my life?"). Lack of decisiveness can diminish an ACOD's academic and vocational success.
- *You possess a hazy sense of identity.* "I don't know who I am or what

I'm capable of." Many ACODs feel this way because no one shaped their sense of identity during childhood. They were left to find their own identity—but failed to do so.

• *You take life either too seriously or not seriously enough.* Some ACODs have been so hurt by their childhood experiences that they now "over-engage" life; everything is "serious business" for them. Others have given up; they are just not going to be caught with too much commitment to ideals, ambitions, or dreams. To keep from feeling emotional pain, they've anesthetized themselves into numbness.

• *You need constant feedback on performance.* The ACOD's need for reassurance (from friends or supervisors) tends to be very strong. In order to keep at a minimum the anxiety of not knowing how they are doing, they constantly seek positive feedback.

A WORD OF HOPE

By this point, you may find yourself asking, "Is there hope? Is it possible to overcome the impact of being a child of divorce?" Perhaps you have lived with the pain of your childhood trauma for twenty, thirty, or even fifty years. Can you possibly reach beyond it?

The damaging effects of divorce on children must not be minimized, but they can be overcome.

I can say with the utmost confidence that there *is* hope. The damaging effects of divorce on children must not be minimized, but they *can* be overcome. Not only can you find relief for the painful psychological and spiritual problems you may be suffering, but, through your own adjustment and healing, you can also avoid passing on to your children the dysfunctional patterns you learned.

What does it take to overcome the damaging effects of divorce? Understanding the various ways your behavior may have been shaped by your experience of divorce is an important first step. It is true, of course, that understanding in itself will not necessarily bring change. But without understanding, it's hard to know where to begin. You can begin your journey toward understanding by filling out Personal Inventory One, which is a brief questionnaire designed to help you get in touch with the *facts* and *feelings* connected with your childhood experience of divorce.

In addition to understanding, there is another important ingredient to overcoming divorce damage. This is the element that a well-known joke emphasizes:

How many psychologists does it takes to change a light bulb?
Only one. But the bulb must really want to change!

Like many good jokes, that one contains a core of truth: Real growth must begin with a willingness to be different. And that is as true for the adult child of divorce as it is for anyone else.

Once you are willing to change, you can benefit from the specific tools for healing and growth that I offer in this book. They are based on my personal experience and that of the many I have seen in therapy. Some of these tools will be spiritual in nature.

In the past ten to twenty years, therapists and researchers have learned a lot about divorce and the impact it has on children. We are learning how to apply this knowledge to the lingering effects of divorce in adult life. Unhappiness, anxiety, and fear can be relieved by attending to the very basic principles I will describe in later chapters. The sooner you begin to apply these principles, the sooner you will achieve a greater sense of well-being. If you are an ACOD, you have every reason to look forward to the future with optimism and hope.

Personal Inventory

1

Getting in Touch with Your Past

These questions are designed to help you get in touch with the *facts* and *feelings* of your childhood divorce experience. Take a moment to jot down your answers on a separate sheet of paper. You may be avoiding facing these facts and feelings, or you may even have suppressed them entirely. Getting these factors into the open where you can reflect on them and face them realistically will help you begin the process of healing.

1. How old were you at the time of your parents' divorce?

2. How many brothers did you have at the time? Sisters?

3. How did you first hear about the divorce?

4. Did you have any warning? What sort of warning was it?

5. What were some of the changes you had to make? (List as many as you can remember—for instance: changed schools, moved to another city, mother began working full time, and so on.)

6. What were your feelings when you *first* heard of the divorce?

7. What were your feelings when the divorce finally occurred?

8. *Who* do you believe was primarily responsible for the marriage breakup?

9. *What* do you believe was the main cause of the breakup?

10. With whom did you live after the divorce?

11. Did your mother remarry?

    a. How did you feel about the remarriage?

    b. How did you respond to your new stepparent?

12. Did your father remarry?

    a. How did you feel about the remarriage?

    b. How did you respond to your new stepparent?

13. What is your clearest memory of an unhappy event following the divorce?

14. What is your clearest happy memory?

15. In retrospect, do you believe that the divorce was for the better, or worse?

    Why do you believe this?

16. Who, of all your family, do you believe was most harmed by the divorce?

   Why?

17. What do you think would have made the divorce less painful or damaging for you?

18. What helped you the most to get through the divorce and its aftermath?

CHAPTER 2

Assessing the Divorce Damage in Your Life

IT IS THANKSGIVING MORNING, and eight-year-old Kathy is alone in her bedroom. She has been awake for some time, but she doesn't want to get out of bed. Her stomach is in knots. She has been dreading this day for several weeks now.

Kathy has pretty much decided how she will spend this Thanksgiving with her mother. No friends—she doesn't want to talk to any of them. They'll just talk about how much fun they're having with their families, and that will make Kathy feel worse. Already she notices that she's jealous of her best friend, Ellen, because Ellen is always talking about her father. Kathy hasn't seen her father for two months, and she isn't going to see him today, either.

Kathy's parents split up six months ago. They didn't fight too much while they were married; her father was the silent type. When he got angry he just left the house, and no one knew where he went. Then one day he left and never came back.

Kathy's father explained to her afterward that he was going to live with someone else because things weren't working out at home. This "someone else" has two children younger than Kathy, and more and more her father does things with them and not with her. That's why Kathy is feeling so down on this Thanksgiving morning. Her father has told her he would come around in the evening to say "hi," but he couldn't come during the day. He would spend the day celebrating with "them."

Kathy can feel the anger churning deep within. She would like to scream and scream and scream. But that wouldn't help much, so she just lies there, dreading the activities her mother has planned and wishing the day would go by quickly.

Kathy's mother enters the room and sits down quietly at the foot of Kathy's bed. She understands the pain and confusion her daughter is feeling. During her separation, as she began to realize her husband was intent on getting a divorce, she took the trouble to get some help for herself. She and the therapist had talked over how difficult holidays can be for children whose parents divorce. She intuitively knows that Kathy is hurting, even now, over her father's absence.

Kathy's mother doesn't criticize her for just lying in bed; in fact, she lies down next to her for a while. They embrace for a moment, and Kathy feels confident enough to talk about the gap in her life that her absent father has created. They both admit it is going to be tough to get through this day.

"I haven't planned anything special," Kathy's mother says. "Doesn't seem to be any point in cooking a big meal for just the two of us. I tell you what, why don't we drive up to Grandma's for the day? She said we could come. You and Granddad can play some games—as long as we are together, I don't really care what else we do."

Kathy smiles. Not only is she pleased by the thought of being with her grandparents, but the deep understanding her mother was able to communicate gives her comfort. She realizes that she isn't alone in her feelings of abandonment. She gets out of bed quickly, and soon they are on the road to Grandma's.

THE LINGERING SCARS OF DIVORCE

When I wrote the book, *Children and Divorce*,[1] I stated quite strongly that divorce hurts children. The trauma of divorce is second only to death, I contended. In some respects it is worse than a death. Death is final; divorce drags on. Death is a single event; divorce is a chain of multiple events. Death is not normally associated with conflict and hostility; divorce invariably is. Death has relatively little social stigma attached to it; divorce nearly always does, even in these days of so-called "enlightenment." We accept the inevitability of death, even as children. But divorce can be avoided, so to a child it almost invariably feels unjust and undeserved.

For awhile I wondered if I had overstated the case in that book. I was speaking personally, as someone who had experienced the pain of divorce as a twelve-year-old child. But after many years in the therapist's chair and much opportunity to reflect on the impact of divorce, I haven't changed my mind. If anything, I am more convinced now than ever before that the children of divorce *are* different. Not on the outside. They laugh, cry, and play games like everyone else. But inside is where the scars are to be found.

I am more convinced now than ever before that the children of divorce are different. Not on the outside. They laugh, cry, and play games like everyone else. But inside is where the scars are to be found.

I remember nearly losing the first finger on my right hand as a child. I was about seven years old. A friend and I were repairing his little sister's tricycle, whose wheel kept coming off. I, the mechanically-minded member of our small group, suggested that we tie some string on the end of the axle to hold it on, but the piece of string we found was too long. "Cut it off with that axe lying there, while I hold the string," I told my friend. His aim was not very good, and I ended up in the emergency room with a partially severed finger. The doctor stitched it back on as best he could, but I can still see the scar—even the little holes made by the needle used to sew it up. Sometimes it itches and even hurts a little, and that's after fifty years.

Believe me, the scars of divorce can do the same. They never completely go away. They may lie quietly for a long time, then one day remind you of their presence.

Of course, we can see physical scars, but we can't see psychological ones. So, as adult children of divorce we cannot always recognize how our early unpleasant experiences are affecting us. This is what this chapter is all about—helping you recognize some of the ways your early experience with divorce may have scarred you.

The scars of divorce never completely go away. They may lie quietly for a long time, then one day remind you of their presence.

Now, I am not saying that you have been irrevocably damaged by your parents' divorce. You may have been one of the lucky ones who bounced back fairly quickly. But chances are that the experience of divorce in your childhood has hurt you in ways you don't recognize.

The truth is that *most* children do not escape the ravages of divorce. And they are directly affected *by the divorce itself,* not by the other components of the marital breakup. Experts used to believe that divorce was a short-lived crisis. "Leave the children alone, they'll get over it," was the common advice. We don't believe that anymore. Most reputable research shows that divorce is a *long-term crisis,* and it is estimated that a significant proportion of the children of divorce develop major, lasting problems.[2] The rest may only have problems that can be classified as "minor," but they nevertheless can leave you feeling robbed of life's full luster.

HOW DIVORCE HURTS CHILDREN

Chances are that you will never again have to face a life event as traumatic as the breakup of your childhood home—except, perhaps, a divorce of your own. The stress, shock, fear, anxiety, depression, insecurity, helplessness, humiliation, and grief changed your life in several significant ways:

1. Divorce may have signaled a collapse in your family structure. Divorce disrupts the security of the family, as well as well as the love and support it provides. From the child's perspective (the parents may not see it this way) there is no longer a "safe haven" to which the child can retreat.

2. You probably lived with months or years of conflict in your home.
Fighting, yelling, and blaming characterize most divorces—before,
during, and even long after the separation. The impact of this conflict on children is devastating.

A cartoon I saw many years ago depicted two young boys sitting
on the pavement talking. One has been away and just returned.

"Hey, Butch! You're back! Didya have a good time?"

"I dunno," Butch replies, his face down and staring at nothing.

"What's the matter?" his friend asks.

"My mom's mad at my dad, and they're not speaking to each
other. But they're both yelling at *me!*"

This is what's really sad about divorce. The conflict eventually
comes to rest on the children.

---

*Chances are that you will never again have to face a life
event as traumatic as the breakup of your childhood home—
except, perhaps, a divorce of your own.*

---

3. Your parents' capacity to parent probably diminished. Parents in
the middle of a divorce tend to be preoccupied with their own conflict. Their emotional turmoil overshadows that of their children,
especially during the critical months or years preceding their
divorce. Once the divorce is over, one or both parents may be preoccupied with dating and finding another partner. For these and
other reasons, many parenting tasks are thus neglected. Adult children of divorce often report that they "raised themselves."

4. Divorce probably confused you by dividing your loyalties.
Children are torn trying to decide whom to believe, whose side to
take, whom to love the most, and whom to live with. They are
pushed and pulled by love and loyalty. Unfortunately, many parents
encourage this—either consciously or unwittingly.

"Who do you love, me or your father?"

"Who provides the money for you to live on, me or your mother?"

Not only is loyalty a dilemma for children in such a situation, but considerable guilt is created by the push and pull of this battle for love.

5. Divorce may have made your future seem bleak and uncertain. Deep-seated insecurity is triggered by the split of a family—and not just emotional insecurity. Most children experience a dramatic drop in their standard of living following a divorce. In particular, divorce often means poverty for divorced mothers and their children. Often the divorce means a move as well, disturbing their established friendships, and forcing them to adapt to a new neighborhood, a new school, new friends—and sometimes, eventually, a new mom or dad. This is simply more change than the average child can cope with.

6. Divorce may have separated you from your father. Ninety percent of the children of divorce live with their mothers, and only one-sixth of these see their fathers at least weekly.[3] A sixth have not seen him for a year. One-third have not seen Daddy for five years. Of any group of thirteen- to fifteen-year-old children of divorce, 40 percent will not have had any visit from their fathers during the past five years.

Without a father, children—especially boys—lack a major ingredient in their developmental formula.

We do not need a major research project to tell us what this lack of fathering does to children. Without a father, children—especially boys—lack a major ingredient in their developmental formula. One major study, which has followed one hundred thirteen children for more than ten years after divorce, has found that these children still have a passionate yearning for elusive or phantom fathers. This need for the absent father is intensified at adolescence.[4]

7. You may have taken on a "parent" role too early in life. Role reversal, even at a very young age, is quite common in divorce situations. Children tend to take upon themselves much anxiety over their parents. They worry about their mothers in particular and become "parental" in attitude and behavior.

8. You may have sustained more losses than you could handle. Divorce is essentially an experience of loss for children. In a divorce, a child may lose a parent (usually the father), a familiar home, a neighborhood, school, church, friends, pets, siblings (when a family is split up), financial resources and—above all—hope for the future. These losses can produce a profound depression at the time of the divorce, as well as a predisposition to become depressed in later life.

TOO MUCH TOO SOON

The long-term impact of your parents' divorce on children was probably influenced by the age you were at the time of the divorce. Children develop through definite, identifiable stages, and a major life disruption at any one stage of development can cause problems related to that stage.

Very early in life, for instance—say, before age six—our primary need is for security. If divorce occurs at this time, we may develop a deep-seated insecurity, a fear of abandonment by those who say they love us. Later childhood (ages seven to ten) is a time when we learn how to communicate outside the home and relate to peers, adults, and even strangers. If the family falls apart at this time, we may fail to master these skills and be slowed down developmentally.

Though there is no really good age at which a child can experience divorce, the period between ten and fourteen years of age is particularly devastating. Children at this age are especially likely to shoulder too much family responsibility just when they need to begin "separating" from the family developmentally.

Bobby was fourteen when his parents divorced. He was quite mature for his age and, when his father left because he was "in love" with a younger woman, Bobby became the replacement "Daddy" for his three younger brothers and sisters. His mother was devastated by the divorce and pretty much immobilized. Bobby was forced to make important decisions for her and acted in many ways as if he were the adult and she one of the kids. He did the disciplining. He gave emotional support.

Because the family was left financially ravaged by the father's failure to pay regular child support, Bobby felt he had to start earning money. Quitting all extramural activities, including his great love, competitive swimming, Bobby lied about his age and landed two part-time jobs. For several years he worked hard and long to help keep the family together.

Finally, Bobby's mother was able to go to work also, but the damage was done. Bobby had turned into a bitter and angry young man. He resented having had to take over the parental role. He was openly hostile toward his father, and he even resented his mother for having taken so long to get her act together.

Now, as an adult, Bobby avoids responsibility. He hates feeling obligated to anyone or having them obligated to him. He never borrows or lends. He has become a loner. The few times he has dated, he pulled back as soon as the relationship started getting serious.

Bobby wants freedom above all. In essence, he has become "stuck" in an adolescent stage of development. His life has been severely damaged by too many responsibilities imposed on him too early in life.

THE FINANCIAL CRUNCH

Bobby was also damaged by a common problem that may have affected you as well—financial insecurity. Whereas the standard of living of a departing ex-husband goes up by 42 percent, that of the ex-wife (and children) usually falls by 73 percent. Furthermore, 60 percent of divorced fathers fail to support their children financially.[5]

This inequitable financial situation, sometimes called the "feminization of poverty," can affect children of all ages in various ways. The very young may be deprived of first-rate day care or schooling and privileges they would otherwise have had. Older children are robbed of many benefits—and even a college education. Financial realities may limit a family's options when it comes to housing, transportation, even food.

I heard of one recently divorced man who told his son that he couldn't send him to college because he was going to marry a woman whose children needed all the financial help he could give them. The father chose to assist his new stepchildren rather than his own son. And although this young man decided to work his way through college, the emotional damage of his father's rejection will take years to heal.

Children, especially very young children, are affected by this financial devastation in another way. Many single parents—again, usually mothers—are forced to work long hours or even take more than one job in order to make ends meet. The combination of extra work and their own emotional pain leaves them little energy for attending to parenting tasks. Too often, the children are left to their own devices.

Perhaps the most devastating aspect of the financial pinch that affects a typical divorced family is the knowledge that the absent father is financially better off, that he refuses to help his children, or both. The lack of financial support often strikes the children as just another form of rejection.

One woman is a "shopoholic"; she snaps up appliances, cars, and especially clothes whether she needs them or not. True, she married well and can afford to spend a lot of money, but she believes her almost insatiable desire for material things is the direct consequence of forced deprivation in her childhood.

IS DIVORCE WORSE FOR BOYS OR GIRLS?

Was the emotional legacy of your parents' divorce affected by whether you are male or female? Probably. The experience of divorce does appear to affect the sexes differently.

Many people would guess that boys have the edge in handling divorce. After all, boys tend to be stoics—reluctant to cry or to let their hurts show. Most boys are skilled at putting on a brave face, acting independent, and adopting a "devil may care" attitude. They also tend to pull away from home life at an earlier age. So boys should do better in divorce situations, right?

Wrong! Studies show that boys of all ages seem to have more difficulties and to adjust more poorly than girls. Schoolwork declines, problem behaviors grow worse; they grow more destructive and hostile, yet more passive and self-critical.

There are several reasons why boys show more harmful effects. Since the father is the parent who usually leaves, boys are more often abandoned by the parent of the same sex, the one who is most instrumental in helping them form their adult gender image.

Daughters who are abandoned by fathers often develop a closer relationship with their mothers. But a boy's resentment at the loss of his father may intensify conflicts with his mother. Since discipline tends to be more difficult for the mother to enforce on sons as they grow older, problem behaviors tend to increase.

Overall, the "boys fare worse than girls" scenario may only be true for the short run. If we look at the longer picture, particularly at the effect of divorce on adult behavior, girls probably suffer equally with boys.

Boys also don't handle emotional pain very well. Unfortunately, our culture teaches them that crying is a sign of weakness and that boys should never show how much they hurt. As a result, they tend to repress their emotional pain, which emerges in the form of rebellion or in other indirect ways.

GIRLS HURT, TOO

But the fact that boys tend to fare worse than girls in a divorce does *not* mean girls escape unscathed. For adolescent girls, especially, it can be devastating to be deprived of love and acceptance from a significant male figure. A father plays an important role in defining a daughter's sense of worth and her sense of herself as a woman. Feeling rejected in this vital relationship can adversely affect a girl's ability to relate to members of the opposite sex in a healthy fashion and can even affect her image of who God is. Although the impact of a father's absence may not immediately affect a girl as much as a boy, in the long run, the loss of this basic male relationship may be equally destructive to the maturation of both sexes.

Even when a father visits his daughter regularly, there is a strain in the relationship that robs it of emotional richness. Shared activities become ritualistic and artificial and lose spontaneity, which is important to a loving relationship.

One twelve-year-old daughter described it this way:

> When dad comes to fetch me, I'm usually excited for the first five minutes. We don't talk much. I just enjoy being with him in the car as we drive. He asks me, "Where shall we go?" I say, "It doesn't matter," but I don't mean it. I want him to take me somewhere new, somewhere special just so that it makes me feel special and shows he cares. So he goes to the same old places. Sometimes it's to a pizza place he likes where the TV is always on a sports program. Sometimes it's to another restaurant that has a bar where he can look at women.
>
> And then we try to talk—but we quickly run out of stories about what happened this past week. I want him to notice my new hairstyle—but he doesn't. I want him to ask me about my friends —but he doesn't. It's like we're slowly becoming strangers. He's not in my life enough to know what's really going on. That's the saddest part. We see each other often, but we don't know each other anymore.

Overall, the "boys fare worse than girls" scenario may only be true for the short run. If we look at the longer picture, particularly at the effect of divorce on adult behavior, girls probably suffer equally with boys,[6] although the damage may manifest itself differently. In a future chapter I will look at the specific "unfinished business" you may have as a man or a woman and suggest strategies for overcoming these gender-specific problems.

THE MYTHS OF CHILDREN AND DIVORCE

Every now and then I come across a book or magazine article that tries to play down the damaging effects of divorce and remarriage on children. Usually written to help ease the consciences of divorcing parents, these treatises emphasize that parents must take care of themselves first and not worry about what effect the divorce will have on their children. And they usually trot out several standard arguments to support their points—arguments I believe are faulty and potentially harmful.

Most children, thank God, can bounce back if they are given the right environment—but that environment is precisely what is missing in many divorce situations.

Now, I certainly am not writing to help you heap additional guilt upon your parents. Most parents feel guilty enough as it is. But denying or minimizing the pain of a divorced child is surely not the most positive way for parents to handle guilt—and it's far from the healthiest way for the adult child of divorce to cope with his or her legacy of hurt. Buying into any one of these myths can slow your recovery significantly.

Allow me to discuss three of the most commonly cited "facts" about children and divorce and show how misleading they can be:

1. Children are resilient; they "bounce back" from experiences such as divorce. This is absolutely true—up to a point. Most children, thank God, *can* bounce back *if* they are given the right environment—but that environment is precisely what is missing in many divorce situations.

In addition, children are not equally resilient. Some are fragile, tender, easily hurt; they tend to be the big losers in a divorce situation. And even the most resilient need consistency, reassurance, and support in order to become healthy adults. Without these things, they may certainly *survive*—but not unscarred.

2. It's better to divorce than remain in an unhappy marriage. The common wisdom here is that the impact of divorce on children is far less severe than the consequences of remaining in an unbroken but troubled home. This idea can be very misleading. Who determines how much "trouble" is too much? Who asks the children? Several studies have shown that the majority of divorcing children would prefer to remain in an intact but conflicted family than to face all the unknowns that divorce brings. My work with ACODs confirms this. Except for severe cases of abuse or mental illness, divorce does *not* mean a better life for children.

This does not mean, of course, that living in a conflicted, unhappy home is *good* for children. By far the best solution, where possible, is to build a better marriage—not dissolve it.

Except for severe cases of abuse or mental illness, divorce does not mean a better life for children.

---

3. Growing up is stormy, anyway—so what's the big deal? Here the idea is that children have to face troubled waters anyway—even that learning to handle problems is a necessary part of growing up—so divorce is not that much of a problem.

I believe this line of thinking is seriously flawed. There is a great difference between divorce and such "normal" problems as peer conflict, moving, and even death. Such typical life storms are weathered by a healthy family's functioning together, with each member supporting the others. A child who has such a haven can face almost any trauma or conflict and come out the better for it. Too often, in divorce, what should be a place of harbor becomes the center of the storm—and the child is cast adrift on that stormy ocean to fend for himself or herself. That kind of emotional "weather" is neither normal nor necessary, and the "storm damage" can be severe.

Personal Inventory

2

Do You Have Divorce Damage?

As you read this first section of the book, you will be asking yourself: Has my childhood experience of divorce affected me in some way? This inventory will help you to evaluate this question and give you an overall sense of how much damage needs repairing. It is *not* intended to make you feel hopeless or overwhelmed by the task ahead, but simply to help you realistically evaluate where you stand today.

To complete the inventory, read each statement carefully and then check either the "yes" or "no" column. If you are unsure about whether the statement applies to you, leave it blank.

1. Did your parents divorce *before* you were fourteen years of age—but after you were four?
   Yes _____   No _____

2. Did your parents quarrel a lot?
   Yes _____   No _____

3. Were your parents physically abusive to each other?
   Yes _____   No _____

4. Were they physically abusive to you?
   Yes _____   No _____

5. Do you find yourself feeling sorry for yourself a lot (say more than once a week)?
   Yes _____   No _____

6. Do you feel depressed more often than you would like?
   Yes _____   No _____

7. Are you aware of a lot of pent-up anger?

    Yes _____ No _____

8. Do you consider childhood (or adolescence) the unhappiest time of your life?

    Yes _____ No _____

9. Would you consider yourself a "high anxiety" type of person?

    Yes _____ No _____

10. Do you feel lonely a lot of the time?

    Yes _____ No _____

11. Do you tend to cry easily or often?

    Yes _____ No _____

12. Are you bothered by thoughts of worthlessness or feelings of low self-esteem?

    Yes _____ No _____

13. Do you have a lot of physical problems, such as gastric discomfort, high blood pressure, headaches, or generalized pain?

    Yes _____ No _____

15. Do you have problems sleeping (either falling asleep or awakening early) that you feel are excessive or abnormal?

    Yes _____ No _____

16. Do you dislike being alone or feel anxious when you must travel by yourself?

    Yes _____ No _____

17. Do you tend to hold grudges and fantasize about "getting even"?

    Yes _____ No _____

18. Are you attracted to forms of entertainment (TV, novels, movies) because they help you escape your problems or avoid boredom?

    Yes _____ No _____

19. Do you daydream a lot—especially about being a hero or someone special?

    Yes _____ No _____

20. Are you often overcome with feelings of helplessness so that you don't attend to important issues in your life?

    Yes _____ No _____

21. Do you have an explosive anger response or have difficulty controlling your temper?

    Yes _____ No _____

22. Do you often have feelings of rejection—a sense that people don't like you or want to be with you?

    Yes _____ No _____

23. Do you try to avoid conflict at all costs?

    Yes _____ No _____

24. Do you pull back from making commitments in relationships?

    Yes _____ No _____

25. Do you overeat or undereat?

    Yes _____ No _____

26. Do you have difficulty making decisions?

    Yes _____ No _____

27. Is your sense of identity very hazy? For instance, do you often feel, "I don't know who I really am"?

    Yes _____ No _____

28. Do you seek feedback on how you are performing (in work, relationships) more than you would like?

    Yes ____   No ____

29. Have you been divorced yourself?

    Yes ____   No ____

30. Are you generally an unhappy person?

    Yes ____   No ____

TOTALS ____   ____

INTERPRETING PERSONAL INVENTORY TWO

In general, the more "yes" answers you gave, the greater the degree of damage you may have experienced as a child. Obviously, however, other childhood experiences besides divorce could have contributed to this damage. Whatever their origin, these unhappy situations can undermine your development as a whole and healthy person. If you are in doubt about your level of adjustment, seek the help of a professional counselor.

Range   Interpretation

0–5   A score below 5 on this inventory could occur when childhood divorce was minimally destructive. Other current life circumstances could be causing you to experience specific distress symptoms.

6–10   Your score indicates some divorce damage, especially if there are no other life circumstances bothering you. Nevertheless, you may have developed better coping skills than average.

11–20 Divorce has most likely affected you quite significantly. The higher your score above 11, the greater is the degree of

Range   Interpretation

damage and the more pressing the need to take remedial action as I describe in this book.

21–30   Clearly, you are experiencing significant personal problems. I would recommend that you explore your personal pain with a counselor or psychologist.

The "Blended Family" Blues

Y OUR PROBLEMS AS A CHILD of divorce may not have been over when the divorce papers were finalized and "arrangements" completed. True, some aspects of the disruption were probably over. The conflict may have subsided somewhat. Financial affairs were probably settled, a new home established, and much uncertainty resolved. But then you may have gone on to face a further challenge. Your custodial parent remarried, and you were forced into a "blended" or "reconstituted" family. (It almost sounds like a group of dehydrated people, mixed with water, and passed off as the real thing!)

I use the word *forced* intentionally because this is how it usually *feels* to the child. Few are consulted about whether they want to be a part of a new family. Most would rather have their old family back together again, no matter how troubled it was. And most would far rather have their custodial parent remain single than be faced with the prospect of living in a house full of strangers.

When my own mother decided to remarry after her divorce, I rather liked my stepfather. And he turned out to be a wonderful man who knew how to be a true friend and never tried to impose himself as a substitute father on me. I came to respect him and to appreciate his loving care of my mother. But if you had asked me at the time my mother remarried whether I was pleased with her choice or whether I would have voted in favor of the marriage, you would have received a blunt "no way."

Nine-year-old Edith felt that way, too, when her mother announced an impending remarriage. Edith's experience of divorce had been a fairly easy one—as divorces go. Edith's parents had more or less agreed that they had married for the wrong reasons—to please their parents—and that they no longer wanted to be married to each other. And they had both worked hard to keep the disruptions in Edith's life to a minimum.

Edith had surprised herself with how quickly she adjusted to a new life alone with her mother in a comfortable new apartment. Her father, unlike so many absent fathers, was regular in his visits. There hadn't been a lot of conflict between her parents to make her anxious. She loved her new school, her new friends, and especially her new relationship with her mother. They were a "team," as Edith's mom put it. Thinking of the two of them that way helped Edith to feel that she belonged with her mom and gave her a sense of importance.

Then the bomb dropped, and the explosion blew Edith's life to smithereens. The news of her mother's remarriage came as a total surprise to Edith. She knew, of course, that her mother had begun dating again and that one man in particular had become a regular visitor at the apartment. Edith even liked the man. He went out of his way to be kind to her. He showed an interest in her schoolwork, her piano lessons, and her collection of dolls. But for some strange reason Edith never quite made the connection between her mom's dating and the possibility of remarriage. The thought that she might someday have a stepfather had never crossed her mind. Now it was a looming reality, and Edith was devastated.

Remarriage after divorce tends to add stress and confusion to an already tense and confused situation, and many children carry into adulthood the scars of being "blended" against their wills.

Edith cried, shouted, and threatened to run away. She kept up the tirade for nearly a month—but nothing changed. Finally she settled down a bit and agreed to stay with her real dad for a few weeks while the wedding took place. She was then to return to her mother's "new" home, which turned out to be her stepfather's "old" house.

Edith's mother had probably told her quite clearly about her new husband's home circumstances, but Edith hadn't paid much attention. Imagine her dismay, when she returned to live with her mother to find out that she now had an "instant" family. In addition to a stepdad, she had a stepbrother and a stepsister, a little older than Edith, but still in their early teens. And she was supposed to share a bedroom with her stepsister.

In telling her story to me many years later, Edith could not get over the suddenness with which life could go from being good to being bad. "One moment I was a happy girl," she recounted. "The next I was a heap of misery. I went from thinking that life was great to feeling that my life was over. I just wanted to die!" She sobbed through many therapy sessions as she reexperienced her childhood feelings.

THE COMPLICATION OF UNREALISTIC EXPECTATIONS

About seven hundred fifty thousand children of divorce enter blended families each year in the United States. The bulk of these new homes are formed by stepfathers whose new wife has custody of her children. About one-ninth of these blended homes have children also from the father. But regardless of the composition of the new family—whether a stepfather moves in with them, they move in with him, or they all move to a new home—combining two homes demands major adjustments of everyone concerned. The longer a single-parent family has existed and the older the children, the more complex the adjustments will be and the greater the likelihood of severe conflicts.

My purpose here is not to discuss the pros and cons of remarriage; it is simply a fact of life for huge numbers of children whose parents divorce. My concern here is with the possible long-term damage this "blending" process can do to children, even under the best of circumstances. Remarriage after divorce tends to add stress and confusion to an already tense and confused situation, and many children carry into adulthood the scars of being "blended" against their wills.

Often parents who remarry feel so guilty about their failed previous marriages that they exaggerate their expectations for the new family. They want it to be everything their first family wasn't. They want to replace everything that was missing or less than perfect. Regrettably, these unrealistic expectations can cause more problems for the children involved, who are called upon to live strained and pressured lives.

Such was the case with Edith. Her mother and her stepfather were idealists. They resolved to turn their new family into one, big, happy "team." (Edith had heard that word before!) "We must pull together. We must look after each other's interests. We must sacrifice our individual needs so that we can all be happy together!" was the theme of dinnertime rallying speeches.

But Edith simply felt depressed. She heard little. She cared little. She felt numb and hopeless. She cried a lot in the privacy of her bed (under the blankets so her stepsister couldn't hear). And life seemed to go downhill for her from then on.

Fortunately, Edith's story does have one happy note. While her home life was miserable, and while she never warmed to her stepfather, she gradually became friends with her stepbrother and stepsister. Today, the three of them are very close, and Edith's stepsiblings form a major emotional support system for her.

Despite this positive outcome, however, Edith's experience in a blended family was a painful one, and it left her with definite scars. Edith's mother and stepfather made many mistakes in trying to combine their households, and Edith bore the brunt of those mistakes. The same is true of many ACODs, who lose far more than they gain in the blended-family game.

NEW FAMILIES, NEW CONFLICTS

Blended families, unfortunately, have much working against them. This may or may not have anything to do with who the parents are. They may be loving, kind, and sensitive—and still have problems. Even under the best of circumstances, several areas of conflict remain intrinsic to blended-family situations. If you were involved in a blended family, any of the following may have contributed to problems in your adult life:

1. You may have resented your stepparent. Most children of divorce resent the intrusion of another person, a total stranger, into the family unit. Their resentment may express itself either through outright anger and rebellion or through passive and subversive sabotage, but the underlying motive is the same: They are reluctant to accept that their natural parent needs a new partner.

Children can also use the stepparent as a target for the hostility felt toward the natural parent. For instance, a child may feel extreme anger toward his mother for divorcing his father. Because the child unconsciously fears hating his mother or showing any of his rage, he directs his anger toward the stepfather. He becomes excessively critical. He insults his new stepfather. He sneers, grunts disapproval, writes nasty notes, and generally acts obnoxious toward the bewildered stepfather. And this habit of "scapegoating" can easily carry over into adult life; he is likely to take out his displaced anger on his friends, his wife, or any other "safe" target.

I once saw a very good example of this scapegoat syndrome in a thirty-year-old mother of two boys. Conflicts with her husband had become quite intense, and she feared facing up to him, so her two sons became the target for her anger. She lashed out at them unreasonably and unexpectedly. She punished them excessively. And her behavior did not stop the moment she became aware of what she was doing. Scapegoating can be a deeply entrenched habit that may require extended therapy to correct.

2. You may have resented the stepparent's new role and felt torn by conflicting loyalties. Children of divorce often resent the fact that a stepparent usurps the place and role of the absent natural parent. Many times I have heard a child say, "He will *never* take the place of my real father" or "No way will I let him discipline me." These are natural reactions by divorced children to the imposition of control by someone they consider an outsider. They feel very deeply the threat of the stepparent's coming between them and their natural parent, and reassurance alone may do little to reduce their fears.

This problem can be further exacerbated by a stepparent who insists that he or she is now the "real" parent to the child. This insistence can be quite strong in couples who idealize their new relationship and want to prove to their ex-spouses that they can make a success of marriage.

With very young children, such an approach may not be much of a problem; the child simply adjusts to the givens of the new situation. With older children it courts disaster. They retain a sense of loyalty to their natural, but absent, parent. And they set up rigid defenses against intruders who threaten to displace the parent. Personality clashes or problems with discipline can further aggravate the sense of intrusion.

3. You may have felt jealous of the stepparent. Very often, a child of divorce will resent the time his or her mother or father spends with the "intruder." Such resentment is understandable. After all, for a while following divorce, the child had his or her custodial parent's full attention. Now he or she has to share that parent with somebody else. Even then, the child may not get a fair share of attention because his or her parent is emotionally preoccupied with the new relationship.

4. Your stepparent may have resented you. Children are not the only ones who feel resentment in a blended family. The stepparent can also resent, dislike, or be jealous of the stepchild. The stepparent may dislike competing for the love of his or her new partner and might even resent his or her new spouse's love for the child.

Such resentment on the part of stepparents is a lot more common than you might suppose, though the resentful stepparents often deny the problem. Instead, they tend to blame their resentment on the child's character, unconsciously searching for minor faults and reasons to reject the child. For example, they might brand the child as "spoiled" or "a brat" as a way of driving a wedge between the child and the natural parent.

Such tactics on the part of a stepparent can create tremendous fear in young children who intuitively feel, but cannot explain, this jealousy. They feel rejected and abused and easily reciprocate the feelings of resentment.

*Personality clashes can occur even in intact families,
but they are more likely in blended families, who share a
household but may not share experiences, values,
expectations, or genetic backgrounds.*

5. Personality conflicts may have divided your household.
Personality clashes can occur even in intact families, but they are
more likely in blended families, who share a household but may not
share experiences, values, expectations, or genetic backgrounds.
These conflicts can be between stepparents and children or
between the stepchildren from each family. It is demanding enough
to adjust to your natural parents and siblings whom, after all, you
resemble a lot anyway. But to be forced to adjust to total strangers
places increased demands on every member of the family. Children
don't always have the capacity to make these adjustments. In the
face of personality conflicts at home, they may either withdraw into
their own world or rebel and become difficult to manage.

6. Discipline may have been an issue. Since each partner has a different history, conflicts over discipline almost invariably arise. When
parents in a blended family disagree over methods of discipline,
they present a divided front to the child, who will then resent the
discipline, no matter how fair it is. The child may even take advantage of the confusion surrounding the discipline and use it to act
out his or her rebellion.

The typical scenario is that the natural parent is much more
lenient and tolerant of his or her own children but critical and
demanding of the stepchildren. They would gladly thrash their partner's kids—"but don't you dare lay a hand on mine." This taking of
sides can polarize a new family into two opposing camps, where
everyone loses.

That is why, as a general rule, discipline should be carried out
only by the natural parent. In other words, with rare exceptions, if a
mother and father each has a child from a previous marriage, the
mother should be responsible for disciplining her child and the

father his. (I also recommend that the absent natural parent not be exempted from the responsibility of discipline.) This avoids the natural feelings of resentment children often feel when being disciplined by anyone but a natural parent. Like it or not, this is how a child's system of justice works.

7. You may have felt confused about where you belonged. Living with a stepfather or stepmother while the biological mother or father lives elsewhere can be very confusing for a child. Young children in particular are bewildered by a system which shuffles them back and forth between dual homes. As an adult they may continue to be confused.

DAMAGE ON TOP OF DAMAGE

Any of the above conflicts—and more—can aggravate the damage children of divorce have already sustained. Not only does divorce itself force children to make major social and emotional adjustments at a stage in life when they are least equipped to do so, but being forced to adjust to a new home with stepparents and stepchildren can be equally or more demanding.

My own situation was not quite so problematic. My stepfather had been single and had no prior experience as a parent. Consequently, he felt so "green" as far as parenting was concerned that he pretty much left all discipline to my mother and set about building a simple friendship with my brother and me.

This helped a lot. But we still had this stranger to contend with in our household. What was he like? Where were his vulnerable points? How much would he take? This caused a lot of insecurity and forced me (I thought) to be extra cautious. And, don't forget, these adjustments were forced on top of the recent separation from my father. My life had already been turned upside down; now, suddenly, a completely new lifestyle was imposed on me.

To a large extent, the impact of living in a blended family depends on your age at the time the remarriage occurred. There is no ideal time to gain a stepparent, just as there is no ideal time to get divorced. But very young children—say, under five years of age—are not yet fully aware of what is going on. Young adults, those in college or who are about to leave home anyway, tend to adjust more easily because they are about to complete the process of separating from home life anyway.

The critically difficult period in terms of long-range damage is from just after puberty to around seventeen or eighteen years of age. At this age, the child is maximally aware of what is going on and is beginning the transition from childhood to adulthood. At this age, children are especially in need of a stable homefront. When the rules are suddenly changed or a new system of discipline is imposed, the normal sequence of development, including the need to individuate or pull away from the rest of the family, is disturbed. Rebellion is likely to intensify during this time, and this attitude of rebellion can carry over to adulthood. Many ACODs, therefore, undergo a protracted "adolescent phase."

Personality conflicts are also greatest at this stage. It is hard enough doing battle with your natural parents as you try to become your own person. A flesh-and-blood connection may allow for more tolerance than you get with stepkin. Emotional withdrawal is likely to be severely punished, or at least viewed unfavorably, and this intensifies a sense of rejection that becomes deeply rooted in your psyche.

I well remember some of the conflicts into which I was thrown. While I did not at first wholeheartedly embrace my stepfather when he married my mother, I soon began to value and respect him. Without realizing it, I would say nice things about him when visiting my father, who would then become openly irritated by this "betrayal." I felt trapped. I did not want my father's disapproval, yet I felt a certain growing loyalty toward my stepfather. This set up an inner dissonance that I had difficulty resolving. After such visits, I found myself trying hard to find fault with my stepfather, feeling the need to pull him down so that he did not appear better than my natural father. To do otherwise felt disloyal, although it did a great disservice to my kind and decent stepfather.

This inner dissonance had its effects on me in later life. I would easily become suspicious of authority figures I respected. I kept feeling I was betraying someone else, someone I should put above others. Not until I saw the connection between what I was doing as an adult and the loyalty conflict between my father and stepfather was I able to stop undermining my relationship with authority figures.

THE STARTING POINT OF HEALING

The evidence is clear: Divorce leaves scars, and facing those scars must be the starting point of healing. In chapters to come I will outline some specific strategies for overcoming the long-term damage divorce leaves on a child. But before I proceed, I want to share a personal word here about the scars my parents' divorce left in me and to point to one very important source of healing—one that in many ways was the key to my own recovery.

My parents divorced when I was twelve. Even though their marriage had always been stormy, the last thing I wanted was for them to separate—let alone divorce. On three occasions they separated briefly before the final breakup of our home, and all three were a taste of hell for me.

The evidence is clear: Divorce leaves scars, and facing those scars must be the starting point of healing.

The anxiety I experienced during those years is impossible to describe in words. Because I had been raised to believe that boys don't show their feelings, I dared not cry or talk about my pain. In moments of weakness or in the privacy of my bedroom, I would allow the tears to flow—often under the blankets so that no one could hear me. But this was always followed by an intense shame at being so weak and a resolve not to be so foolish.

Over the months and years that followed I developed an abhorrence for tears. I tried to avoid sad movies or seeing injured animals because I was tenderhearted by nature and easily moved by the pain of others. If crying caught me unawares and a tear trickled down my face, I would quickly dab it away and make sure no one saw me doing it. I became quite deft at tear wiping.

Going to church was a particular problem. For one period of my adolescence we had a preacher at our little church who always ended his sermons with a "tear-jerker." He obviously believed that his sermon would have more spiritual impact if he could suck a few tears from the congregation. He never ended with a happy story.

And that man was good! How he did it still amazes me today. He must have had the largest collection of "sob stories" (as I called them) in the entire world.

I used to cringe when this preacher began to wind up his message. I could smell it coming. As soon as he started his sob story, I would distract myself and try not to listen. I counted window panes high up at the front. I counted bricks in the side walls. I looked for flies (and we had lots of them in South Africa) to divert my thoughts. I tried to guess how high the ceiling was—anything to get my mind off his story.

Most of the time, despite my efforts at distraction, I would get hooked, and a tear or two would begin to roll embarrassingly down my cheek. How thankful I was that the preacher always prayed immediately after his sob stories! He did it to drive his point home. But for me, those prayers afforded a welcome opportunity to flick away any tears and put on my "I'm too strong to cry" face.

IT'S NEVER TOO LATE TO CRY

Why did I find it so hard to cry? My resistance to tears was a way of denying my emotional pain. I didn't want to face how much I hurt. In retrospect I see that I was probably depressed all through my adolescent years, following the disintegration of our home, but I would never admit it myself or to anyone else.

Then I began my career as a psychotherapist and discovered that by repressing this pain I was making it worse. I began to deal with it more directly. One day I just decided that crying was healthy. I realized that to cry publicly was a strength, not a weakness, and I determined to overcome my aversion to tears. Gradually I learned to respond to incipient tears with less shame and more courage. Then my mother died after a brief struggle with cancer, and I finally gave up the struggle to suppress my tears. Healing was on its way.

Today I see that the freedom to cry is a great tonic. I cry when I need to and recommend this response to my patients as a healthy and necessary component of complete wholeness. I cry publicly if I am moved, and I don't feel ashamed of it, as many of my students will attest. I also cry about my childhood experience of divorce.

I have discovered that *it is never too late to cry*. Crying is a part of the grieving process. It helps us to let go of the past. Most children of divorce spend their time and energy trying to recover that which was lost in their childhoods. They seek love from surrogate parents and affirmation from bosses who have replaced their mothers or fathers as authority figures. They scramble for self-respect, trying to please everyone who demands something from them. They waste many hours fantasizing that somehow their parents will get together again or wishing that the divorce had never happened.

What they really need to do is grieve their losses and *cry*. Cry over what they have lost as a child—then let it go. Cry over an absent father—then stop trying to replace him. Cry over the help that they never received—and find it now in new relationships. Cry over the changes they were forced to make as children—and forgive those who forced the changes. Cry over their shattered dreams, their lost hopes, their moments of despair—and create new ones for themselves.

I believe that as a culture we have lost our ability to grieve, and thus we deprive ourselves of a great healing force. We rush to replace our losses or to find substitutes for what we have lost before we have truly let go or mourned our loss. This is the cause of much resentment—the cancer of the emotions.

Crying does many good things for us. In a sense, it "washes away" our hurts. It restores balance. Most important, it helps bring us to the place that we can "let go" of lost dreams or shattered hopes.

This is the starting point of healing for the adult child of divorce. You must begin by facing your scars—admitting, as honestly as you can, the sadness of all that has happened to you. You must bring it out into the light where it can no longer frighten you and where you can feel your anger, resentment, hopelessness, and despair.

Then take the time to cry over what you have lost. Don't rush to make up for your losses. Don't dream of a day when all will be right again. Don't short-circuit your grieving. Just accept that what is past is past. Your mourning will soon give way to new life, just as winter gives way to spring.

I take great comfort in recalling that Jesus knew how to cry over his sorrows also. Grief and mourning were part of his human experience. He wept over the death of Lazarus, the brother of Mary (John 11:35) and over the city of Jerusalem (Luke 19:41). To me, this fact attests to the truth that Jesus was an emotionally healthy person. Some have called Jesus' mourning the "divine sympathy." I think it is more. I think Jesus wanted to give us a model for healthy grieving.

If Jesus can cry, so can I. And so can you. Grieving may well need to be your first step in learning how to let go of your unfortunate past.

Personal Inventory

3

How Do You Feel about Your Parents or Stepparents?

Deep down, how do you feel about your parents? Many ACODs avoid confronting these feelings because they are negative and too painful to bear. Others have never stopped to reflect on how they really feel about their mother, father, stepmother, or stepfather. For years they have suppressed or even repressed these feelings.

The purpose of this personal inventory is to help you get in touch with these feelings. The better you understand them, the quicker your recovery will be. Don't be afraid to confront how you really feel—only good will come from it.

As you read the statements below, reflect on what you are *feeling*, not just on the facts about your childhood. Don't rush the test. If, after some reflection on a particular item, you feel overwhelmed by your emotion, set the book aside for a while and give yourself the chance to let your feelings sink in. Then return to the personal inventory and continue.

Respond to each item as carefully as you can, first for your father (or stepfather) and then for your mother (or stepmother). Use the following rating scale and enter the number that best fits your feelings:

    0 = Rarely or none of the time
    1 = Some of the time
    2 = Most of the time

    Rating for Mother _____ Rating for Father_____

1. My father/mother embarrassed me with his/her behavior.
    Mother _____ Father _____

2. I feel angry whenever I think about my father/mother.

   Mother _____   Father _____

3. My father/mother is very demanding and overpowering.

   Mother _____   Father _____

4. I am always worrying about what my father/mother would think about my behaviors or accomplishments.

   Mother _____   Father _____

5. I believe that my father/mother really doesn't understand me.

   Mother _____   Father _____

6. I really believe that I hate or hated my father/mother.

   Mother _____   Father _____

7. I often wish I had had a different father/mother.

   Mother _____   Father _____

8. I feel that I have no love feelings for my father/mother.

   Mother _____   Father _____

9. My father/mother listened to and took my feelings into account when making decisions.

   Mother _____   Father _____

10. I did not enjoy being with my father/mother.

    Mother _____   Father _____

11. I feel that I could not really trust my father/mother.

    Mother _____   Father _____

12. I believe or believed that everyone else had a father/mother who was more loving, accepting, and understanding than mine.

    Mother _____   Father _____

TOTAL SCORE :

Mother _____   Father _____

INTERPRETING PERSONAL INVENTORY THREE

There is really no one way to determine what a "safe" score is on this inventory. Its purpose is to help you reflect on your feelings rather than to measure them precisely. For your guidance, however, the following interpretations can be made for various score levels.

Range   Interpretation

0–4   This score is so low that either you had a near-perfect parent—or you are not being honest about how you feel toward him or her.

5–8   Your feelings about this parent are quite normal. Your score indicates that you only occasionally became angry toward him/her or experienced mild feelings of disillusionment.

9–12   Your feelings are somewhat negative and may reflect some residual animosity or disappointment toward this parent.

13–18   Your feelings indicate a moderate level of anger and several unresolved issues surrounding your relationship with your parent or stepparent. You may need some help in resolving your feelings.

19–24   You are acknowledging a high level of anger and resentment toward your parent or stepparent. Your relationship may be so severely strained that you need professional help in resolving your feelings.

Part Two

Beginning Your Recovery

ALL HEALING HAS A BEGINNING, a point in time when you resolve to start the recovery process. You make the conscious choice—a commitment of your will—to find a way out of your present state. That point, that decision, is the beginning of a lifelong process of growth.

Are you willing to start? I suggest that you write down, in your Bible or diary, a commencement statement: "Today, (date and time), I choose to begin my healing." Look back at this written commitment from time to time; you will find it carries you through some rough spots. Whatever happens, however painful the discoveries you make about yourself, no matter how tough the going gets, remind yourself of your decision and resolve to see it through. You *can* make it!

Now, on to recovery. In this part of the book I will focus on its beginning stages. First, as an ACOD you probably have a lot of unfinished business to attend to. Your growth may have been temporarily halted. Your development may have been sidetracked. You may have learned a few bad emotional habits. Whatever the problem, healing begins when you use psychological *and* spiritual resources to pinpoint your unfinished business and begin to take care of it. Then you can move on to resolving your hurt, anger, and shame and learning to take care of yourself in a healthy and responsible way.

But I urge you—don't try to do it by yourself. Instead, reach out and grasp the hand of the "Man of sorrows" who was also "acquainted with grief" (see Isaiah 53:3). Once you have grasped his hand, you'll discover that he holds on to you more firmly than you could ever hold on to him.

CHAPTER 4

Facing Your Unfinished Business

E VERY ADULT CHILD OF divorce has unfinished business in his or her life. One of the major reasons childhood divorce has such an impact on adult life is that it begins a process but doesn't finish it. It turns your life topsy-turvy and then leaves you dangling in midair with many issues remaining unresolved. This state of "incompleteness" often carries over into adulthood.

Having unfinished business doesn't mean you are unable to function. You may even be a high achiever, successful in your chosen pursuit and powerful in influence. Nevertheless, the unfinished business of your parents' divorce is no doubt lurking in the shadows of your life, waiting for your attention. Only when you attend to this business will you be complete and healthy again.

Why are you as an ACOD especially likely to have unfinished business in your life?

First, the *pain* of your family's disintegration probably hit you at an age when you didn't have the resources to handle it. In order to cope, chances are that you either denied your pain or pushed it deep within your psyche so that it was out of your awareness. Either way, that pain is probably still around because it was never handled adequately. I will explore some of the likely consequences of denial and repression in the next chapter.

Second, you were probably forced to make more adjustments than you could handle before, during, and after the divorce. You had to accept new circumstances, change homes, go to a new school, meet new friends, lose old ones. You began the process of making adjustments, but chances are there were too many to process. There were too many loose ends; too much was left unfinished. As a result, memories remain unhealed. After all the turmoil of that period of your life, you are left with more questions than answers.

The unfinished business of your parents' divorce is no doubt lurking in the shadows of your life, waiting for your attention. Only when you attend to this business will you be complete and healthy again.

I remember these feelings well. Too much happened too fast.

"Pack your things; we're leaving," my mother said to me. "It's not the end of the world," she reassured me as I started crying. Her decision to leave my father seemed very much on the spur of the moment, although she told me in later years that she had thought about it for a long time. But I was left with deep feelings of confusion and bewilderment.

It was all too sudden. I had homework to do, things to get ready for school the next day, friends waiting for me to come and play, plans for the weekend. How could these all be dumped like this? I knew my mother had been unhappy for a long time. So had I, but how was running away going to solve anything? I tried pleading with her. Would she reconsider her actions? Couldn't she see I was frightened? All I got was, "You are too young to understand these matters—pack your suitcase."

I can still feel the pain in my chest when I recall that day. My heart still aches, even though it happened so long ago. This is part of the *unfinished business* I am still struggling with.

My mother, younger brother, and I moved to a hotel temporarily, then finally to another house in another neighborhood. Every move forced a new set of adjustments, and I was never given the time or support I needed to work through the separation from old friends, old habits, old games, and old routines. There was just too much change, too much anxiety.

Even today, I don't like change very much. I prefer things to be stable, even boring. I become anxious when the boat of life rocks too much. The many unfinished tasks and experiences of my childhood divorce have left their imprint on my life.

Your story may be much the same as mine. You, too, may be limping through your life with the feeling that many issues are waiting for closure, waiting to be completed. Chances are, your development as a child was interrupted. Your emotional security did not jell. You still don't have answers to so many old "whys." And you feel somehow incomplete, not fully grown up—like you've gotten stuck somewhere. You have! That's the whole point of beginning your recovery by facing unfinished business.

DIVORCE DISRUPTS NORMAL DEVELOPMENT

Still another reason you as an ACOD are likely to have unfinished business is that normal human development proceeds step by step, in stages, and divorce often interrupts this process. Healthy emotional growth requires us to complete the developmental demands of one stage of life before moving to the next. If the developmental issues of a particular stage are not handled satisfactorily, this form of "unfinished business" will interfere with our progress in the next stage. We may even "get stuck" at a particular point and be unable to grow any further emotionally.

Every adolescent, for instance, has to go through a period where he or she begins to develop a sense of separation from the rest of the family. Psychologists call this "individuation," the process of becoming one's individual self. If this separation doesn't take place at the right time (usually between fourteen and sixteen years of age) the adolescent moves into young adulthood too dependent on the parents and family.

It's the same when learning any skill or sport. You begin with the basics, master them, then move to master the next level of skill. If you fail to master the skills of one level, the next level will be almost impossible to achieve.

This "sequential mastery" of life skills and emotional development is absolutely essential to achieving emotional maturity.

Unfortunately, divorce can interfere with this normal development in children, leaving uncompleted issues from one stage that carry over and interfere with the next.

If the developmental issues of a particular stage are not handled satisfactorily, this form of "unfinished business" will interfere with our progress in the next stage. We may even "get stuck" at a particular point and be unable to grow any further emotionally.

CASANDRA'S STORY

I recall several years ago reading the personal diary of a patient who was an adult child of divorce. All through her parents' divorce, starting at age ten, Casandra kept a careful record of her emotions and experiences, and she continued to write about them until she was well into her twenties. She showed them to me, hoping that it would help me understand her life story.

Casandra was an attractive, expressive child. She describes herself as having had long brown hair, an impish glint in her eyes, a quick wit, and a sensitive spirit—that is, she felt things deeply. Here is a selection of her diary entries immediately following her parents' separation:

July 20, 1977. It is a beautiful summer day. School is out, so I thought we would go to the beach. Mommy promised we would, because she likes the beach also, but she was sad all day, so I didn't ask to go. I sat in my room most of the time and played with my dolls. Then Mommy came and told me that Daddy wasn't coming home today. He doesn't want to live with us anymore. He's living somewhere else. I really don't understand why. Doesn't he love me? I thought things were getting better. They used to fight a lot, but it's been better lately. I cried and cried in my room. I need my dad, but maybe I did something he didn't like.

August 15, 1977. I haven't seen my dad for a week. He used to come by every day after work. I rushed to finish my schoolwork, tidy my room, and wait for him, but he didn't come. Every day I waited. Then he called to say he was sorry. "Too much work," he said. "Wasn't feeling well," he said. I hurt so bad I'm going to die. Why do people I love always leave?

December 16, 1977. It's getting near Christmas. Dad came by to give me some Christmas shopping money yesterday, but he didn't stay long. Says that he gets uncomfortable being in our house. I said we could go eat out, but he was in a hurry. He only comes once a week or every two weeks. He doesn't like to talk much. He fidgets and moves around a lot. I want to tell him how I hurt—about the pain in my heart. I want him to know how I don't sleep at nights and how I dream that he is home again. I want to ask him whether he thinks it's all Mommy's fault. I think about him a lot, so it's hard to concentrate on school stuff.

April 10, 1978. I'm beginning to think that I made Mommy and Daddy get a divorce. Mommy says it was because Daddy got a girlfriend, but I think if I hadn't been a problem, Daddy would have stayed. I've been thinking a lot about the bad things I did, like never cleaning my room, throwing things about, or screaming a lot. Maybe I gave Daddy too much to worry about. It still hurts. When will it go away? I think I'm starting to hate my dad. He doesn't care anymore. His girlfriend has children, and he seems to spend more time with them.

June 4, 1978. I had a dream last night. It was that Daddy came to the door all dressed up in a black dress suit like you see in the movies. We had a date. I put on a new dress and we went out to a movie and dinner. He treated me like I was grownup. We talked and laughed—then something woke me up. I tried to get back to sleep and go back to my dream. You can't ever do that. It doesn't work. I lay awake thinking about Dad. I don't know if I love him or hate him. He's left me for someone else. I don't understand this. Mommy tells me Daddy isn't paying for my expenses like he said he would. How does he think this makes me feel? I wonder if God is like my dad. Does he say he loves you and then throw you away? Does he say he will come and visit you and then never come? If God doesn't love you, then I guess nobody really loves you.

As you can see, Casandra's focus at this point was on her father and his absence. She was struggling to figure out how he could say he loved her, yet not be in her life. Slowly she was learning to distrust all men, to believe that they promise one thing but deliver another. She was also beginning to generalize this distrust to God—a very important point to remember. In later life, this was to be a significant piece of "unfinished business" for her. Lumping both God and men together as untrustworthy, unloving, and unapproachable got in the way of her personal life and her spiritual pilgrimage. In her mid-twenties her diary had the following entry:

> *March 3, 1988.* God, where are you when I need you? You say you will always be there for me, but I don't think I can ever recall a time when I really called out to you that you rescued me. I know that the stuff I gripe about is petty, but I always feel like I'm dealing with my real father. Oh God, how it hurts not to have someone who really loves you. Mom is there, I know, but I sort of take her love for granted. After all, she gave birth to me, so what else could she do? But to have someone really love you—and be there whenever you need them—seems so hard. What makes me even angrier is that you say you love me. I've tried to please you all my life. Sunday School. Church. I pray. I give what I can. What more must I do to make you happy with me? Why do I keep mixing you up with my dad? His face is what I see every time I try to pray to you.

This confusion of identity and projection of the blame and shortcomings of an absent father onto God is quite common. Unfortunately, its dynamic lies deep within the personality. Several years of therapy may be required before Casandra feels like she can separate God from her father. And then she will have the work of coming to understand that her father is not representative of all men and that it is possible to build a loving, trusting relationship with a man that is free of distrust. For Casandra this will open up a whole new life. She will literally feel that she has been "born anew."

In a sense, this whole book is about healing the unfinished business of divorce. Some of this unfinished business is serious enough to warrant more in-depth treatment in separate chapters. At this point, however, I want to outline some of the more general issues of unfinished business and to point the way toward their resolution.

COMING TO TERMS WITH
YOUR MALE OR FEMALE IDENTITY

As I discussed in chapter 2, divorce tends to affect the sexes differently, and these effects have to do primarily with the absence of the father. Even if the divorce or separation is mutually agreed upon or if the wife is the instigator of the divorce, custody is normally granted to the mother. And this leaves children without a strong male figure with whom to identify.

UNFINISHED BUSINESS FOR BOYS AND MEN

Much has been written on the psychological problems a boy can develop because of the absence of either parent. Any of these can become unfinished business for him as an adult.

---

*Even in this enlightened age, boys are taught to be "tough"
and not to show their feelings. As a consequence, they are
especially prone to have unfinished business that involves
unacknowledged feelings.*

In addition to these specific difficulties, men may have special problems coping with other kinds of unfinished business because of the way they are socialized. Even in this "enlightened" age, boys are taught to be "tough" and not to show their feelings. As a consequence, boys often go to great lengths to avoid expressing their pain. Instead, they push their feelings under, even to the point that they themselves are no longer aware of them. Men are especially

---

How Divorce Can Affect Boys

1. He may develop gender-identity problems, displaying either "feminine" or effeminate traits (such as preoccupation with dolls, talking in a high voice, or dressing in girls' clothes) or exaggerated "masculine" ones (resorting to "macho" talk and behavior).
2. He may develop homosexual feelings or orientation.
3. He may become overly dependent on mother ("mama's boy").
4. He may overidentify with other males, becoming involved in gangs or men's clubs.
5. He may repress significant feelings and become unable to show (or even feel) emotion.
6. He may lack a clear understanding about how to function as a healthy male.
7. He may have great difficulty relating to women.
8. He may become intolerant of negative emotions and natural expressions of pain (such as crying).
9. Resentment of the mother's role may lead to a distorted view of women.
10. He may overidentify with the absent father by becoming totally like him, mimicking his style and behavior.
11. He may harbor feelings of anger and resentment toward his father.

---

prone to have unfinished business that involves unacknowledged feelings—grief work, intimacy problems, and so forth. I will address some of these issues later in this chapter.

UNFINISHED BUSINESS FOR WOMEN AND GIRLS

Women, too, need exposure to both parents in order to mature naturally—to help them learn how to relate to men and to learn about themselves as women. A father's comments, touch, feedback,

How Divorce Can Affect Girls

1. She may incessantly seek affirmation from loving males to bolster her sagging sense of identity as a woman.
2. She may use sex as a way of obtaining love from men.
3. She may sabotage her friendships with men by becoming jealous or suspicious.
4. She may have difficulty establishing lasting, gratifying, adult, heterosexual relationships, assuming that only female relationships can be trusted.
5. She may develop a pervasive feeling of rejection, assuming that because she is not smart, pretty, sporty, or good enough to warrant a father's acceptance, she is not good enough to be accepted by anyone else.
6. She may later reject identification with her mother, even though they were close at the time of the divorce, blaming her mother for what she is now experiencing as a deficit in her relationships. "I don't want to be like my mother" is a common complaint.
7. She may generally have difficulties relating to males—seeking male attention too often, becoming inappropriately "forward," prematurely rejecting relationships, lacking confidence in her ability to have a lasting marriage, or having difficulty working through conflicts with her spouse.[1]
8. She may be more prone to substance abuse, to running away from home, or to engaging in delinquent or self-destructive behaviors such as truancy, shoplifting, or eating disorders.[2]

and demonstrated love are all important for a girl's complete psychological development. A mother's presence models appropriate feminine behavior and reactions.

A girl brought up without a father because of a divorce may have the tendencies listed above.

A particularly devastating source of "unfinished business" arises when a mother leaves her marriage for another relationship and abandons the daughter, so to speak, to the father. Since this is not the "typical" pattern, it communicates a particularly serious rejection. Such scenarios are becoming more common as women feel the need to pursue their own careers or seek "a life for themselves."

When a girl is deprived of her mother, and especially if there are no other significant female mentors in her life, she can develop any of several problems.

Girls without Mothers

1. She may experience deep feelings of intense rejection and fears of further rejection all through life. (The mother-daughter bond is so fundamental that no amount of logic or rational explanation can overcome a deficiency here.)
2. She may feel strong hostility toward all mother figures.
3. She may suffer intense guilt feelings based on the fear that she was the cause of her mother's rejection.
4. She may become overdependent on all mother figures, unrealistically expecting that they will become substitute mothers for her.
5. She may be especially prone to anxiety states, especially panic disorders that involve sweating, palpitations, trembling, and agitation.
6. She may develop assorted fears about becoming sick or incapacitated and having no one to care for her.
7. She may become obsessed with mothers and mothering and display intense anger at any mother she sees as inadequate.
8. She may overcompensate as a mother herself, suppressing even the slightest thought that she might want to run away from her own children.
9. She may be unable to cope with separation anxiety, becoming intensely fearful whenever a husband or child comes home later than expected or feeling extremely uncomfortable when visiting strange places or finding herself alone.

TENDING TO UNFINISHED "GENDER BUSINESS"

The damage done to a child of either sex by the absence of or rejection by a parent is not easily undone. Confusion regarding male-female roles is almost certain to develop, and formal therapy may be required to correct serious problems of gender identification. Nevertheless, just making the connection between what happened then and what is happening now can mark the start of healing. The suggestions contained in chapter 7, "Rewriting Your Life-Script" can help you come to terms with your identity as a man or a woman.

Women, too, need exposure to both parents in order to mature naturally—to help them learn how to relate to men and to learn about themselves as women.

COPING WITH GRIEF

Most unfinished business for the ACOD, of course, is not inherently gender-related, although some problems do pose particular problems for one sex or the other. Grief-related problems, for instance, can develop in either men or women, although men may have particular difficulty in this area because they are more likely to deny or bury their feelings.

The grief that follows divorce is not the same as the grief that follows death. In many ways, I think it is worse. The grief following the death of a parent is shared by many. In divorce, it is borne disproportionately by the children. Death involves an identifiable mourning ritual and a grief process that is supported by our culture. This is not true for divorce, even though the loss may be just as severe. In addition, the finality of death forces the grieving response. In divorce, the "death" may drag on over months and years and be compounded by loss after loss, so actual grieving never has a chance to get underway. In addition, the child's ongoing wish to restore the marriage may put off the onset of grieving or prevent its completion altogether.

To be emotionally healthy, one must grieve life's losses—and divorce certainly represents a loss to children. Mourning is a process of "letting go." As we reflect upon the loss, become sad, and grieve, we slowly come to accept the reality of the loss. This helps us release the lost object or person and eventually move on with our lives.

The grief that follows divorce is not the same as the grief that follows death. In many ways, I think it is worse.

Every loss, therefore, whether it is real and tangible (like the loss of a loved one in death) or abstract and symbolic (like the loss of someone's esteem or love), needs to be grieved. If we don't grieve our losses in a healthy way, we unconsciously cling to them, and over time these ungrieved losses accumulate in unconscious memory. They may compound and exaggerate other, minor losses, causing them to loom as major tragedies. And they invariably trigger depression and feed self-pity: "Life is terrible, God doesn't love me. Everything bad always happens to me. Look how I'm always the one to get hurt."

It is quite common for boys and girls who experience divorce to reach adulthood with "grief work" to be done. Until they have taken care of this unfinished business, they may be unable to grieve any loss. At the same time, without realizing it, they may become more prone to sadness and depression, yet lack the ability to identify the source of their sadness and thus put it behind them.

Much has been written elsewhere about the grieving process, so I will not go into detail about it here. The unfinished business for you as an ACOD has to do with recognizing your grief, facing the reality of your loss or losses, and allowing yourself to mourn them. The suggestions listed later in this chapter under "Recovering the Sense That Your Feelings Count" can help you do this.

BUILDING INTIMACY

Fear of rejection is a very real and pervasive consequence that divorce has on children. After all, if one parent has already left, it's natural for a child to fear that the remaining parent may leave also.

I clearly remember lying awake at night, worrying whether my mother would still be there in the morning. My twelve-year-old mind couldn't quite figure out all the ramifications of the separation. All I knew was anxiety and the fear of being abandoned again.

This fear of abandonment may lead some children to "test" their parents' tolerance for disobedient behavior. To gain reassurance that they are not going to be abandoned, they push disruptive behavior to the limit.

Another and perhaps more pervasive way of handling the fear of further rejection, especially in boys, is to initiate the rejection yourself. I recall doing this myself. The game is to "keep people at a distance," including parents, friends, and relatives. This way you don't have to fear abandonment because you are already abandoned; you try to make your worst fear a reality so that it no longer has power over you. Besides, being the one who does the rejecting always feels better than being the one who is rejected.

A pervasive way of handling the fear of further rejection is to initiate the rejection yourself. The game is to "keep people at a distance."

But there is a price for this pseudo-security. It prevents you from learning how to build intimacy and how to risk the pain of close relationships. Having been "burned" once, you are not about to be burned again, so you push everybody away.

Such tactics, of course, can have serious consequences for dating, marrying, parenting, and generally being happy. And here, also, the suggestions contained in chapter 7 and elsewhere in this book can help you take steps toward avoiding defensive, intimacy-destroying behavior.

REPAIRING YOUR SELF-ESTEEM

Problems of self-esteem are among the most common challenges adult children of divorce must face, and I will address self-esteem issues at several points throughout the book. But the term self-esteem has been so widely used and misused over the past few decades that I want to clarify exactly what I mean when I use it.

Building a sense of personal value is hard enough for any child in our Western world. Value tends to be measured either by how a person looks or by how he or she performs. Very few of us enter adulthood with an honest "self-picture" or are entirely free from hateful or rejecting feelings about ourselves. We grow up convinced that somehow we just don't pass muster—and that assumption is inherently unhealthy.

The foundations of healthy self-esteem are laid in childhood. Unfortunately, our negative self-perceptions also begin early in our lives, and the experience of divorce can be especially damaging to how we see ourselves.

But it is equally unhealthy to spend all our energy searching for a special, exalted feeling about ourselves. And that is exactly how our culture tends to interpret self-esteem. Too often, the search for "self-esteem" borders on narcissism—it becomes a quest to feel that we are important and popular and have the potential to achieve anything we like. Such an effort leads to excessive interest in our own appearance or performance, inordinate competitiveness, and a reduced ability to love and accept others. A self-esteem based on an exaggerated self-importance cannot be healthy.

So what is healthy self-esteem? I propose that we think of it as the *absence of self-hate and self-rejection, accompanied by a high level of self-acceptance.*[3] We have a healthy self-esteem when we stop trying to be someone else, when we are content to be who God has created us to be. This is the import of the biblical advice, found in Romans 12:3, that we are not to think of ourselves "more highly than [we] ought," but to think "soberly," or honestly. We must be *truthful* in our self-thoughts.

Healthy self-esteem, therefore, must involve two essential feelings about ourselves: *an accurate self-image* with no distortions—either positive or negative, and *complete self-acceptance.*

The foundations of such healthy self-esteem are laid in childhood. Unfortunately, our negative self-perceptions also begin early in life, and the experience of divorce can be especially damaging to how we see ourselves. Divorce can harm our self-esteem in several ways.

Divorce and Self-Esteem

1. The divorce experience may distort a child's image of his or her own value.
2. A child may believe that he or she caused the divorce and must therefore be an unworthy person. (This assumption is quite common and is related to a child's natural self-centeredness; children tend to assume that everything that happens is directly related to them.)
3. Parents are often too much in conflict with each other to work at helping the child develop an accurate sense of who he or she really is.
4. A child often feels "different" because of the divorce. This difference is interpreted as "inferior," no matter how many other children are in the same predicament.
5. Economic hardships may cause a child to feel rejected by others or not able to live up to the standards of peers.
6. If one parent develops a bad reputation in the community because of antisocial or "scandalous" behavior, the divorce may draw attention in a way that makes the child feel stigmatized. The child may feel ashamed to be connected to such a parent.
7. Since young children judge their worth by what a parent thinks of them, parents who are too wrapped up in their own problems to communicate a sense that they are valued can cause a child to undervalue himself or herself.
8. The divorce may be so full of conflict that the parents project anger and displeasure onto the children, leading the children to assume something must be wrong with them.
9. Separation unavoidably conveys feelings of rejection to a child.

At this point in my life, I can clearly identify a key set of events that severely disturbed the development of my own self-esteem. For several years following my parents' divorce, I had to rely on friends and relatives for help in many areas of my life because my mother was overwhelmed by her own problems. I had to depend on other people to take me to school activities, holiday outings, special family gatherings, and even on vacation.

During that time, I was learning to play the classical guitar. A special competition was being held in a large city thirty miles away, and several of us boys were to participate. My mother couldn't take me, so she arranged for me to go along with one of the other parents. I hardly knew the other boy—I didn't even like him—but I had no choice but to tag along.

We left early in the morning, and I felt like an intruder from the beginning. The family stopped to visit an aunt on the way, and I sat in the back of the car by myself. I felt that nobody wanted me—that I didn't belong anywhere. After we performed at the morning concert, we went to lunch. I didn't have enough money to pay for myself, so the other mother paid for me. Between the afternoon and evening sessions, we went to someone's house (I never found out whose house it was). And once again I felt like an outcast—the most unwanted kid in all the world.

There were several such events during the period following my parents' separation. They all had the same effect: they left me feeling that I didn't belong, that something was wrong with me, that I didn't deserve anything good. Over a period of time, these feelings began to erode my sense of value, to turn my self-esteem to self-rejection and self-hate. Undoing that damage has taken most of a lifetime—and I still have work to do in this area.

As an adult child of divorce, you are almost certain to have some difficulties in the area of self-esteem. Personal Inventory Four at the end of this chapter can help you gain a better understanding of your self-feelings. It covers several important aspects of your self-image, as well as your feelings about this image. It also explores how your parents may have contributed to your distorted self-image and how you compare yourself to others. The interpretation of your score is quite straightforward and will help you get a feel for what your particular self-image problems may be. Then, once you have this improved self-understanding, you can begin to do some repair work on your self-esteem.

Now, I do not want to give the impression that fixing a serious self-esteem problem is easy; it's not. Building a truthful picture of yourself and a higher level of self-acceptance will take some hard work, and it will not happen overnight. But conscientiously applying the following principles can take you a long way toward raising the level of your self-esteem.

1. Begin by facing facts and "owning" the problem. Admit to yourself that your damaged self-image had its origin in your childhood, but that it's your problem now. Don't waste time trying to explain it in terms of your present problems. And resist the temptation either to make excuses for your parents or to hold them responsible for your present feelings. Just face facts: Your parents could have been more sensitive to how you were feeling. They could have corrected the distortions that were taking shape by encouraging you to talk about your self-feelings. But they didn't! If you have any anger toward your parents for failing you in this regard, then consider your anger another piece of unfinished business and read my discussion in the next chapter about handling anger. But your main task at this point is to take responsibility for how you feel about yourself now. *You* are the only one who can begin to reshape your self-image.

Building a true self-image requires that you be honest about yourself. Consciously set aside both false modesty and hypercriticism and let the true picture of a human being with both weaknesses and strengths emerge.

2. Then start to build a more accurate internal picture of yourself. Our self-esteem is derived from our self-image, that picture we carry of ourselves in our heads. A distorted self-image (usually negative) lies at the root of much self-hate.

There are several ways you can work to develop a more accurate self-image. Group therapy is usually the most powerful technique. In the relative safety of a small group of honest and accepting peers, you can begin to explore who you really are and develop the courage to be honest about yourself. But formal group therapy is not the only route to a clearer self-image. A support group, a close friend, or a loving spouse can also help you get a better idea of who you are. The one thing you do need is the insight of at least one other person; you can't paint a realistic self-portrait without a "mirror."

You will probably find that developing a more accurate self-image involves the following tasks. You must:

- set aside the distorted messages you received from your parents,
- correct the negative images you have internalized about yourself,
- understand that there are things about yourself you can't change,
- challenge irrational feelings that have developed about not being wanted or valued by others,
- discard negative mental "tapes" you keep playing for yourself: "Nobody really cares about me" or "I'm not worthy enough for others to love me."

In short, building a true self-image requires that you *be honest about yourself.* Consciously set aside both false modesty and hypercriticism and let the true picture of a human being with both weaknesses and strengths emerge.

3. As you discover more about who you really are, try to be more self-accepting. You need to work at becoming more comfortable with who you are. The more self-accepting you are, the more beautiful you will become to others.

Just look around you. Who do you know that you like very much? Who do you admire as being healthy and open? My guess is that it is someone who is basically self-accepting, who stands tall and says, in effect, "This is who I am—take it or leave it!" You will never have a healthy self-esteem until you become more self-accepting, especially about aspects of yourself that you can't change.

This admonition applies just as much to physical or external characteristics as it does to aspects of personality. Most problems of low self-esteem are contaminated by a wish that one could be taller, shorter, thinner, fatter, smarter, faster, stronger, prettier, handsomer, or wealthier. A few of these changes are possible, but most of them are not—at least without inordinate effort. If you *can* change something about yourself that you don't like—without sacrificing something else that is equally important to you—by all means go ahead and make the change. But stop fighting those aspects of yourself over which you have no control.

If your genes have made you too short for your liking, for example, what benefit is there in saying to yourself, "I will only be a valuable person if I am taller"? Instead, make it a point to stand tall in your spirit. Thank God for who you are.

4. Claim your spiritual identity. The Bible contains some basic information and advice concerning self-identify that can transform your life if you accept it. You are a child of God. This means you are worthwhile not because you are good or accomplished or successful, but *because God loves you.* In fact, you and I are so precious to God that he chose to share our human plight and then to sacrifice his life for the sole purpose of rescuing us from the mess we had made of things. I urge you to claim this privileged position as the foundation for your self-esteem. Once you internalize how much you are worth to God, you will have much more difficulty holding on to self-hate.

RECOVERING A SENSE THAT YOUR FEELINGS COUNT

Divorcing parents who are preoccupied with their own physical and emotional survival often neglect the feelings of their children. Their energies are drained by the many demands of the divorce conflict. This neglect sends a powerful message to the children: "Your feelings are not as important as my feelings. As soon as I have taken care of myself, I may be able to take care of you."

The children, deprived of time, care, attention, and especially a listening ear, begin to feel discounted. "What I feel doesn't really matter," I recall saying to myself many times. "If it did, my folks would pay attention." So I began to feel insignificant—not only at home, but everywhere. And not just insignificant—I also felt that somehow my feelings were *not valid*, that they didn't count at all. And if that were true, I might as well not exist.

"What I feel doesn't really matter,"
I recall saying to myself many times. "If it did,
my folks would pay attention to my feelings." So I began to
feel insignificant—not only at home, but everywhere.

I learned later, as an adult, that our feelings *are* a major part of who we are. Everything we do and think will affect our feelings, and our feelings in turn influence our thoughts and actions. In other words, we cannot ignore our feelings without "shutting down" a portion of ourselves. But how are we supposed to reconcile a life full of feelings with the deep-seated belief that whatever we feel doesn't matter?

That was a dilemma that haunted me for many years. And as a consequence, I entered adulthood with a reluctance to talk about myself; I didn't trust revealing myself to others. I even tried to avoid feeling anything at all. As a result, I had great difficulty defining my own identity. I would have intense feelings about something but be utterly unable to experience or express those feelings accurately. When I wanted to talk about, say, my sadness over some incident, I would just "clam up" and try to ignore the feeling.

But such feelings don't go away. They continue to affect us in ways that sometimes seem puzzling. Over time, the habit of discounting feelings results in a deep sense of estrangement. Independent thought becomes difficult because we lose faith in our own judgment and perception. And assertiveness is next to impossible, because we never really feel we have a right to express our thoughts or emotions in action.

How can you make your feelings count? Here are some suggestions:

1. Give up trying to recover your childhood feelings so you can express them now. There are those therapists who focus on this, believing that you can gain a new freedom by belatedly expressing your feelings. It's too late. They have lain there unrecognized too long and have already done their damage. Move on!

2. Learn how to recognize what you are feeling now and get these feelings into the open. Feelings *are* important. They are *signals,* important messengers about what is happening in your life. Once their message is delivered, they have served their purpose and can be forgotten. But first you must *hear them out.* This may be difficult if you've developed the habit of discounting your feelings. For this reason, you may need to follow a seemingly artificial process of analyzing what you feel and the possible reasons for it. For instance, you may feel vaguely troubled about what someone has said to you, and your first instinct may be to dismiss your unease. Instead, say to yourself—out loud, if necessary—"I am feeling down about something... now, let me discover what the problem is." Then go back over the conversation and see if you can pinpoint what triggered your feelings.

After a short exploration, you may realize that the uneasy feelings began right after your friend told you she was moving away. You are feeling sad because of an impending loss, and that sadness is a call for you to begin grieving this loss. If you heed its message—and that of other feelings you identify, you will gradually come to trust yourself more.

3. Get into the habit of talking about your feelings. I don't mean dump them unwittingly on everyone you encounter. No one likes people who dominate conversations with long catalogs of their emotions! But it is a good idea to seek out a close friend, a family member, or counselor for help in "talking out" what you are experiencing. You may also find it beneficial to write about what you are feeling. Expressing or "externalizing" our feelings maximizes their value as messengers; for some reason, they make more sense to us as we try to explain them to someone else or put them down on paper.

Sometimes it may help to talk about your feelings to the person causing them—especially if you are trying to build or maintain a relationship by improving your communication. But this is not always possible or advisable, nor is it necessary for your purposes here. What you really need is a sounding board, someone to help you understand your feelings and reinforce their validity.

An important part of learning to talk about your feelings is building a *vocabulary* for expressing them. Try to find the most accurate words to describe what you are feeling. If you feel deficient in this area, try using a thesaurus or other "word builder" to help you expand your feeling vocabulary. Start with one of the basic emotions, such as depression. Look up other words under this heading, then follow up by looking at some of the suggested alternative words. Look up the words; try to understand their nuances. Then write down some of the best ones and practice applying them to the way you feel.

Expressing or "externalizing" our feelings maximizes their value as messengers; for some reason, they make more sense to us as we try to explain them to someone else or put them down on paper.

---

4. Then move beyond the feeling into action. Remember, the point of expressing your feelings is to *clarify the reasons behind them and hear the message they bring.* There is a reason you feel the way you do. Ask yourself what it is. Then ask, "Does knowing the reason point me to a course of action?" If you are feeling frustrated because your life isn't going anywhere, continuing to feel frustrated has no purpose in itself whatsoever. Find out the cause of the frustration—then make some choices or initiate an action that will remove the frustration.

BALANCING AUTONOMY AND DEPENDENCE

Given the fact that most children of divorce are forced to individuate early—that is, their family breakup forces them to fend for themselves at an earlier stage than other children—you might expect them to be more independent, autonomous, self-reliant, and confident. This is not the case.

Most ACODs feign autonomy or self-reliance, when, in fact,
they desperately want to cling to others or be taken care of.

Most ACODs feign autonomy or self-reliance, when, in fact, they desperately want to cling to others or be taken care of. But because they feel cut off and isolated, they are afraid to let others know they are needy. Instead, they push people away, pretend nothing is wrong, and "go it alone."

We all need a *balance* between autonomy and dependence in our lives. There are times when we need to be self-reliant and times when we must lean on others. We should never be so rigid or defensive that we cannot reach out to touch or be touched by others, nor should we be so helpless that we cling to others and force them to make our decisions for us—either extreme is unhealthy.

But ACODs typically have difficulty finding the balance between the two extremes. To find out if this is true of you, why not work through Personal Inventory Five, at the end of this chapter, which is designed to give you an idea where you stand on the autonomy-dependence scale. Once you've done that, you can take action to make your life more balanced. Here are some suggestions to help you do that:

1. Try to balance your own needs. When you feel strong, make a point of reaching out to someone else who is hurting. When you feel weak, call up a friend and ask if you can share your feelings and get some help.

2. Be willing to assume the dependent role more often. Admitting need is not a sign of weakness. Men, especially, may need to open up the dependent side of their personality.

3. Be clear about what you need when you ask someone to help you or to just "be there" for you. Resist the temptation to dump your entire life in someone else's lap. Set boundaries for other people's time, advice, or presence, and let them know what those boundaries are.

4. Don't do unreasonable things when seeking to be dependent. For instance, the middle of the night is not the right time to call a friend and say, "I need to talk." Be considerate of the other person's needs as well.

5. Try to be as honest as you can when you are either seeking help or giving it. A true friend is an honest friend. But remember that honesty must be tempered with love.

6. Remember that the greatest comforter of all is God. If you have absolutely no one else to turn to—God is there for you. Even if you have lots of support—he is still there. According to the biblical record, he *longs* to give you comfort, but even here you must be willing to receive his comfort: "casting all your care upon him, for he cares for you" (1 Peter 5:7).

REDEFINING LOVE

Perhaps the most important bit of unfinished business for ACODs is that of rediscovering or redefining love. This is because the most significant damage divorce can do to a child is to damage the meaning of love.

Perhaps the most important bit of unfinished business for ACODs is that of rediscovering or redefining love.

Now, I am *not* saying that parents who divorce don't love their children! Most parents going through a divorce would adamantly assert their love, and many do their best to act it out through what they tell their children, what they give them, how much they sacrifice for them. Unfortunately, other aspects of divorce often combine to sabotage the child's *experience* of love. As a result, most ACODs say they have always felt unloved. And here they are referring to to the fact that many love messages are contradictory.

Children of divorce grow up in an environment that sends confusing messages about love. The parents might talk about love, but they don't model it well because of their own conflicts. In their pain, they may even do unloving things to each other and to their children, who are often dragged into the conflict and used as pawns in the battle. They are told they are loved but then used in selfish ways by parents. As a result, children learn that "love" is chaotic, confusing, painful, and sick. This sort of love pulls you apart, grinds you down, keeps you unbalanced, breeds resentment. And when that kind of love is your childhood model, you will find it very difficult to reach adulthood with a healthy understanding of love.

Healthy love builds a sense of stability and safety and sets the stage for warmth, inner peace, and happiness as an adult. If this understanding of love has been distorted by childhood experiences, it will need a lot of repair. Here are two ways you can start to rediscover and repair a damaged sense of love:

1. Begin by realizing that what you experienced as a child may not have been healthy love. Chances are, your parents couldn't or didn't know how to be loving or their pain and conflict prevented them from being loving parents. So admit this fact and then try to set it aside. Wipe the slate clean and start again.

2. Then concentrate on being loving to others. The best way to redefine or rediscover love is to start acting in a loving way to others. You pretty well know how you would like to be treated, so start by treating others that way.

This is important for two reasons: First, if you are preoccupied with receiving love from others, you will learn very little about how love works, and so you may continue to feel disappointed. Second, the psychological payoff of giving love to others reinforces loving behavior. You quickly learn what works and what doesn't. And people tend to respond to love *with love*. This has a synergistic effect and quickly builds a healthier understanding of what love is all about.

Now, I don't mean you should love others just so you can be loved back. But it is true that being loved is one of the tremendous bonuses of being a loving person. And when someone you love loves you back, you feel accepted, valued, cared for, and respected. These are the ingredients of deep and abiding joy.

A lot of people—ACODs included—fail to realize that love is first of all a behavior, not a feeling. It is no accident that God commands us to love but never needs to tell us to receive love. We are told in 1 John 3:18, "Let us not love in word, or in tongue, but in deed and in truth." Simply put, this means that love is not really love until it is put into action. Love has more to do with what we *do* for one another than what we feel for one another. But the good news is that loving feelings often come *after* we have acted in a loving way.

A lot of people—ACODs included—fail to realize that love is first of all a behavior, not a feeling.

God knows how we are made—after all, he made us both to love and be loved. And that is why we can heal all the distortions of love by obeying his command about love. It is my primary prescription for healing this component of your unfinished business.

GETTING CLOSURE ON YOUR DIVORCE EXPERIENCE

There are many things that ACODs typically do not understand and want to know about their particular experience of divorce, remarriage, or both. For instance, when a father has had no contact with his daughter all through high school, college, and into adulthood, she may be haunted by such questions as "Why have you avoided me?" "What did I do to chase you away?" "Don't you love me?" Recovery may be thwarted until she has some answers to these and many other questions.

You may also have unfinished business with a stepparent and may need to seek an opportunity to clear the air with him or her. For instance, you may need to discuss why your stepmother resented your love for your father, why she deliberately sabotaged your relationship with your natural mother, or why she encouraged her own children to "keep you out" of the extended family. Your healing may require many explanations, and even some apologies, before you can expect to make any progress.

In any case, it's a good idea, when possible, to attempt to find answers to your questions by approaching your parents or stepparents. Be cautious, however, not to inflame or attack. Try to discuss your hurts or confusion in a calm, matter-of-fact way, explaining that your only desire is to bring healing. It is very possible, especially if some time has elapsed since the divorce or remarriage, that your parents or stepparents will be happy to answer your questions the best they can.

Here are some rules for ensuring that you do not "blow it" as you seek to confront issues from your childhood.

Confronting Parents or Stepparents

1. Choose the right time and place.
2. Affirm all the good things you experienced from your parent or stepparent.
3. Be positive and not critical.
4. Take responsibility for your own feelings; don't blame them on others.
5. Listen to what the other person has to say.
6. Don't press for everyone to accept your position, just ask that they hear you.
7. Don't attack or put anyone down.
8. Try to avoid anger. If you get angry, pull back and hold off on any further action until you have your anger under control.

An important part of getting closure on your divorce experience will involve resolving some of your feelings toward your parents or stepparents. This may mean you must work to:

1. Resolve divided loyalties. As I have indicated in earlier chapters, divorce and remarriage often cause children to be torn between their feelings for mother and father, parent and stepparent. These divided loyalties must be sorted out. You can't be everything to everybody, so you must *choose* what you will be to whom! Often this means you must ignore petty jealousies and plant your affection where you find the greatest love.

This *may* mean choosing to be more loving and loyal to one parent—or even to a stepparent over your natural parent. There is nothing wrong with this. If a stepparent has proven his or her love to you over many years, why would you want to discard it in favor of someone, though blood related, who hasn't given you the time of day?

Try to be objective here. The test of love is behavior, not feelings. Be true to yourself and honest with your emotions. What is most important is that you resolve your conflicts and stop fighting inner battles that leave you overstressed and unable to move forward with your life.

2. Avoid projecting your negative feelings onto others. Children invariably emerge from their parents' divorce or remarriage with feelings of suspicion, fear, anxiety, and resentfulness. As adults, they may continue to carry these feelings of suspicion, fear, anxiety, and resentfulness into other relationships without being aware of what they are doing.

Recovery demands, therefore, that you become aware of such "transferences" so that you can stop doing it. There is no magic therapy that can stop you from doing this—just plain hard work. Formal therapy might increase your awareness of these feelings, but you must still be the one to direct them back to where they belong so that they don't destroy your present relationships.

Resolving your feelings toward your parents and stepparents, as outlined above, can help you detach your negative feelings from other relationships. If you no longer fear or resent your parents or stepparents, you will be less likely to transfer these feelings onto others.

3. Get closure on your past feelings, if possible, then claim freedom from your past. Experiencing grief and pain is sometimes a necessary part of recovery from the devastating effects of childhood divorce. You need to confront your painful feelings—your fears, anxieties, resentments, and rejections—if only to ensure that they are reattached where they belong—to key figures from your childhood.

But this exploration of one's painful past can easily go awry, and you can become locked into either a deep depression or uncontrollable anger. And there will be times when you are unable to confront old hurts or when someone from whom you are seeking closure will not cooperate. Be assured that your healing can proceed despite this incompleteness. You must simply make the decision to leave it where it is and move beyond it.

There will be times when you are unable to confront old hurts or when someone from whom you are seeking closure will not cooperate. Be assured that your healing can proceed despite this incompleteness.

We can't control others, and we certainly can't force them to be good to us on our terms. If you have tried your best to effect healing in a relationship with a parent or stepparent but are unable to make any progress, pack your emotional bags and move on. You cannot limit your recovery because someone else refuses to go along with it.

There's a sound biblical basis for this advice; it is contained in Matthew 18:15-17. While the specific context has to do with church discipline, the principle can easily be applied to other situations as well. This is how I paraphrase the passage:

When someone has harmed you, try to talk about it with him or her alone. If that person will not hear you, check it out with another. If necessary, ask this other person to go with you to talk it over with the one who has hurt you. If nothing comes of this, *then you are free*. Walk away from this person. You no longer have any obligation to put matters right. And this is *not* a violation of the law of love.

I believe that this makes sound spiritual and psychological sense. We cannot go through life feeling guilty or obligated to everyone who has hurt us. There must come a time, after we have tried everything reasonable to confront our hurt feelings, when we must *claim our freedom*. It is our God-given right, and our healing depends on it.

A young Christian man once came to talk to me. His father, a highly respected Christian businessman, had taken up with his secretary and divorced his ailing wife, leaving her to fend for herself after thirty years of marriage. The young man was furious, and he was even angrier that his father would not listen to him. For more than a year, he had tried to tell his father about his disappointment, his disillusionment, his disgust that his father, whom he had idealized, had destroyed their lives. He knew he couldn't change a thing—"But Dad, please let me tell you how I feel." The father had refused every approach. He insisted that he had a right to be happy and to do anything he chose. He would not give a moment of time to listen to his son's feelings.

What options does the son have in such a situation? To go on punishing himself, or to punish his father? Neither path offers real hope for recovery. His only hopeful option is to grieve, forgive, and *move on!* That is what the young man chose to do. And in the course of time, his hurts started to heal.

A FINAL WORD ON UNFINISHED BUSINESS

ACODs who are trying to take care of unfinished business must realize that we cannot have everything perfectly arranged in this life. Chances are, many questions will go unanswered. Many feelings will not have the satisfaction of expression. Many hurts will go unexplained. You may have to build your recovery upon a heap of broken promises and sacrificed hopes.

Honesty with yourself and others will be the key to your progress. And here I must address a special note to my fellow Christians: Hiding behind religious clichés won't help. If you are part of a Christian community that leans toward denial and overvalues perfection or forces you to hide your true feelings for fear of being exposed as a hypocrite, you may need to find a healthier and more accepting support group.

I find it sad to give such an admonition, but it is necessary. There is a form of Christian practice that can be very distressful and that I believe has the potential to do great harm. It ignores our humanity and undervalues honest struggle. It minimizes negative human emotions such as sadness or depression, even condemning them as "unchristian." And it mistreats believers because it forces them to pretend that they are spiritual, spirit-filled, and victorious rather than admitting their frailty, struggles, or doubts. I believe recovery is all but impossible in such an atmosphere of artificial spirituality.

Honesty with yourself and others will be the key to your progress.

Many pastors and scores of devout Christians pass through my consulting room with deep resentment toward those who perpetrate this religious abuse, often practiced in the name of Christ. They have no one else to talk to about their pain. They sometimes even fear that "others" will discover that they are "in therapy." Needing help is the ultimate stigma for those who believe in the effortless, totally "victorious," life.

Jesus, for such people, is not the sensitive listener of the Damascus road or the passionate savior of the Garden of Gethsemane. This compassionate Christ has been replaced by the false picture of a tyrant who lacks empathy, who makes impossible demands on his followers, and who is eager to punish them the moment they fall.

As an adult child of divorce, you don't need that kind of God—who is a false god, anyway. You need a God who is full of grace and kindness, who forgives failure and restores you the moment you turn back to him in contrition. In other words, you need the God of the Bible. With him you can be ruthlessly honest. In him you will find not judgment and condemnation—but a rich resource for real and lasting healing.

Personal Inventory

4

What Are Your Feelings about Yourself?

Answer the following questions about yourself as carefully as possible. Reflect on your "gut feelings" in these matters and then enter your score in the column using the following rating scale:

0 = Rarely or never do I feel this way
1 = Sometimes I feel this way
2 = Most of the time I feel this way

SCORE

_____ 1. People don't really like me.

_____ 2. I wish I were more popular than I am.

_____ 3. My parents didn't really try to understand me.

_____ 4. My parents were never proud of any of my accomplishments.

_____ 5. I don't like to learn something new, because I believe it won't matter.

_____ 6. When I compare myself with almost anyone else, I feel inferior.

_____ 7. I don't like to speak out in a group because I feel that what I have to say is not important.

_____ 8. Compared with most other people I know, I am not a very nice person.

_____ 9. I don't really like the way I look.

_____ 10. I think most people find me a difficult person to like or to have good feelings about.

_____ 11. I think that even God would have some difficulty liking me.

_____ 12. I have a long way to go before I become the person I want to be.

_____ 13. I easily give in to what other people believe or say because I think they know more than I do.

_____ 14. I become very uncomfortable whenever I am with people I think are smarter than me.

_____ 15. There are many things about me I wish I could change.

_____ TOTAL SCORE

INTERPRETING PERSONAL INVENTORY FOUR

Theoretically, your score on this personal inventory can range from 0 to 30, but I consider a score of less than 5 to be impossible, if you are really honest with yourself. If your score was that low, try again. Think about your feelings more carefully. There has got to be a time when you genuinely did not feel good about some aspect of yourself, at least for a brief period of time. If you scored more than 5, then proceed with the interpretation:

Range   Interpretation

0–5   You did not take the test seriously enough or you are denying *normal* feelings of dissatisfaction about yourself. You should have felt some dissatisfaction on a few of the measures.

6–10   Your feelings are perfectly normal. No one feels absolutely comfortable with every aspect of him or herself, and you are feeling about as good as anyone really does. You may need to reconcile yourself to wishing occasionally that you could be a better person; these feelings help to keep you on your toes.

11–16   You feel discontented about yourself. This score means you acknowledged occasional negative feelings about yourself on almost every measure in the test. You may need to do some repair to your self-image.

17–24   You clearly have a more serious self-image or self—acceptance problem. You do not have appropriate value feelings about yourself. Repair work is almost certainly needed.

25–30   You have a serious self-esteem problem that needs urgent attention. You probably should seek professional help immediately.

Personal Inventory

5

What Is Your Autonomy-Dependency Balance?

ACODs often feel socially isolated and tend to become either excessively attached to others or distant or isolated. Both of these extremes are problematic. We all need a balance between being dependent on others and being independent or autonomous. The following inventory will help you measure this balance in your own life. Using the following scale (and watch the wording carefully), enter a score for each question that best reflects your experience with others:

> 0 = I hardly ever feel this way.
> 1 = I sometimes have felt this way.
> 2 = I feel this way more often than I would like.
> 3 = I frequently or almost always feel this way.

SCORE

_____ 1. If given a choice, I would rather be with other people than be by myself.

_____ 2. I don't mind asking people for help or advice.

_____ 3. I really like other people to offer me sympathy.

_____ 4. I long for someone special in my life.

_____ 5. I like parties, social occasions, or getting together with friends.

_____ 6. I need support and help from others and cannot cope without it.

_____ 7. It bothers me to think about losing a close friend or spouse through death.

_____ 8. I don't mind putting my trust in others and don't fear being disappointed if they let me down.

_____ 9. It bothers me to be left alone for an evening or a weekend (such as when my spouse or close friend goes away).

_____ 10. I get upset when someone close to me comes home later than I expect him or her to.

_____ 11. I feel uncomfortable when visiting a strange city by myself and I don't know anyone.

_____ 12. I need other people's approval or affirmation for what I do.

_____ 13. I hate being alone when I am sick and prefer to have someone with me.

_____ 14. I feel a need to explain things to people so they won't misunderstand me.

_____ 15. I need to talk things over with friends or family before I make decisions affecting my life.

_____ TOTAL SCORE

INTERPRETING PERSONAL INVENTORY FIVE

Range   *Interpretation*

0–8   You are probably too independent. You probably feel that other people are too much of a bother.

Range   Interpretation

9–15   You tend toward too much independence. You may not be open enough to other people.

16–25   If you've answered honestly, you probably strike a healthy balance between autonomy and dependency—being able to act for yourself but reaching out for others when you need them.

26–35   You tend toward too much dependency. You rely too much on other people and need to be your own person more.

36–45   You are too dependent; you need other people too much. You probably can't make decisions on your own, and you look to other people too much for support and advice.

CHAPTER 5

Resolving Your Hurt, Anger, Guilt, and Shame

Seldom have I seen a patient as angry as Robert. I couldn't get him to sit still for more than ten seconds at a time. He paced backward and forward. He stomped his feet. If I hadn't removed the delicate dried-flower arrangement from my office coffee table, I'm sure he would have pounded it flat with his fist. Robert had just begun getting in touch with the very deep resentment he felt toward his divorced parents.

Finally Robert shouted out, "I can't understand how parents can hurt kids the way they do. What's wrong with them? Don't they have any idea how cruel it can be to ignore a hurting child who is too young to know how to stop the hurt?

"I can understand a parent who gets angry and beats a child," Robert went on. "Anger makes you lose control, and you just lash out without thinking. But just to check out... to ignore a kid and make him fend for himself—I'm damned if I can accept it."

Robert doesn't usually use that kind of language. But Robert was hurting very deeply. Until now, he had never realized just how deeply. It was not so much what his parents had done to him, but what they hadn't; theirs were sins of omission rather than commission. This is why it had taken him so long to realize that his deep feelings of hurt and bitterness were connected to his experience of

115

divorce as a child. It was hard to point to a particular reprehensible act and say, "They did that, and it makes me angry."

To make matters worse, both of Robert's parents were so troubled themselves that they easily evoked pity. All through his teenage years, Robert had excused his parents, jumped to their defense, apologized on their behalf—and was left carrying the burden of blame all by himself. No wonder he was angry!

When our hurts remain unrecognized and thus unforgiven, they become a part of us, shaping our personalities, altering our outlooks, and changing the course of our personal histories.

What were the "sins of omission" Robert's parents had committed? They included such things as keeping their son completely in the dark about what was going on in their home. (They rationalized that this would be less painful for him.) For instance, the day his mother left home, abandoning the seven-year-old Robert to a passive, helpless, and inadequate father, no one told Robert she wouldn't be returning. He waited several days, worrying about where his mother was. When he asked his father about it, the helpless man just shrugged his shoulders and walked away.

Robert's parents also abdicated their responsibilities for parenting him. They stopped all discipline, set no boundaries, paid little attention to him at all. As a result, Robert grew up confused, bewildered, uncertain—and all the time telling himself, "They didn't mean any harm" or "They did the best they could."

Deep down, however, Robert didn't really believe the excuses. And his hurt ran deep. Over the years, buried resentment festered and gradually turned him into a bitter person. In fact, anger and resentment had become so embedded in his psyche that he found it hard to conceive of living without it. How was he ever going to shake off all this deep bitterness? What would be left of him? To him, it felt like trying to remake his personality all over again.

Robert was discovering the hard way that anger and resentment are major components in the legacy of pain that a divorce leaves behind it. When our hurts remain unrecognized and thus unforgiven, they become a part of us. They grow on us like parasites, shaping our personalities, altering our outlooks, and changing the course of our personal histories. A significant part of the work of recovery, therefore, is learning to cope with the anger and resentment that may cloud our lives.

WHO'S REALLY RESPONSIBLE?

Many ACODs, like Robert, feel reluctant to put any blame or assign any responsibility to their parents for their problems.

They excuse them: "They didn't really love each other."

They apologize for them: "They were hurting so much themselves that they didn't have any energy left to attend to us kids."

They even lie about them: "Their intentions toward us were good. There's no way they could have realized how much we were hurting."

If no one else is to blame, then these children assume that they themselves must be the culprit. So many children of divorce end up blaming themselves for what happened in their families and carrying a load of neurotic guilt into their adulthood.

No one—least of all an adult child of divorce—wants to find fault with his or her parents. Doing so feels disloyal, almost like a betrayal. But in many cases, recovery cannot begin until the ACOD is honest enough to own up to where he or she thinks the blame really lies. If you allow sympathy for your parents' struggles to get in the way of your honest assessment, you will invariably *short-circuit* the healing process.

You can only forgive a hurt that you understand, and you can only forgive someone who you admit has hurt you.

Sooner or later you must be willing to forgive your parents, and anyone else who has hurt you, for their role in the divorce. But *you can only forgive a hurt that you understand, and you can only forgive someone who you admit has hurt you.* While you may sympathize with and excuse the perpetrator, you cannot forgive without, in effect, holding him or her responsible. After all, if he or she did nothing to harm you, what is there to forgive?

Denying, excusing, apologizing, regretting, or prematurely pardoning the hurts you have suffered is a dead-end trap. Instead of moving you toward forgiveness and recovery, making excuses for others simply diverts the blame back to yourself.

A vital step in healing resentment, therefore, is clearly to understand and accept the nature of your hurt—and that includes *placing blame where blame is due*. This permits you to experience anger in a way that opens you fully and completely to the need to give and to receive forgiveness.

Robert lay awake many nights mulling over his childhood and all its pain. He rediscovered how his parents had used silence to avoid confrontation and how they had put up a massive wall of denial. And Robert had to stop convincing himself that they did this for *his* sake. "They were protecting me because I was so vulnerable," he had told himself. "If only I had been tougher, they would have told me the truth." Robert had to face the fact that his parents had been at fault. It was their weakness, their neurosis, their helplessness, their fragility that caused many of his childhood problems.

"Stop blaming yourself, Robert," I would tell him. "Stop trying to protect your parents. You know deep down what the real score is. The sooner you accept that they really were to blame, the sooner you can move to the place of forgiveness."

Often we are afraid to blame our parents (and I am intentionally using the stronger word *blame* rather than *hold responsible*) because we feel that in doing so we are accusing them of harmful intent. But no normal parent, even a troubled one, is intentionally harmful. And in any case, speculating on intent is a waste of time. What counts in the long run are the results; if harm was done, it was done. The cause can be identified and those responsible must be held responsible, at least in your own thinking.

Remember, inadequate parents are responsible both for what they do and for what they don't do. Some parents leave such a legacy of fear and anxiety that they can be described as "toxic." By failing to attend to the physical and emotional needs of their children, such parents may be causing severe damage. Why shouldn't they be held responsible for this neglect?

For the one who has been hurt, "holding them responsible" is the first step toward forgiveness. You have to fully understand both the hurt you have experienced and who it is that did the hurting.

"Blame your parents," I encouraged Robert. "Feel it as blame. Don't minimize it. Don't water it down. Blame is the only emotionally appropriate label for it."

Thus began Robert's first steps toward recovery. As I described at the beginning of this chapter, he began consciously to feel what he had unconsciously known all along—that intentionally or not, his parents had abdicated their responsibilities toward him. They had cast him adrift on a stormy sea without any life preserver. Later in this chapter I will discuss the next steps in the process of forgiveness and healing. First, however, I want to explore further how understanding the nature of your hurts, anger, and shame that arise can help you understand your particular distress as an adult child of divorce.

HIDING FROM YOUR HURT—
UNDERSTANDING COPING MECHANISMS

To a child, divorce hurts—there's no way around it. The divorce does injury to your sense of security, your self-esteem, your self-respect, your confidence in the future. The distress can throb in your chest like real pain or explode in your head with a violent headache. Sometimes it makes you quiet and gloomy. Other times you keep yourself busy and distracted by becoming engrossed in some activity just to escape it. *Hurt*—no other word can adequately describe the way divorce feels to a child, and the hurt doesn't necessarily go away once that child has become an adult.

ACODs start hiding from their hurt as children because they simply don't know how to cope with it.

But not all ACODs are in touch with their hurt feelings. They've learned how to anesthetize them—how to make them numb. They've learned how to ignore their bad feelings to the point that they become unconscious of the hurt. Some have repressed their hurts so deeply that their stress has emerged in the form of high blood pressure, ulcers, or other psychosomatic illnesses. (Every physician knows that much physical illness has roots in emotional pain.)

ACODs start hiding from their hurt as children because they simply don't know how to cope with it. How does a six-year-old, a ten-year-old, or even a young teenager cope with the overwhelming distress of seeing a parent pack and leave? What do they know about handling grief or melancholy? Where do they take their sadness to get comfort? They are still too young to have learned what to do with their pain.

"Well, then, perhaps this is a good time for them to begin to learn," someone might say. "Kids must realize that life isn't a bed of roses. A person has to experience some knocks in order to toughen up. Let's stop coddling our kids; they need to be exposed to the real issues of life."

There is a grain of truth to this assertion. Children who have been constantly sheltered from life's painful realities don't necessarily turn out to be well-adjusted adults. But the pain of divorce is overkill—a kind of baptism by fire (and a raging one at that). Children should learn life's painful lessons gradually, and should never have more adjustment forced upon them than their level of maturity can tolerate. The hurts of divorce can be more than some children can tolerate.

How do we try to cope with our hurt? Here are several of the unhealthy ways:

1. Denial, which is often the first coping mechanism a child learns, takes one of two forms: "Nothing is wrong," and "Something was wrong, but it won't happen again." To cope with their emotional pain, children minimize, joke about, rationalize, or discount what is happening to them. Or they just refuse to face up to reality.

"My dad will come back tomorrow; just you wait and see," one ten-year-old once told me. "He's just gone to look at a new car he wants to buy. He hasn't left. He wouldn't go away without me." I really felt sad for that little boy, whose father had already moved in with another woman. In refusing to face up to reality, this child may have been successfully avoiding conscious feelings of hurt. But deep down, perhaps even unconsciously, his little heart was about to disintegrate with fear.

That's the trouble with denial: it doesn't really make the hurt go away. Sooner or later, the hurt will emerge, perhaps in an even more painful form, and the denial will continue to stand in the way of healing. This coping mechanism tends to become more rigid and harder to break the longer it is used. Later in life this boy may continue to use denial whenever he is faced with a painful reality. Unfortunately, boys tend to use it more than girls, which means that men use denial more frequently than women.

Fantasy is only healthy if your feet are firmly on the ground. Otherwise, it only provides an imitation peace.

---

2. Fantasy. The imagination is a God-given resource, meant to enrich our lives, make us more creative, and provide healthy relief from humdrum routine. And yet imagination, in the form of fantasy, can easily become an unhealthy defense mechanism as well.

I clearly remember how I used to retreat to a fantasy world to cope with my hurting heart after my parents divorced. I would lie on my bed with my eyes closed and let my imagination run freely. I could fantasize that my parents were reconciled and we were all happy. I could imagine that my grandparents let me stay with them in the countryside to begin a new and exciting life. My fantasy could make me a star in the movies or a great preacher. Even though these daydreams had nothing to do with our home situation, they provided relief from pain and an escape into never-never land where life was happy and pain absent.

As a young adult I continued to use fantasy to escape pain, aided by a very good imagination. I have almost broken the habit now, but it was a struggle. Retreating into fantasy is a habitual coping mechanism that can easily become a permanent part of you.

"So what's wrong with having fantasies?" one middle-aged man challenged me once. "It doesn't do any harm. No one gets hurt. I can accomplish anything I want to in my imagination. I can be a great football player or a great orchestra conductor. People applaud me, and I feel good about myself. What's wrong with fantasy?"

He was insistent. He did not want me to take away the only defense he had against hurt.

"It's just not reality," I told him. "Sooner or later, you have to open your eyes and realize it isn't true. Fantasy is only healthy if your feet are firmly on the ground. Otherwise, it only provides an *imitation peace*. It takes living in full awareness of reality, with God's power in your life, to provide *real peace*." But he wasn't convinced, and he remains an unhappy person today.

3. Regression. One of the more damaging effects of divorce on a young child is chronic fear. Many of these children always feel "scared"—there's no other word to describe the feeling. They're scared of the conflicts that are going on. They're afraid of the future. Their fear of "normally" fearful situations such as being alone, going into a dark room, or going to the dentist is intensified.

One way children cope with this general fear (as with many childhood disruptions) is to regress—to go back to an earlier and more primitive way of coping. This means the child displays behavior he or she has already grown out of. One child might go back to being excessively dependent on his mother. Another may revert to using a comfort blanket or go to bed holding on to a favorite doll. Older children sometimes find a discarded pacifier and secretly suck it.

Adult forms of regression—childish behaviors—are quite common among ACODs. It includes using temper tantrums to intimidate ("I must get what I want on my terms"), pouting ("I'll punish you for hurting me"), and self-pity ("Everyone must love me on my terms"). Some may even revert to sucking their thumbs—but this would not really be much of a problem if it was all they did!

Each of these coping mechanisms leads to greater misery, not less. Strangely enough, the avoidance of pain that these behaviors encourage actually *sensitizes* you to pain. Adult stress is exaggerated because your regressive behaviors have made you more sensitive to emotional pain.

4. Anger. The natural consequence of hurt is anger. You can't avoid becoming angry. Your body and mind are so designed that you become angry whenever you are exposed to hurt, either physical or emotional. The deeper the hurt, the stronger the anger.

The natural consequence of hurt is anger. The only truly effective antidote for hurt and anger is forgiveness.

Now, the actual feeling of anger does not stay with you permanently; the feeling subsides. But your mind has the ability to accumulate the memories of your hurts, and these memories have the ability to recreate the anger long after the hurtful events have been forgotten. This is how we become angry people. Our personalities become diffused with anger. And we get in the habit of using our anger to handle any further hurt.

The hurt of divorce is deep enough to cause major anger problems for ACODs. How does this anger show itself in adulthood?

Anger and the ACOD

1. You may become extremely sensitive and "touchy"; you blow up at the slightest provocation.
2. You develop a low tolerance for hurt. You've had enough hurt for one lifetime already. Any further hurt evokes an exaggerated anger response.
3. You develop an acute sense of fairness and justice, and you react with extreme anger to even minor violations of your "rights."
4. You become suspicious of the motives of others. You fear that most people are out to hurt you—or at least that if you don't look after yourself, no one else will.
5. You become generally hostile, causing others to fear your temper or your overreactions.
6. You bear grudges; you don't easily forget the hurts done to you.
7. You expect people to apologize whenever they've hurt you, and you refuse to forgive them until they do.
8. You see anger in everyone else but seldom acknowledge it in yourself.

HEALING YOUR HURT AND ANGER

The coping mechanisms I have described above are all essentially unhealthy. None of them really do anything to make the hurt go away, and all of them tend to result in more pain over the long haul.

Is there a better way? Absolutely. The only truly effective antidote for hurt and anger is *forgiveness.*

As you probably know, forgiveness isn't easy. In fact, I have always reacted rather strongly against the popular idea that one should "forgive and forget." How can we possibly *forget* the painful things that have happened to us?

If I can forget a hurt done to me, I really don't need to forgive it. It is precisely because I *cannot* forget my hurts that I am called—both by God and by psychological common sense—to forgive them.

We all experience hurt every day of our lives—a critical remark by a friend, an angry outburst by a spouse or child, an offense by a neighbor or shopkeeper. Many of these don't bother us because they are not important enough to register in our minds. Thank God that our brains were not designed to retain everything. Every night when we sleep, our wonderful minds work a miracle on the many hurts we've experienced. We really do forget them; they are gone! They don't need the healing balm of forgiveness—healing has taken place naturally.

But some hurts cannot be forgotten. They are too important, too deep. They were caused by someone we cared about—someone who should have known better. Or they pressed one of our "buttons," reviving old feelings of rejection. Such hurts remain in our memories and work their damage like a hidden cancer. These hurts are not always *consciously* remembered; they can simmer below the level of our awareness or lie dormant as if in hibernation, waiting for the right moment to come alive to disturb our peace or create angry feelings.

The very fact that you are an ACOD means you have many of these unforgotten hurts that need to be healed. This is unavoidable. Within you there is a child that has been damaged—a child that aches because of fear, neglect, anxiety, and feelings of abandonment. A child that is deeply hostile and resentful.

How can we heal this deep inner hurt? Here are the steps that I have personally found helpful:

1. Force your hurts into the open. It is precisely because your hurts lie dormant and unconscious that they have power over you. Because you don't see them for what they are, they disrupt your peace, disturb your relationships, and intrude into your life. They may cause you to be angry at the slightest provocation, or sensitive to the smallest slight. Because you don't know they are there, you cannot deal with them constructively—and as a result, they don't go away.

Writing out your memories can be especially helpful; somehow the act of putting pen to paper can uncover long-buried experiences.

So make an effort to unearth and confront your hurts. Take some time to reflect upon your past. Talk to a trusted friend about your memories—or get into therapy if necessary. Consciously reflect on how painful it was to go through a divorce as a child—and even try to relive in your imagination some of the significant events of your childhood. Try to identify as many hurts as you can and to expose them to your consciousness.

Writing out your memories can be especially helpful; somehow the act of putting pen to paper can uncover long-buried experiences. Even writing your own childhood autobiography can be helpful in getting you to expose your hurt feelings and understand where they come from so that you can let them go.

At one time, when I was struggling with some of my resentments, I took the time to write out a narrative reconstructing some conversations I had with my father in my early teens. These conversations concerned some of my early childhood fears. He didn't seem to understand how I felt, and he really didn't pay attention to what I was trying to tell him. But in writing out the story and remembering those fears years later, I was able to see that my father had experienced some of those very same fears. This helped me to "release" my anger toward my father for not being understanding.

2. Refuse to minimize or excuse your hurts. And here we are back where we started—with the need to face your hurts squarely and own up to who caused them! As we have seen, our desire to avoid painful memories or even misguided sympathy for our parents may cause us to downplay our hurts. This is not constructive.

Now, I don't mean you should forever hold your parents responsible for all your unhappiness or problems! We tend to do this a lot in our culture. Parents are not perfect, and your parents probably did the best they could, given their circumstances. You have to take responsibility for how you react to your childhood pain and repair the damage to the best of your ability.

For your own sake, you must learn to forgive your parents. But forgiving hurts is never the same thing as excusing or minimizing them! Making excuses for others only short-circuits the process of forgiveness.

3. Deliberately move to the place of forgiveness. Forgiveness is both an act and a process. It is an act of your will in which *you choose* to surrender your right to hurt those who have hurt you, and it is a continual process of choosing forgiveness until you finally *feel* forgiveness.

It is critical that you understand this distinction. Making the decision to forgive someone does not mean that you will magically be free of your resentment. Long-term healing of deep hurts will almost always require more than one shot.

The act of forgiveness means taking your hurts and saying to them, "No longer do I give you the power to affect me. I surrender you to God. I forgive those who have hurt me by his power, and I give up any need to continue holding on to my resentment."

This act of choosing is the first step in forgiving. The next step is a process. You *continue to choose forgiveness.* Every time the hurt arises—and it will—you remind yourself, "I have already forgiven this hurt." And then you deliberately *behave as if you have already forgiven.* This action will reinforce your original decision to forgive.

The process I have described is very important from both a spiritual and a psychological point of view. Spiritually, you are exercising faith. You are saying to yourself, "I have forgiven. This is a fact. Now I have faith that I have forgiven the one who has hurt me." You are also recognizing that not to forgive is going to harm your spirit. The very essence of your being needs to feel "clean" and free of resentment. Choosing to forgive those who have hurt you *begins* the process of spiritual healing. It opens you to receiving God's forgivenss.

Psychologically, you are reinforcing the right attitude of forgiveness. It's a demonstrable fact that behavior helps to reinforce beliefs. At first you may not feel any different. But as you begin to behave in a forgiving way toward the one who has hurt you, you will slowly start to feel the forgiveness also.

4. Don't let your forgiveness depend on the response of those who have hurt you. Too often we take the first step of forgiveness, then wait to see if those who have hurt us will apologize or even acknowledge their role in our pain. If they don't respond to our overtures the "right" way, we pull back again to the place of our hurt.

It is vital that you look at forgiveness as *your* choice—an action you choose independent of what others do. Don't expect that those who have hurt you will acknowledge their actions. Don't think, just because you have taken the first step toward forgiveness, that they will jump to admit their guilt. Don't wait to see if they or anyone else will applaud you for your magnanimity. Instead, concentrate on forgiving because God commands you to forgive—"For if you forgive others their trespasses, your heavenly Father will also forgive you"—and because you accept the reality that forgiveness is necessary for your own healing.

Since your personality is likely to have been shaped toward anger by years of unresolved hurt feelings, the next step is to begin changing your angry behavior.

---

5. Continue to change your angry behavior. Since your personality is likely to have been shaped toward anger by years of unresolved hurt feelings, the next step is to begin changing your angry behavior. It is very possible that your anger is out of control. If you don't know how angry you are, ask a trusted friend to give you an honest picture of the role anger plays in your life.

To change your behavior, first recognize that angry behavior destroys the one who is angry. It is like a boomerang—it comes back to you. Unlike the boomerang, however, it hurts the one who throws it more than the intended target. Once you have recognized that angry behavior is not good for you, try these specific changes to help you reduce your angry behavior:

- *Try to be aware of your tendency to "scapegoat" others.* Scapegoating is unhealthy because it hurts innocent people—like your spouse, children, or even pets, often those who least deserve your anger. In the process, it tends to alienate those whose support you need most. "You always hurt the one you love" is a sad observation, not a prescription for healthy growth!

- *Try to focus your anger on its real source.* Make an effort to be more assertive (in a gentle, not bullying way). If possible, when something makes you angry, confront the cause of your anger directly. Talk to the one who has provoked you and try to resolve your conflict.

- *Refuse to argue.* Angry people are always ready to do battle with words, if not with deeds. But it takes two people to create an emotional war. If you decline to become involved in an argument, the battle will fizzle out. Then you will be able to resolve the conflict in an atmosphere of calm.

- *However, make sure that you don't avoid conflict.* Some people resist overt conflict but adopt "passive-aggressive" tactics; they sabotage communication and use subtle and indirect ways to express their anger. Tackling conflict situations head-on is a much more effective way of resolving your anger.

- *If you are a parent, be very careful not to project your anger onto your children.* For some strange reason, ACODs tend to redirect their anger onto their own children. It's like a reverse reaction. You were angry at your parents as a child, so now as a parent you aim your own anger toward your children. It doesn't make sense—but since when does any neurotic behavior make sense?

- *Finally, resist responding to anger with anger.* Angry people know how to meet anger with anger. They are also conditioned to becoming angry—it is an emotional habit. When someone is angry at them, they tend to get angry back. They think that the best defense against anger is more anger. This only makes matters worse, so try to develop a gentle way of reacting. When someone displays anger, respond with a plea for objective calm. In fact, ask yourself how Christ would act in your situation—and do the same.

UNDERSTANDING YOUR GUILT AND SHAME

Children of divorce have more than anger and resentment to get under control. They must also resolve their *shame* and *guilt*.

Shame is not the same thing as guilt, although the two are often confused. Guilt arises out of a sense of wrongdoing and a fear of punishment. But shame involves a feeling of inferiority—a gut-deep sense that something is inherently wrong with you as a person.

It is true that ACODs feel a lot of guilt—guilt over "causing" their parents' divorce, guilt over the anger or even hatred they feel toward their parents, guilt over desperately wanting something they fear may be wrong for someone else. But I don't believe guilt is half as damaging to the adult child of divorce as the shame he or she accumulates through the experience.

Guilt arises out of a sense of wrongdoing and a fear of punishment. But shame involves a feeling of inferiority—a gut-deep sense that something is inherently wrong with you as a person.

Shame is a *very private* emotion that is inherently difficult to communicate—and the confusion of divorce makes that difficulty worse. It is the deep and painful feeling you get when you think you've lost the respect of others. It is the mindset that something is wrong *with you*. It is dishonor, disgrace, and humiliation all rolled up into one. It makes you want to hide your face even from God.

Many ACODs develop the body language of shame—folding their arms a lot (so as to hide behind this shield); failing to make eye contact; covering their faces with their hands, handkerchiefs, or books or simply hiding behind pillows, doors, or any other convenient object. They feel the need to "hide" their shamefulness.

What does an abiding sense of shame do to you as an adult? All of the following are possibilities.

Shame and Its Effects

1. You develop a shame-based way of looking at yourself, seeing everything through the spectacles of shame.
2. You feel inferior to everyone else—no matter how bad they are or how many mistakes they make.
3. You find it difficult to assert yourself or stand up for your own rights.
4. You become a martyr to your own needs. In other words, you allow yourself to be hurt for the sake of your own needs.
5. You develop a shyness born of the belief that others are constantly evaluating you and seeing you as an outcast.
6. You come to prefer isolation rather than the company of others. Being with people increases your shamefulness.
7. Your self-esteem and self-respect self-destruct.
8. You cannot be spontaneous because you are always wondering what others are thinking.
9. You criticize yourself incessantly because you are always worrying about making the right impression.
10. You judge yourself very harshly whenever you feel a sense of failure.
11. You are terrified of being "found out."
12. You avoid even moderately challenging tasks for fear of not succeeding.
13. You never seem to be free from a feeling of embarrassment.

What can you do to resolve your shame and guilt? A lot! And it's important to do everything you can to put the twin specters of guilt and shame to rest.

FREEING YOURSELF FROM GUILT

There is a positive side to guilt; one can be and feel guilty in a healthy way. This is the healthy guilt that you feel when you really have done something wrong. For instance, you have lashed out in anger at one of your children. Or you have deliberately lied to your spouse.

In such a case, your guilt feelings can fulfill the healthy function of spurring you to set things right. How? The process is simple, although it is not always easy:

1. You must repent of what you have done. This simply means coming to the point that you are truly sorry for what you have done and have made the decision to act differently. Repentance, in a sense, is the act of heeding the message of your guilt feelings and taking responsibility for your wrong actions. To repent is to turn, to turn away from wrong behavior and to turn toward what is right.

2. You must tell God what you've done wrong and, preferably, tell another human being as well. This act of getting your wrongdoing out in the open reinforces your repentance and moves you on toward healing. It may or may not be appropriate to confess to someone you have wronged. In some cases, doing that may relieve your guilt feelings only at the price of the other person's sense of trust or peace of mind. If that is genuinely the case (and you are not just rationalizing to avoid the other person's anger), it is better to consider confessing to a trustworthy third party—a close friend, a clergyman, or even a therapist. But whether or not you actually confess to another person, it is vital that you confess to yourself and to God. Admit the specific nature of what you have done, and face the reality of its consequences.

3. Next, ask for forgiveness. If you have chosen to speak directly to someone you have wronged, ask that person to forgive you. But whether or not that is possible, it is important to ask God for forgiveness. The act of asking is inherent in the healing process.

4. Do what you can to make restitution. Make a genuine effort to rectify any wrong you have done to others. This may be as simple as replacing lost property or as difficult as repairing broken relationships. You may find that full restitution is not possible, but it is important that you make a good-faith effort to do what you can.

People who suffer from neurotic guilt don't really want forgiveness; they want to keep on feeling bad about what they have done.

---

5. Accept your forgiveness. Even if restitution is not possible, or if the person you have wronged refuses to forgive you, you must eventually accept the fact that you have done what you could. You must then make the effort to forgive yourself and then move on. If you are truly sorry for what you have done and have sincerely asked God's forgiveness, you can be confident you are forgiven: "If we confess our sins," Scripture assures us, "He is faithful and just to forgive us our sins and to cleanse us from all unrighteousness" (1 John 1:9).

Regardless of the other person's actions, therefore, you will truly be forgiven if you ask. But it is up to you to accept the fact that you are forgiven. You must choose to let go of your guilt feelings and move on.

Every one of these steps is essential to healing true guilt. But they won't work with another kind of guilt feeling—what I call false or neurotic guilt. This kind of guilt feeling resists resolution because it is really a form of self-punishment. People who suffer from neurotic guilt don't really *want* forgiveness; they want to keep on feeling bad about what they have done. Neurotic guilt needs professional help to make it whole again.

OVERCOMING SHAME

As I have said, some guilt can be healthy. But there is nothing good or healthy in an ACOD's shame. Shame, you see, is always created by a set of *false or erroneous beliefs,* adopted as a child, about what it means to be a valuable person. What are some of these false beliefs?

- You believe that your value was diminished by the unsatisfactory behavior of your parents.
- You believe that your life has been, and forever will be, dishonored by divorce.
- You believe that the humiliation you felt is permanent.
- You believe that somehow everyone you now meet automatically knows everything there is to know about you—that you can hide nothing from the world.
- You believe that if one person looks down on you, this person must be right, and that everyone else feels the same way.

I am sure you can add to this list your own erroneous, shame-filled beliefs. In fact, why don't you? Take a sheet of paper and write down some of your own shameful feelings. Putting your assumptions down on paper will help you to see how ridiculous they really are.

Shame is always created by a set of false or erroneous beliefs.

Now remember, these beliefs are *false,* erroneous, and irrational. They are distortions and misinterpretations of the truth. There is nothing honest in them.

To heal your shame, then, three things must happen:

- You must counter these false beliefs with truthful ones.
- You must increase your awareness of when you feel shame and when your behavior is being controlled by this shame. When you feel shame, you can immediately challenge these feelings.
- You must avoid reinforcing the thoughts or feelings of shame that will unavoidably arise at times.

Allow me to elaborate briefly on each of these points.

STEP #1: COUNTER FALSE BELIEFS

The belief that you are unworthy, disgraceful, or whatever else it is you feel about yourself was probably formed before, during, and after your parents' divorce. You didn't create it; it was forced upon you by circumstances. It probably grew out of little things—a hurt here, an angry word there, a slight or rejection somewhere else. It may have been subtle or covert. Or it may even have been deliberate and to your face.

No matter! Your task is to get these ideas into the open where you can see and challenge them.

Challenge your faulty beliefs and replace them with healthier, honest alternatives.

You may find it helpful to take the list of erroneous beliefs that you listed in the exercise above and to examine them closely, one by one. Find their lies. Ask yourself, "Can this possibly be true? Can it all be true?" If it is not *all* true, then there is enough distortion to warrant that you challenge the statement and counter it with a more truthful one.

Take, for example, the idea that because one or both of your parents embarrassed themselves by their behavior or through their divorce, your value as a person has been contaminated. Many ACODs feel this. But is it true? Absolutely not. No matter how disgraceful the behavior of your parents was, it was theirs and not yours! You need to become your own person enough to cut the emotional umbilical cord and say, "I will not take your shame upon me. I will not feel this way about myself." Consciously make some space for yourself.

Now keep reasoning with yourself this way. Challenge your faulty beliefs and replace them with healthier, honest alternatives. Say to yourself, "Even though my parents were dishonored, disgraced, and even ostracized, I am my own person and will be judged *only* by my own standards and actions. I will forgive them, where appropriate, but I will not be scarred by their mistakes. I choose not to take this shame on me."

I have found it helps to remind myself regularly that the only opinion that really counts is God's. He knows everything. He understands perfectly. When I am healthy in mind and spirit, I don't feel shame toward him. I assure myself that I don't need to feel this way with others, either. I deliberately place myself only under his judgment.

STEP #2: INCREASE YOUR AWARENESS OF WHEN YOU FEEL SHAME

So that you can further counter the false beliefs that feed your sense of shame, you need to be much more aware of when these beliefs are at work in you and when you are actually feeling shameful. There are a couple of ways you can do this:

1. You can anticipate situations in which your shame will be felt. For instance, you may know from experience that you feel uncomfortable at social gatherings. You may have feelings that you don't belong there or that you are being rejected in some subtle way. Since you know that such situations trigger your shame feelings, you should begin ahead of time to challenge the beliefs that underlie these feelings. As you anticipate going to a party, ask yourself some probing questions: "Why would I be invited if I wasn't worthy? What evidence is there that I am not wanted?" Challenge your beliefs—get them into the open and confront them.

2. You can build your understanding of what your shame feels like and make a habit of labeling it when you feel it. How do we feel shame? We blush, fidget, and want to escape. We feel embarrassed, shy, disgraced. We may even feel dirty, indecent, or evil. We want to hide and not have anyone look at us. Our self-consciousness increases dramatically. We constantly ask ourselves, "What are others thinking? What are they saying?"

Unfortunately, at the moment we feel our shame, we are usually so caught up in it that we don't stop to label it. So develop a habit of asking yourself often whether what you are feeling is shame. Ask your friends to tell you when they see you acting embarrassed. Check yourself in a mirror to see if you're blushing. Do *anything* that will help you admit your shame to yourself.

STEP #3: AVOID REINFORCING THE SHAME

There will be times when your shame will not be a hangover from your childhood. It will arise because you genuinely made a mistake, overstepped a boundary, blundered, botched, mismanaged, or failed to do something. And if you think you can go through life without any errors, think again. Failure of some sort at some time is inevitable. You cannot escape it. And your feelings are based not on erroneous beliefs, but on a real mistake or ridiculous action.

But consider for a moment:

- *How often* does this happen? Seldom!
- *How much* shame should one feel? As little as possible, provided you acknowledge your mistake and take steps to apologize or correct it.
- *Why* does one feel excessive shame even here? Because human nature loves to wallow in self-pity and because, as ACODs, we have developed an excessive shame response.
- *What* should you do about this shame? Get rid of it as soon as you can. There is *no value* in perpetrating shame feelings. Accept your failure for what it is, make amends, and get on with life. *You're not perfect.* Stop punishing yourself for your imperfection.

We are so programmed by childhood experiences of embarrassment that we experience an excessive reaction of shame even when our mistakes are small, insignificant, and unnoticed by others.

Shame, like guilt, is in the cards for all of us. It is part of being human, and it cannot be totally avoided, even with healthy childhoods. And yet some of us make a meal of shame. We are so programmed by childhood experiences of embarrassment that we experience an excessive reaction of shame even when our mistakes are small, insignificant, and unnoticed by others. Our reaction goes way beyond the reasonable. Every time we overreact in this way, we reinforce the excessive shame mechanism within us and thus perpetuate our shamefulness. What is the result?

- We cannot tolerate any sign of weakness in ourselves. We strive to be perfect in everything.
- We go to pieces whenever we make a mistake.
- We cannot take criticism or any feedback on negative performance.
- We must always appear to be perfectly in control and free of any error.
- We play games to avoid being found at fault in anything.

All of this, of course, is designed to avoid shame. Unfortunately, it has the opposite effect; it increases our experience of shame even over little, insignificant things.

To stop this reinforcement of shame you can do the following:

1. Remind yourself that shame is an emotion always aroused by seeing yourself as you imagine others are seeing you. In other words, shame is not something you normally feel when you make a mistake by yourself. You feel shame when *someone else sees you* as you don't want them to see you.

Now, if this is so, then you can break the reinforcement cycle in two ways:

- You can choose not to let the opinions of others have so much power over you.
- You can ask for feedback in order to discover whether this is how they actually see you.

Here's an example of what I mean: For many years I felt very self-conscious because of my physical shortness. I believed (irrationally) that people would not respect me if I were not six-foot-six and able to tower over them. Height, for me, was power. Whenever I could not accomplish some task that required height—such as reaching up and taking something off a high shelf—I felt acute embarrassment. When someone tall would say (quite loudly, it seemed to me),

"Let me help you," my embarrassment turned to shame. Somehow I felt that I had failed, that I had lost the respect of others because I was short.

Then, one day, I decided that my shame was affecting me too much. I began to tell myself that God made me as I am. I determined to work at accepting myself the way I am and even praising him for it. That shift in attitude began to do the trick. I discovered, through conversations with my friends and through times of earnest prayer, that the problem was within *me,* not in others. My shame had no basis in reality. As I kept reminding myself of this reality, my shame began to subside.

2. Remind yourself, whenever you feel inordinate or irrational shame, that its real cause lies in your childhood experiences. You are projecting on to your present circumstances feelings that really belong "back there" somewhere. I often say to myself, "Come on now, you are reacting to the shame of your childhood. There is no reason for you to be feeling this way now. Send it back to where it belongs."

We often "feel from the past." Our earliest feelings happened in response to certain circumstances in childhood, and similar (but not identical) circumstances can recreate those feelings in the present. Just to know this and to remind yourself of it can help to send your feelings back to where they belong and restore your perspective on the present.

3. Finally, whenever you feel unreasonable shame, you can stop reinforcing your shame by what I call "stepping over." Like false guilt (where you are feeling very guilty even though you've done nothing wrong) shame feelings cannot just be stopped. They are real feelings. They may not have a basis in reality, but they exist anyway. It is possible, however, to consciously "step over" your feelings and go on with your life.

This is *not* the same thing as repressing or hiding from your feelings. You have listened to a particular feeling or set of feelings and changed whatever needs changing. It doesn't serve any purpose now. Now it just lies there in your pathway, preventing you from moving forward. So "step over" it—ignore it, set it aside, behave as if it isn't there, get on with whatever it is you are doing. Doing so will keep you from reinforcing the shame.

Let's assume, for example, that you are at a party with your husband (or wife, friend, child, parent, or anyone close to you). In conversation with some friends, this loved one says something that really embarrasses you. He or she exposes some intimate detail about your life together that is sensitive and that you would rather keep private. You sense your feeling of shame. You want to hide your face. You are even angry at him for saying it. What should you do?

- You acknowledge to yourself that you are feeling shame.
- You challenge your beliefs about this shame. Did you do something wrong? No! *He* is the one who is making a fool of himself. Your friends will understand; they might even value his transparency. You could be overreacting (you've done it before).
- You still feel ashamed, once you have cleared away all the irrational thoughts.
- Consciously step over your shame. Behave as if it were not there. Continue with your own conversation, knowing that by so doing you are refusing to reinforce your shame. In time, your feelings of shame over this situation will weaken and disappear.

Shame may be a powerful emotion in the adult child of divorce, but it does not have to control you. You are not powerless to prevent it; you *can* overcome it. Winning the battle will take some discipline and persistence—and possibly some help from God and from other people. But this is a battle you can win.

Even small gains in this area, while you are still at the beginning of your healing, can give you the courage to continue fighting the battle against shame by building your confidence and helping you trust the process. Take a moment to celebrate your accomplishment whenever you make a step forward in conquering your shame. Rewarding yourself with self-praise will help to break the habit of always thinking about your failures and not acknowledging your successes.

Personal Inventory

6

Was Your Family Dysfunctional?

The degree of family dysfunction you experienced as a child, before or after a divorce, can be a major factor in determining how you are affected by being an ACOD. Use the following scale to answer the questions about your family (choose whether you want to rate your predivorce or postdivorce family situation):

0 = I almost never experienced this.
1 = I sometimes experienced this.
2 = I often experienced this.

SCORE

_____ 1. My family tried to solve problems by screaming and shouting *rather* than by discussing them.

_____ 2. Family members resisted asking each other for help.

_____ 3. My parents (one or both) did not tell me they loved me; I was just expected to know that they did.

_____ 4. As children, we had no say in the way we were disciplined.

_____ 5. Rules about discipline or behavior were nonexistent or changed often.

_____ 6. We all went our separate ways without a sense of togetherness.

_____ 7. One or more members of my family used silence or sulking to punish or control others.

_____ 8. We seldom talked about our feelings at home.

_____ 9. We did not do things together as a family.

_____ 10. I could not express how I felt about things to my family.

_____ 11. We misunderstood each other and could not communicate clearly.

_____ 12. Tenderness between family members was avoided and even discouraged.

_____ 13. Family members had bad feelings about each other.

_____ 14. I dreaded going home after a weekend away because the family was tense and angry.

_____ 15. Discipline at home went too far, and I felt that I was being punished more than others.

_____ TOTAL SCORE

INTERPRETING PERSONAL INVENTORY SIX

Every family has *some* dysfunctional elements, because neither parents nor children are perfect. So don't be surprised if you discover that your family was partially dysfunctional. At a certain point, however, family dysfunction becomes a problem. This "crossover" point may vary from situation to situation and depends very much on the personalities of all those involved.

As a general guide, the following interpretation of your family's dysfunction can be made:

Range   Interpretation

0–5   This is a very low dysfunctional score. Are you sure you are being honest?

Range   Interpretation

6–10   This is a normal dysfunctional score. Occasionally your parents lapsed, but mostly they functioned in a healthy way.

11–15   Your family evidenced some dysfunctional patterns. They may have been more severe and damaging in some areas than in others.

16–20   Your family was clearly dysfunctional in some areas. Your childhood was probably quite conflict-ridden.

21–30   This range of score evidences fairly severe dysfunctional patterns in most areas of functioning. It is very likely that you have been significantly affected by this dysfunction as an adult.

CHAPTER 6

Taking Care of Your ACOD Self

"**I** KNOW THAT SOMETHING'S wrong in my life; I just can't put my finger on what it is," sighs twenty-two-year-old-Cindy. "I know it sounds like a cliché, but I just can't seem to find myself!"

Cindy's parents divorced when she was two and her mother remarried two years after that. And ever since those early days of her life, Cindy has struggled with feelings of confusion—the sense that something "just isn't right" with her.

For one thing, she feels somehow "closed down." She knows she holds back a lot, whether in relationships or at work. She wants to move forward with her life, but instead finds herself retreating. She tends to play the martyr, assuming that if she wants something for herself she is being selfish. And she doesn't feel she has any right to her own opinions or even her own feelings. As a result, she can never say no to others' requests; she allows others to manipulate and control her.

Even though she rationalizes her inability to stand up for herself, Cindy deeply resents being manipulated. Often she fantasizes about running away to some other part of the world where she can get lost in the crowd. She has even considered becoming a missionary—not from a deep desire to spread the gospel, but just to get away from her unsatisfactory life.

ACODS AS SELF-NEGLECTERS

Cindy, like many other ACODs, has a problem with taking care of her "self." Because of the unpleasant and sometimes threatening experiences of her unsettled childhood, she has never developed a clear sense of who she is and what her rights are as a person.

In other words, Cindy's "self" has been wounded. Growing up, she became trapped between her natural, God-given desire to become a fully functioning person and the many hidden messages she received about how everyone else's needs must come first and that it is better to surrender your rights than claim them. Her childhood experience of divorce did not prepare her well for adulthood.

One of Cindy's primary problems is that of *boundaries*. We all have to learn those invisible barriers that tell us where *we* end and *others* begin. Boundaries help define who we are and allow us to claim a certain space in the world—a place where we belong. But Cindy has no clear sense of what rightfully belongs to her.

ACODs easily become "self-neglecters" with a totally distorted notion of what it means to be "selfish."

Cindy hardly knew her natural father while she was growing up, and she never felt close to her stepfather. And this was partly because her mother often reminded Cindy that she was only "a guest" in the new home. Her motive was to emphasize that Cindy should work especially hard to behave herself. Unfortunately the message Cindy received was that she was a second-class person and an intruder. Her mother feared being rejected again; she said another marriage failure "would be the death of her." And she kept projecting this insecurity onto Cindy.

This tendency is quite common in second marriages, where the responsibility for preventing problems in the new home falls on the stepchildren. "Be good." "Don't fight with her children." "Don't make your stepfather mad." "It's got to be your fault—you really don't belong here!" Cruel sentiments. And they are conveyed by both word and deed.

I remember this pressure well, although my mother never stated it overtly. I was smart enough to figure out (although it may only have been my perception) that *I* was the intruder who was being tolerated so that my mother could have a happy second marriage. My behavior had to be impeccable. I mustn't rock the boat. Instead, I must keep the peace at all costs, or else this marriage (and our future security) would be in jeopardy.

But it's not just children from blended families who feel the burden of responsibility for "holding things together." Many divorced children are cast into caretaker roles that leave them confused about their roles and their rights. When the custodial parent is unable to function adequately, for instance, children may end up taking on household, child care, or even wage-earning responsibilities beyond their years.

There is only one way (and it is unhealthy) you can meet those kind of unusual demands as a child: Surrender your right to be yourself. You must let the other people have their way. Let them stomp all over you. Give up your natural desire to be different—to be yourself—and become what everyone else wants you to be!

Under this kind of pressure, some children rebel, but others capitulate. That is what happened to Cindy—and it happens to many other ACODs as well. We easily become "self-neglecters" with a totally distorted notion of what it means to be "selfish." The sense of who we are as persons (which is what we mean when we talk about the "self") becomes distorted and a distinct "ACOD self" emerges.

In essence, the ACOD self is a self with no rights. What are other typical characteristics of children of divorce?

1. They are confused about the appropriateness of "self-care." ACODS often lack a clear sense of why and how to look after themselves.

2. They lack adequate self-esteem. This deficit could range all the way from intense self-hate and self-rejection to utter confusion about one's rights and responsibilities.

3. They have a distorted self-image, which is often the cause of self-esteem problems. ACODs with "self problems" tend to see themselves as bad people—inadequate, defective, and undeserving of any of life's prizes. A self-image is formed during the childhood years, and a healthy one is shaped by love and understanding. Even in the best of circumstances, there is much we discover about ourselves we don't like. We need an environment of acceptance from others (especially parents) to help us accept ourselves. This acceptance tends to be limited or absent in conflict-ridden homes.

4. They are immobilized by a fear of failure. Many ACOD fears have to do with failure. The marriage was a failure. The home may have been a failure as well. Love has failed, and even God seems to have failed. Failure—and avoiding failure—therefore becomes a major life issue.

5. They have difficulty trusting others and taking risks in love or relationships. This is closely related to the fear of failure. ACODs have experienced firsthand how love can turn sour. They have seen the down side of romance. No wonder they become skeptical about marriage and mistrustful of love. Deep down, many ACODs believe that there is only one predictable human trait—people turn on you eventually. So why bother? It's safer to just stay away from love and people. So you pull back and play it safe. You've been hurt so much, especially in relationships that were supposed to be safe, that it's hard for you to trust anyone.

6. They feel somehow defective. "What's wrong with me? I know I'm not right. Something feels wrong all over." Cindy's words are typical of many other ACODs. The self has been deeply distorted while it was still in its formative stage. It began as pliable clay waiting to be shaped into something very special, but its earlier experiences knocked it out of shape.

YOUR RIGHT TO BE A "SELF"

What's wrong with your *self?* Nothing that can't be fixed. It will take a little work, but please believe that your basic, *real* self is still as precious as anything in the universe. Healing, as we will see, is more a matter of *removing* the inhibitions that prevent you from becoming your true self than of creating a new self.

Healing a defective sense of self and building a foundation for better self-care must begin with some reflection on what it means to be a self. Our culture tends to be very confused about the appropriateness of focusing on the self. The virtues of self-sacrifice often are touted right in the midst of a glorification of self-indulgence. We hear both "Do anything for love" and "Do what's right for you."

Our culture tends to be very confused about the appropriateness of focusing on the self. We hear both "Do anything for love" and "Do what's right for you."

This confusion is heightened for those of us who live in the Christian subculture. We fear being narcissistic. We want to avoid selfishness or too much preoccupation with ourselves. We are cautioned against the errors of humanism and applauded whenever we surrender our rights to others in the name of "humility."

ACODs have enough problems developing a clear and uncontaminated sense of who they are as it is. These confusing messages tend to magnify their problems immensely.

Recently I started seeing a thirty-nine-year-old man—let's call him Frank—who is struggling with severe anxiety and depression problems. Frank is a classic, if rather extreme, example of an ACOD. He described to me how "imprisoned" he feels. His "boring" job, his "nagging" wife, his "out-of-control" kids, his "helpless" mother, his alcoholic father—all represent oppressive burdens to him. Every month he drives four hundred miles to visit his ailing parents (who, although long-divorced, still live in the same town) because "It is my duty as a son." When I challenged his motive for doing this, he challenged me in return with, "But I was always taught that this is what a good son should do. Isn't this what Jesus would do?"

"No," I told Frank, "I don't think Jesus would do what you are doing." I pointed out to Frank that his visits were motivated more by guilt than by love. His parents never appreciated the visits, and they used the opportunity to continue their embattled relationship by attacking each other in his presence. In addition, Frank's wife and children had begun to resent his frequent absences and complained that the expense of these trips as causing them to suffer as well. What was the point of his going? He was only inflaming his parents' hostility, robbing his wife and children of both time and money, and making himself miserable in the process. But as with so many ACODs, Frank's distorted sense of self was keeping him on a path toward physical, psychological, and spiritual destruction.

I finally convinced Frank that he had to give priority to his own family and to himself. His first task was to correct his ideas of what it meant to be a "healthy self." This meant he had to undo his many faulty ideas about "self-sacrifice" and stop creating false guilt. He had to come to understand that God had given him the right to be a self. In other words, while Frank keeps feeling guilty because his natural urge is to "be himself" and claim all the privileges of being a person—including happiness—he should begin to feel guilty about *not* being a true self. He should feel uneasy when he neurotically and persistently surrenders his rights. He should see God as urging him to be more aware of his own needs and feel the freedom to take care of these needs. This is *healthy guilt.* It helps us to be true to ourselves.

Once Frank has stopped denying himself the right to be a true self, he will discover that he *has the freedom to sacrifice his rights,* in love and without resentment, whenever he chooses to do so. This is the great paradox of unselfishness. It only comes when you know you have the right to be your own person.

Some preachers insist that we must endlessly and relentlessly sacrifice our "selves." But I am convinced that this is not what we are called to do as Christians.

A case in point is the interpretation of Matthew 16:24, in which Jesus says, "If anyone desires to come after me, let him deny himself, and take up his cross, and follow me." The words *deny himself* here can be taken to mean many things. And some people use those words as a gateway to self-abasement, self-judgment, and self-rejection. They equate the "self" with selfishness, self-seeking, and self-aggrandizement.

But there is a self that is none of these things. Psychologists refer to it as the "ego," a term which simply means the "I." In this sense, our selves are simply who we are—and that is a gift from God, not a temptation we must deny.

Matthew 16:24 is a call to discipleship, not a call to self-degradation or self-hate. It is a call to deny the desires, distortions, and unhealthy appetites that inevitably beset human beings. It is not a call to self-flagellation but to spiritual living, to patient suffering, and to hard lessons. Finally, it is a call to accept God's grace enabling us to do these things—a call away from our "do it yourself" lives.

What Christ calls us to is the task (often strenuous and difficult) of *balancing* our rights against the rights of others. This means that we *must* consider our own needs (and the needs of our family) against those of others. We are not to allow our needs to dominate those of others—but we are also not to surrender our needs completely.

Self-sacrifice, if it is to be healthy,
must come from a self that is secure and strong.
Otherwise it is an act of cowardice,
not of love and grace.

And here is the bonus: When we are able to claim our right to be a self, we give others the right to be themselves. It is when we feel we have to constantly step aside for the benefit of others that we become resentful and bitter.

Slowly, Frank came to see this. What helped him tremendously was Jesus' story commonly called the "parable of the talents." (It is found in Matthew 25:14-30.) He realized that God had given him certain gifts and that he was called to be a "good and faithful servant" (see v. 21) in developing those gifts. By neurotically letting everyone else control his life, he was not fulfilling his responsibility as a steward of what God had given him. He needed to learn how to say no to the inner and outer pressures in order to say yes to his Lord. With that revelation—and some hard work—a new and happier Frank began to emerge.

Let me emphasize: Being true to your self is *not* the same as being selfish or self-indulgent. Selfishness and self-indulgence arise out of *distortions* of what it means to be a true self. Self-sacrifice, if it is to be healthy, must come from a self that is secure and strong. Otherwise it is an act of cowardice, not of love and grace.

UNDERSTANDING THE PROBLEM AREAS

Divorce invariably involves a dysfunctional family system—one characterized by emotional repressiveness or estrangement, intense anxiety, deep-seated insecurity, inadequate communication, excessive criticism, and distortions of the meaning of pleasure. And such dysfunctions all contribute to a distorted sense of self. Of course, these problems can exist in intact family situations as well as in broken ones. And other factors besides marital discord can work to distort a child's sense of self—the parents' emotional health (or lack of it), life circumstances such as poverty or unemployment, and the personalities of all the parties concerned.

What this means, of course, is that a child can develop "self problems" in a variety of family situations, not just in divorce. However, I believe that the potential for a distorted sense of self is greater when there is a background of divorce. Often, in fact, divorce is the culminating crisis that is superimposed on these other self-destroying problems. It is often the straw that breaks the camel's back and causes the collapse of the self.

Adults who have a background of divorce tend to develop "self problems" in several important areas:

- self-criticism,
- relationships,
- self-esteem, and
- spiritual identity.

Let's now look briefly at each of these distortions of the self.

PROBLEMS WITH SELF-CRITICISM

Because ACODs typically grow up feeling deficient and unloved, they tend to turn on themselves and use self-criticism as a form of punishment.

This self-punishment is often rationalized. "Oh, I criticize myself every time I make a mistake at work because this helps to keep me on my toes and avoid mistakes," one young woman told me recently. She believed that she would become more error-prone if she allowed herself any margin for error. But the truth was that her habit of punishing herself resulted in *more* errors. I tried to show her that her self-criticism only made her more tense and so afraid of making mistakes that she probably made them three or four times more often. If she concentrated on her work and stopped being so self-critical, she would be more far more efficient.

Because ACODs typically grow up feeling deficient and unloved, they tend to turn on themselves and use self-criticism as a form of punishment.

Self-criticism can take several forms. Some people develop the habit of always comparing themselves with other people—and, of course, always coming off second best. Other ACODs blame themselves for everything that happens.

One young woman I worked with, for example, worked in a large office where many desks were placed close together. Whenever she overheard someone else being reprimanded by a supervisor, she would get very upset, feeling that somehow *she* was to blame. She reacted the same way at home. Whenever one of her kids got into trouble, for instance, she blamed herself: "I didn't teach Peter properly. I'm sure I made a mistake when I told him what to do." Such self-blame, whether excessive or even mild but frequent, can lead to a host of other problems, including depression and chronic resentment.

Why do problems of excessive self-criticism arise? Usually because there is too much *blaming* in the family. Parents who are in conflict typically throw a lot of blame around, and the children often take some of this blame upon themselves. Children tend to think in simplistic terms and are essentially self-centered; this means they have an inherent tendency to apply any problem they observe directly to themselves. The younger the child, the more likely he or she is to do this.

Parents who feel the need to present themselves as perfect are especially likely to blame others excessively and to do a lot of harm to their children. Their facade of perfection shifts the blame to their kids, who then may develop supersensitive self-critical mechanisms.

The healing of your self-critical tendencies, like so many other problems, will probably require some careful rethinking. First, you must become convinced *that there is no value whatsoever in self-punishment.* And then you might find it necessary to do some detective work into how and why your habit of self-criticism developed. New freedom can emerge from a deep understanding of how you were shaped to take blame when you are not at fault or why you have a need to punish yourself excessively. Once you understand *why* you tend to blame yourself, you can *choose* not to do it.

Do you grasp this point? Your self-criticism is so deeply ingrained in your personality that all you can do at this stage in your life is to *decide* not to indulge it. You will probably have some successes and some failures as you attempt this. But in time, your need to criticize yourself will begin to lose its power over you. If your self-blame is very severe, you may want to seek professional help.

PROBLEMS WITH RELATIONSHIPS

I recently met with a pastor who began the conversation with a litany of woes: "I am nearly thirty-five years old and still single. I've had lots of dates, and many women are interested in me, but I just can't seem to move forward in any dating relationship. I seem to be overly picky and critical. No one seems to measure up to my expectations."

He paused when he saw my smile. "You must know something I don't know," he ventured.

"No," I replied, "It's just that I hear that same story so often I'm beginning to think the problem is contagious. Please continue."

"Well, it's just that I was wondering whether coming from a divorced home has anything to do with my problem. I can't believe that out of all the women I've met, there's not one I can build a

---

*The more secure you feel in your self-identity and the more
confident you are that you can claim your rights as a person,
the more willing you will be to risk relationships.*

---

happy life with! I crave intimacy. I enjoy women's company. I'm very
normal sexually. Why can't I choose a wife?"

He then went on to tell me his family's history. His parents divorced when he was six years of age. His mother, who never remarried, had carried her bitterness over being rejected through the
rest of her life. His father had married again, but the second marriage also flopped. And now this young pastor was experiencing a
very common consequence of childhood divorce: problems building secure relationships, including deep feelings of uncertainty
about getting married.

Over the next few weeks, as we explored his feelings, several factors emerged that are typical of many ACODs when it comes to
establishing relationships:

- Deep down, he had become disillusioned with the whole marriage business.
- He seriously doubted his ability to make a sound decision
  regarding a spouse.
- He questioned his own ability to maintain a marriage relationship.
- As he thought about marriage, he kept flashing back to his
  own unhappy home. In his imagination he relived the fights,
  the shouting, and the unpleasantness, and was afraid of
  repeating those experiences.
- He frankly admitted that, not having grown up in a normal,
  intact home, he had no idea what one was like—much less
  how it could be created or maintained. He lacked an adequate
  model of a normal marital relationship.

There are other factors, unconscious at this stage, that we will yet
explore, but these are sufficient for the moment to illustrate some
of the difficulties you may have in relationships.

Fortunately, many self-related relationship difficulties can be overcome. Interestingly enough, one way to do this is to work on the *other* "self areas" such as self-esteem and spirituality. The more secure you feel in your self-identity and the more confident you are that you can claim your rights as a person, the more willing you will be to risk relationships. But developing specific "relationship skills" can also be very helpful in fine tuning your sense of balance between yourself and other people. I will suggest some of these skills in chapter 8 and show how they can be developed.

PROBLEMS WITH SELF-ESTEEM

This aspect of the ACOD's healing has and will come up several times throughout this book. It is unavoidable because self-esteem is an absolutely foundational issue. Many of the difficulties I have discussed can be traced back to the primary problem of inadequate self-esteem.

Just what is self-esteem? First of all, as I have already made clear, it is *not* some special feeling of love one has toward oneself.

What Self-Esteem Involves

1. Not hating yourself for just being who you are.
2. Not rejecting yourself when you fail.
3. Not punishing yourself for being imperfect.
4. Not wanting to be someone else you admire.
5. Accepting that you are who you are.
6. Being "transparent" about yourself to others.
7. Seeing yourself as just as valuable as anyone else—no more and no less.
8. Being willing to own up to your strengths as well as your weaknesses.
9. Knowing that you are deeply loved and valued by your Creator.

Of course, everyone, not just ACODs, experiences feelings of inadequacy or inferiority from time to time. But several factors make children of divorce especially prone to developing feelings of low self-esteem that will carry over to adulthood:

- Despite its increased acceptance in our society, divorce *still* carries a stigma. Children of divorce still tend to feel "different" and disgraced.
- The indignities of other people's reactions (humiliating, demeaning, or even pitying comments) can create feelings of inferiority.
- The divorce process (settlements, custody battles, and so on) often batters a child emotionally, disrupting the formation of an adequate self-image.
- The dissolution of the family, often accompanied by a sense of abandonment, undermines the very foundation on which self-esteem is built: healthy child-parent interactions.
- Love is likely to become more conditional in times of parental conflict. The withdrawal of parental love is more likely to be used as punishment in times when a parent is too distracted to use healthier means of discipline, and this can devastate a child's self-esteem.
- The losses associated with the divorce (loss of home, friends, social standing, security, parent, school, and so forth) create depression in the child. Depression breeds lowered self-esteem, since lowered self-esteem is one of the natural symptoms accompanying depression.

Deep-seated self-hate that is created in childhood almost always carries over into adult life—where it usually wreaks havoc. If your self-esteem is low, you probably also lack confidence, you feel inferior, you become excessively self-critical. You fear failure and therefore avoid risks. And healthy assertiveness is a real problem for you. You are unable to stand up for your own rights or your family's rights, and you cannot say no to demands made of you or set limits to other people's intrusions in your life. In fact, the only time you can assert yourself may be when you are angry—but you have probably built up enough resentment and hostility toward those who take advantage of you that you are angry much of the time, anyway. And if you are not angry, chances are that you're depressed.

The suggestions for building self-esteem outlined in chapter 4 can go a long way toward restoring a healthy sense of self. In addition, here are several projects you can work on:

1. Build your sense of competence in one specific area of your life. You cannot feel good about yourself if you try to be a jack of all trades and master of none. There *must* be something special about yourself—some skill, knowledge, or ability that is uniquely yours. Find it. Ask those close to you to help you discover your "specialness," or explore it through counseling or taking personality tests. Pray for insight in this matter.

You *are* special. Focus on that. Value it. Develop it. And I am not just talking about intellect or athletic ability. I mean examine your character. Look inward to find your real strengths. Can you be a true friend to someone? Can you develop compassion for hurting people? Do you have the ability to focus outwardly? Are you a giving or godly person? Your sense of self-worth will grow very rapidly if you begin to value these qualities about yourself.

Many children of divorce experienced some deficiency in their sense of being loved. To compensate for this, we have to work now at building more stable, accepting, and secure relationships.

---

2. Work on your love relationships. The feeling that one is genuinely loved by someone else (and I don't mean just romantic love) is absolutely crucial to maintaining a sense of self-worth. For this reason, the effort of building loving relationships can be one of the most rewarding in terms of self-esteem.

Many children of divorce experienced some deficiency in their sense of being loved. The love we did receive was often conditional; it depended on our being good or not "making waves"—or it depended on our parents' current emotional state. We may even have felt that our parents wanted to abandon us or that their expressions of love were simply a manipulative ploy!

To compensate for this, we have to work at building more stable, accepting, and secure relationships—relationships in which love is unconditional. I will make some suggestions later about how this can be accomplished.

3. Stop making impossible demands on yourself. It is very common for ACODs to work out their unfinished childhood business by placing extraordinary demands on themselves and others. They set their expectations so high that they cannot be met. As a result, they are constantly falling short—and thus perpetuating a sense of failure and nonaccomplishment.

Why do we do this to ourselves? Sometimes we are unconsciously trying to appease our consciences. Sometimes we are desperately trying to earn the respect of others. Sometimes we are trying to compensate for many losses. There are many possible reasons. But whatever the reason, living under the hardest taskmaster of all—yourself—can undermine feelings of self-worth. If you appoint yourself as sole judge and jury for your conduct, you probably will never measure up to your own standards.

A young woman recently came to see me because her job as a legal secretary was driving her crazy. As we explored her situation, what emerged was a problem that is quite common for ACODs. She felt worthwhile only if she could master everything given to her. She would never refuse a work assignment. Nor could she admit to her supervisor that she was overloaded or that a particular job was beyond her training. She took all the work that was given to her, so more and more was piled on. Her self-esteem depended on meeting impossible and unrealistic expectations that she had internalized: "If only I could be the world's greatest secretary, I'll feel okay about myself." This irrational belief and her efforts to act on it were driving her more and more deeply into depression and despair.

Once this woman was able to see what she was doing, she began to change. Quite quickly she connected her self-loathing with her childhood experiences. She saw how absurdly she had connected her self-esteem with meeting the impossible demands she placed on herself. She also realized that being swamped by these unreasonable expectations was only eroding her self-worth further.

I knew she was well on the road to recovery when several weeks later she made this statement: "I am finally seeing that I'm not the world's greatest secretary, and that feels okay. I'm also beginning to realize that I'm probably just as good as anyone else I know. I don't have to be better—just the same!"

PROBLEMS WITH YOUR SPIRITUAL SELF

I have always had a deep interest in spiritual matters. After a very unhappy childhood, clouded by the conflicted marriage of my parents, I became a Christian at the age of seventeen. That commitment made all the difference in the world for me. I found out what it was like to have my deepest, most personal self—my spiritual self—transformed and renewed. For the first time in my life, joy became a reality for me.

Now, many years later, I make no apologies for identifying myself as a Christian psychologist. And after years as a therapist, I really believe that true recovery must reach deeper than the mind and the emotions, into the realm of the spirit. We cannot truly be right with ourselves until we become right with God.

Of course, there are those who might define "mental health" or "emotional health" so narrowly that it excludes anything spiritual. But I believe that definition is too limited; it doesn't take into account the whole of what it means to be a human being. How can I separate, say, my emotion of guilt from my deep yearnings to be a good and godly person? How can I cope with grief if I do not consider the possibility of some existence beyond the grave? Psychological and spiritual health cannot be separated.

For this reason, I believe that secular psychotherapy—despite its many benefits—is inherently limited in its ability to bring healing into people's lives. That is not to say that secular psychotherapy is not valuable. It can provide some dignity and freedom from incapacitating anxiety and worry. It can help people feel more competent and restore a modicum of self-esteem. It can even teach us to be better parents and to live together with less conflict. But there are some things it cannot give us. It cannot bring us joy at the deepest level of our beings.

After years as a therapist, I really believe that true recovery must reach deeper than the mind and the emotions, into the realm of the spirit. We cannot truly be right with ourselves until we become right with God.

Sigmund Freud admitted these limitations when he said that psychoanalysis could cure the miseries of the neurotic—only to open that person up to the *normal* miseries of life. In other words, there's a level of existence that is beyond the reach of psychotherapy alone.

To put it another way, secular psychotherapy can make the barn of life look pretty good on the outside by giving it a coat of paint, and it can even clean up the inside of the barn so that it looks clean and tidy. But the basic structure of the barn—the wood that actually makes it a barn—may still be rotten! In the course of time, the paint will fade. Horse droppings and rusty pieces of farm equipment may once again litter the inside floor. But more important, unless something is done to the wood of that barn—boards replaced, termites exterminated, whatever is necessary—the whole structure will eventually collapse. All of this means that the process of "taking care of ourselves" must involve attending to the needs of our spiritual selves.

What are some of these spiritual needs?

- We need to feel in harmony with our Creator. Deep down, all of us yearn to be joined to God in love.
- We need to have a sense of destiny—to know that this life is not the beginning and end of existence.
- We need to know that no matter how much we fail in life or how wayward our path, God offers forgiveness for all our sinfulness. This comforting reality addresses the human guilt problem at its very source.
- We intuitively know that to be able to relate healthily with others, we must be spiritually restored.
- Consciously or unconsciously, we all long to give expression to the image of God within us.

What spiritual resources are available to help us satisfy these spiritual needs?

- We all have the capacity to reach out in faith and touch God.
- We have Scripture to instruct us in who God is and how to accept God's offer of grace.
- We have the wonderful, though mysterious, gift of prayer that makes it possible for us to communicate with God.
- We have God's offer of forgiveness, full and free, if we will turn to him and accept it.

But being an adult child of divorce can sometimes make it difficult for us either to recognize our spiritual needs or to make use of our spiritual resources. It is very easy for children of divorce to develop problems that prevent them from meeting their spiritual needs. One of the most common and significant, as I have mentioned several times, is a distortion in our view of God—a distortion that tends to keep us at a distance from the Source of all healing.

Our early view of God (or our "God concept") is based largely upon images shaped by our parents. The father's role is particularly important, although I don't believe, as some therapists do, that the father is the sole or even the primary influence. Many significant adults help shape a child's image of God—especially at the feeling level. Nevertheless, the influence of parents is critical at this point.

If your parents were largely responsible for your developing God-concept, it follows that abusive or inadequate parenting may have severely distorted your understanding of who God really is.

If your parents were largely responsible for your developing God-concept, it follows that abusive or inadequate parenting may have severely distorted your understanding of who God really is. You may have grown up thinking of God as harsh, punitive, or judgmental—or as remote, uncaring, or just "not there." All of this will affect how you view your own behavior, your relationships, and especially yourself. It also affects how you relate to God. If you see him as a tyrant, you will fear him. If you see him as unreliable, you won't trust him.

Whether you see him as a hard taskmaster, an absent and uncaring landlord, a critical judge out to trap you in some mistake, or a well-meaning but ineffectual guide—your spiritual life will be compromised by your distorted view.

This is what happened to Jodi. Her father was a deacon in a local fundamentalist church—a pillar of the congregation. He taught in the Sunday school, visited the sick, and would do anything for anybody in need. But Jodi he criticized. Nothing she could do seemed to please him. She often thought it was because he had wanted a boy and got a girl.

Jodi's father's excessive and persistent criticism about her schoolwork, the way she wore her hair and clothes, her manners, her attitude, her friends, and even her basic looks (he said she "wasn't very pretty") created horrendous obstacles for Jodi's spiritual life. In later years she felt so guilt-ridden that she couldn't resist an altar call. She always went forward, even if she knew she didn't need to. She also had great difficulty in saying the Lord's Prayer—or even listening to it. Just hearing "Our Father" would make a knot tighten up in her stomach.

"Who was God? Is he a man? Can't I just think of him as an angel?" These were the questions Jodi struggled with as she tried to put her spiritual life in order. To this day, her father denies that her problems have anything to do with his critical nature.

You may consider this case a little extreme, but let me assure you that I have frequently encountered such distortions in adult children of divorce. Children who experience emotional abandonment (which is very common in divorce) can come to view God as unloving, super-judgmental, distant, indifferent, unapproachable, and "against" them. They feel unworthy of such a God, and the last thing they want to do is to take their problems to him. "The heavens have shut me out," is how one man described his feelings about God. I have encountered scores of people who feel this way. It seems to go along with a history of parental difficulties.

How can one heal one's spiritual self from such distortions?

1. Work at developing an accurate mental picture of God. There are many resources for doing this. Read your Bible. Reflect on God's compassion (Psalm 78:38), his love (John 3:16), his majesty (Job

37:22), and his wisdom (1 Corinthians 1:25). Talk to "veteran" Christians whose understanding you respect. Study literature that helps to describe who God is. J.B. Phillips' classic, *Your God Is Too Small*,[1] is an excellent remedy for a distorted image of God. And Philip Yancey's, *Disappointment With God*,[2] is an excellent resource for reducing the huge gap between what people *expect* from God and what they actually experience. Having had inadequate parenting, you may find yourself expecting the wrong things from God. After all, you've never had an adequate model, so what do you know about how he works? Yancey paints a very clear and biblical picture of what you can rightly expect from God by "letting God speak for himself."

2. Work at separating your image of God from that of your parents or other living persons. By increasing your awareness of when you project onto God the images of your parents, you should be able to effect a separation. Keep reminding yourself, "God is not like people—certainly not like my mother or father. God reaches beyond human boundaries. He is everything I could possibly desire in the perfect parent, friend, or spouse." Reinforce this separation by continuing to work on your mental image.

3. Resist giving "holy excuses" for your self-problems. It is far from uncommon for ACODs to project their confusions about their selves onto God—to use their faulty God-concepts to excuse their own unhealthy behavior. For example, ACODs easily fall into the trap of becoming perfectionists as a way of proving to themselves and others they are worthy—and then rationalizing that *God* is demanding this perfectionism. Other ACODs, as we saw earlier in the chapter, explain their inability to assert themselves in terms of God-ordained "self-sacrifice."

The problem with such mental games, of course, is that they short-circuit the healing process. If we define our failure to take care of ourselves as God-ordained, then the act of challenging our unhealthy behavior seems like sacrilege. We end up using our God-concept as a barrier to healing rather than depending on the living God to help us recover.

Once again, working to correct our faulty ideas about God and ourselves is the first line of defense against using these ideas as "holy excuses." "Holy perfectionists," for example, need to get their heads straight about the reality of forgiveness. The very reason that forgiveness figures so prominently in the New Testament is that God knows we cannot go through life without making some mistakes. I'm not saying that we cannot achieve the utmost for him, just that forgiveness is there when we fail. Part of the genius of Christianity is that it teaches forgiveness for imperfection, not salvation through perfectionism. And internalizing that reality can go a long way toward helping us pull down the self-erected barriers of rationalization.

ACODs easily fall into the trap becoming perfectionists as a way of proving they are worthy—and then rationalizing that God is demanding this perfectionism. Other ACODs explain their inability to assert themselves in terms of God-ordained "self-sacrifice."

---

4. Make a point of developing your spiritual awareness. Because many ACODs see God negatively, they tend to avoid him—consciously or unconsciously—by shutting off their spiritual awareness. After all, if you believe God is intolerant of failure, punishing and judgmental, or even just cold and distant, you will naturally try to protect yourself from him.

There are many ways this can happen. You may overintellectualize your religion, avoid religion altogether, or just shut God out of your everyday life. But no matter how you cut yourself off from God, you end up hurting yourself, because in the process you are cutting yourself off from the very Source of healing you need most.

I often hear ACODs complain that they just cannot "feel" God. Their feelings about God are numbed, and this lack of feeling may seriously hamper their spiritual development.

ACODs in particular may have difficultly "feeling" that God has forgiven them. There are several possible reasons for this. One of the most important is that the experience of forgiveness is very foreign to some ACODs simply because it is not a feature of most conflict-ridden homes; the parents are at war precisely because they can't manage forgiveness. No wonder their grown children may find it hard to handle the reality of God's forgiveness.

In such a situation, I find it helpful to assure my patients that the *fact* of forgiveness does not depend on the *feeling* of forgiveness. And this is true of other ways of experiencing God as well. You may need to begin by realizing that your emotional problems and your faulty God-concept may make it difficult for you to tune in to spiritual reality. But your difficulty in "feeling" God has nothing to do with the reality of who God is.

I often hear ACODs complain that they just cannot "feel" God. Their feelings about God are numbed, and this lack of feeling may seriously hamper their spiritual development.

Once you have accepted that your feelings are not necessarily a reflection of reality, you can begin the work of developing your spiritual awareness. Many resources are available to help you do this. Talk to a clergyman or to another person who seems to have a vital spiritual awareness. Learn to meditate and admit to God that you have difficulty feeling his presence, and ask him to make himself real to you.

Over time, these things can help pull down the barriers you have unconsciously erected against God. As you carry them out, remind yourself that they have worked for many people over the centuries. Also remind yourself that your feelings aren't necessarily the best indication of reality. And don't give up your work on other areas of your recovery. As you struggle to find healing for your other self-problems, your spiritual awareness will likely improve—and you will receive the transforming power you need to rise above your problems as an ACOD.

5. Work at increasing your trust in God. Most spiritual problems for adults who have experienced divorce as children center on issues of trust. After all, their trust was violated from their earliest years. They trusted that their parents would provide a secure home, that they would be taken care of, and that life would always be good. That trust was broken by the most important people in their lives. No wonder trust is a problem for them!

"Since I couldn't trust my father, how can you expect me to trust you—or God?" one feisty teenager challenged me once. And to a point he was right. One of the essential ingredients for building trust is that things happen when they are supposed to happen and that people keep their promises. And when divorce happens, life becomes anything but predictable. People disappear, promises are broken, you learn that the people you love just cannot be relied upon. In such a situation, how can you be expected to learn trust?

My answer to that teenager is the same answer I have given myself many times when confronted with my own feelings of distrust: once again, feelings are not necessarily reality, and our childhood experience does not necessarily give us an accurate picture of God. My father may not have been reliable or trustworthy, but God is not like my father—or anyone else. He *can* be trusted simply because he is God.

One last thought on the subject of trust. Often when we say to ourselves that we cannot trust God, we are really saying that we are *angry* at God for something or other. Our refusal to trust is an act of defiance brought on by anger.

Being angry at God is never helpful—spiritually or psychologically. In fact, the psalmist tells us that only a "foolish man" or woman gets angry at God daily (Psalms 74:22). I know that some Christian psychologists encourage their patients to verbalize and experience their anger toward God, but I have always seen this as a futile and counterproductive exercise. What point is there in storming the gates of heaven? Such misdirected anger has to be the ultimate in scapegoating.

More important, directing our anger at God does further damage to our God-concept by imputing unworthy motives to him. Why would God harm you intentionally? Why would he hurt you when you don't deserve it? To be angry at him is to believe that he doesn't care about you. It is far better to direct your anger at the *real* source of your hurt than to project it at God, which cuts *you* off from the very power you need to deal with your hurt.

Fortunately, God understands when we vent our anger on him.

*Often when we say to ourselves that we cannot trust God,
we are really saying that we are angry at God for
something or other.*

He knows how our minds play tricks on us. If we really need a scapegoat, he is always willing to oblige. So there is no penalty for feeling this anger or for even expressing it. But recovery requires that you pull your angry feelings back from God as soon as you possibly can and attach them to their real source. When you do that, you can continue to build the spiritual resources you need as you learn to take care of your ACOD self.

CHAPTER 7

Rewriting Your Life-Script

WHETHER OR NOT YOU are aware of it, you live your life from a master "script." The choices you make, your decisions, your actions, and even many of your feelings derive from a set of deeply established beliefs, attitudes, and assumptions that guide and direct your life. These are the minor scripts that together make up the master plan for your life.

In a sense, a "life-script" is like a plot in a play. It is a plan for how things will be done, a sort of prescription for living. And it contains within its emotional pages the patterns for future actions, reactions, and emotions. Your life-script determines how you will react when certain things happen to you and what you will do when confronted by certain circumstances. Ultimately, therefore, it influences what you make of your life.

Many people find their lives to be unmanageable because of unsatisfactory "life-scripts." They have been programmed to think, feel, and act in such a way that they create their own unhappiness and emotional pain. They repeat the same ineffective behavior over and over without learning from their mistakes. They keep going back to the same old way of doing or thinking, and they seem doomed to duplicate their ineffective behavior patterns for the rest of their lives. If they never stop to analyze and rewrite their "scripts," these scripts are destined to follow them to the grave.

Although life-scripts can be formed at any stage of life, most of them have their origin in early life. And that is one reason divorce can be so damaging to children. When childhood is disrupted by a major trauma such as divorce, decisions are made, beliefs are established, and attitudes are formed that become a *life plan* for that child. Adult children of divorce, therefore, tend to have *special* life-scripts. Unless they are challenged and changed, they easily determine who that child is as an adult. Every ACOD should, therefore, take some time to examine his or her life-scripts.

Many people find their lives to be unmanageable because of unsatisfactory "life-scripts." If they never stop to analyze and rewrite their "scripts," these scripts are destined to follow them to the grave.

This chapter will examine a few of the most common life-scripts that ACODs develop. I will analyze some general scripts, then look at a few that affect only males or only females, then I will share some thoughts on how that life-script can be rewritten.

EXAMPLES OF GENERAL ACOD LIFE-SCRIPTS

Claude Steiner, a follower of Eric Berne and proponent of a therapeutic approach called Transactional Analysis, believes that there are three basic life-scripts that cause misery in life[1]:

- depression—the "no love" script,
- madness—the "no mind" script, and
- addiction—the "no joy" script.

I find his analysis very helpful. However, I have found that these three universal scripts take particular forms in the ACOD. So let me examine these three basic "misery scripts" in the context of childhood divorce.

"NOBODY LOVES ME"

Lovelessness is a universal ACOD life-script. It arises because as a child you believed that one or both of your parents didn't love you. How could they have loved you? They didn't take care of your needs!

Our need for love is so foundational to emotional health that thwarting or violating it has an impact on every aspect of our lives. We need love like we do air; it is the only emotional "atmosphere" that fosters wholeness and happiness.

If you grow up without feeling unconditional love, you may well end up feeling like an emotional cripple as an adult. You want love, but don't feel lovable. You might even reject love because you can't trust it, or you may feel the constant need to test love to see if it's genuine. Because you believe that nobody can really love you, you sabotage whatever love comes your way—and you end up not being loved at all. Your life-script thus becomes a self-fulfilling prophecy.

Some ACODs make a vow in childhood: "I'll never get married." And vows, of course, are powerful life-scripts; they determine exactly how we plan to live our lives. Fortunately, most vows like this are made in a fit of anger and lose their power over time. For some, however, a childhood vow of this kind shapes unconscious fears of intimacy and bonding.

If you believe that nobody can really love you, you sabotage whatever love comes your way—and you end up not being loved at all. Your life-script thus becomes a self-fulfilling prophecy.

Is it possible to break a "no love" life script? Absolutely. And not only is it possible—it is absolutely necessary if you're going to be whole again. With a mature attitude and a sensible review of your particular "script" variation, you can begin to shape a new attitude toward love and marriage. Talking over your feelings with someone else can be especially helpful. Bringing your unstated assumptions out in the open will often show clearly how untrue they are. In particular, you must understand how irrational it is to believe you are unlovable.

"I THINK I MUST BE CRAZY"

If you follow this life script, you live with the ever-present fear that something is wrong with your mind. And this script, like the others, can take any of several forms.

In its most extreme form, this script may lead you to fear you are actually "going crazy." Dysfunctional families have a way of creating these fears. After all, you may be told that you have no right to feel the way you do, or that what you observe is not really happening at all. In some divorcing families, blame is dispensed left, right, and center with little regard for truth. There is little consistency or predictability. No wonder these children grow up so confused that they literally believe something is wrong with their minds!

If as a child you live continuously under unhappy circumstances you cannot control, you may develop a deep-rooted belief that you are at the mercy of life.

Another variation of the "I'm crazy" life-script is the "learned helplessness" scenario. This is perhaps the most damaging of all life-scripts. If as a child you live continuously under unhappy circumstances you cannot control, you may develop a deep-rooted *belief* that you are at the mercy of life. You come to assume that everything that happens is determined by forces outside of your control and that you can change nothing. As a result, you continue in your distress, making no effort to get out of it. Your sense of helplessness, therefore, leads naturally to chronic feelings of hopelessness and depression.

Not too long ago, I counseled Cynthia, a twenty-seven-year-old who still lived at home. Cynthia's parents had divorced when she was fifteen, and her mother, an ineffectual sort of person, had fallen apart. As a result, Cynthia had to take control and become the "strong" person in the family.

As years rolled by, Cynthia found herself unwillingly cast in the role of her mother's caretaker. Helplessness had become Cynthia's life-script in this matter. She had came to believe that her mother (who was only in her late forties) could not live without her help and that therefore she had no choice but to take care of her. Cynthia worked, kept house, and even denied herself a normal dating life so that she could stay at home with her mother. Gradually, however, a deep resentment set in, and Cynthia became more and more depressed.

I recall Cynthia's first words to me as she sat in my office: "I think I'm going crazy. I have no mind of my own. My life is wasting away." She had lived so long under the life-script of learned helplessness that she had no idea how to change her life.

The beliefs underlying Cynthia's self-destructive behavior were far from rational, but they were so deeply entrenched in her personality that they "felt" reasonable to her. What were some of these beliefs? Reduced to their stark and ridiculous reality, they sounded like this:

- Nobody loves me, so I must do everything possible to please my mother because she is the only one I can expect love from.
- If I do not take care of my mother, she will not survive, and I will be responsible.
- My mother couldn't possibly get a job at her stage of life, since she has never worked before. Even though she is still quite young, she is frail and incapable of taking care of herself.
- It is a child's duty to sacrifice everything for the sake of a parent, because parents do the same for children.
- If I leave my mother and live my own life, she will feel abandoned and rejected and will never forgive me.

As I helped Cynthia to put her underlying beliefs into words like this, she became very excited because she had begun to realize that *none of them were true!* The life-script she had been following so slavishly was based on ideas that had no basis in reality.

The process of therapy is unavoidably slow in many cases, but Cynthia's recovery was quick. All she needed was for someone to reassure her that she wasn't crazy, that she had a right to her own life, that her mother would survive if forced to care for herself, that life could be beautiful if she tackled it courageously. She quickly got rid of her helpless feelings, and together we planned her phased withdrawal from her mother's control.

Within a year, Cynthia's mother had a job, was living on her own, and was quite happy. Cynthia's helplessness had been feeding her mother's helplessness. As she began to withdraw from her caretaker role, however, her mother responded by being less helpless herself. With some counseling, she got over her grief and resentment at being abandoned by her husband and started a new life.

And Cynthia? She's a lot happier. Instead of fearing that she might be crazy, she feels strong, purposeful, in charge of her life— and she is busy writing out a new life-script.

"I WILL NEVER BE HAPPY"

This script, in effect, is controlled by the belief that you simply are not programmed for happiness or joy in this life. And unfortunately this life-script, like the other two, easily becomes a self-fulfilling prophecy. In addition to robbing you of the joy of living, this life-script often contributes to the development of addictions. Because your life-script prohibits you from being naturally happy, you seek comfort or distraction in an external substance or behavior. The "no joy" life-script is especially likely to form the basis for many of the so-called "hidden addictions"—workaholism, compulsive shopping, excessive TV watching, overeating, compulsive gambling, and sexual compulsions.

The "I will never be happy" script operates to produce unhappiness in several ways:

1. You "define" what it is that makes you happy and what doesn't. In other words, you tell yourself exactly what will or will not make you happy, and you don't allow for any substitutions. "If I can meet the right person," you say, "then I'll be happy." Or, "If you give me what

I want, then I'll be happy." The problem is that when you lay down such specific qualifications for happiness, you set yourself up to be *unhappy* if what you expected doesn't happen.

Adult children of divorce are especially vulnerable to doing this because our early experiences set us up for confused expectations. Our discordant home life makes it hard for us to know what we can reasonably count on. On one hand, we are so deprived of happiness as children that we never quite figure out how to be happy. At the same time, the daydreams and fantasies to which we retreat for comfort may lead us into unrealistic expectations.

Since you believe you are not programmed for happiness,
then you are likely to make decisions that will
guarantee unhappiness.

---

2. You become negative and pessimistic, always looking on the dark side of your circumstances. Since your script specifies, "You couldn't possibly be happy, no matter how good life is to you," you become incapable of seeing just how good your life really is. And since you believe you are not programmed for happiness, then you are likely to make decisions that will guarantee unhappiness.

This particular life pattern clearly arises out of the unhappiness of a conflict-ridden childhood. Children of divorce typically have been let down so often that they play it safe by always expecting the worst. They protect themselves from disappointment by ceasing to believe that life can be good.

3. Another source for the unhappiness life-script is faulty messages from parents. These messages, which originate in the parents' own bitterness and confusion, may be imparted directly, in the form of bad advice, or indirectly, through passing comments or even body language. Quite often they are directed at the ex-spouse and concern the opposite sex: "All men are rats; you can't trust any of them." But they can also be about life in general: "I don't know why I don't just give up! What's the point, anyway? You work and work and have nothing to show for it."

Unhappy parents inculcate many distressing attitudes, often without realizing it. If children accept these pronouncements uncritically, they easily form the basis for unhappy life-scripts.

Has your own life-script been shaped by bad advice that set you up to be unhappy? Take a moment and see how many of your own bad attitudes you can trace back to faulty messages from a parent. Try to understand what these messages *really* meant in terms of your parent's own life and how these have become part of the scripts that control your life today. Here are a few for you to explore:

- *"You can't trust anybody."* What your mother really means is that she can't trust your father. Her attitude is based on her experience of him. It cannot apply to every other living person.

- *"You try your best, but you cannot please anyone."* What your father really means is that he tried to please your mother but failed. Again, you cannot generalize this to everyone.

- *"Never let them see you cry."* Other variations of this message include "Hide your feelings"; "Never show you are weak"; "Emotions are not real"; "Don't give people any advantage over you." This faulty message indicates that *self-concealment* is the only way to survive. Actually, the exact *opposite* is true. Being open with your feelings brings healing, while closing them off breeds further emotional turmoil.

- *"Don't tell..."* This bad advice advocates *secrecy* over openness, and it can take many different forms. Often it is directed at the ex-spouse in an effort to control him or her: "Don't tell your father I bought a new pair of shoes." "Don't tell your mother I came home." Or it can take the more general form: "Don't tell anyone about our private affair." When children are urged to participate in disguising the truth and even in deception they become confused, ashamed, torn between loyalties. In adulthood they may become downright dishonest or at least unable to face trouble head-on.

SEX-ROLE DIFFERENCES IN LIFE-SCRIPTS

Men and women are socialized in most cultures to develop certain parts of their personalities while suppressing others. This socialization interacts with physical and genetic factors to produce the final life pattern of each of the sexes. While some life-roles (such as mothering) are controlled by sex genes, many are not. They are taught—or "caught" through observation.

By overemphasizing sex-role differences in our culture, especially at the emotional level, we create personality "gaps" that limit people's potential to become whole human beings.

For instance, girls are typically taught how to develop their nurturing selves. Building upon their instinctive roles as future mothers, they play with dolls, and they give hugs. They are also allowed to cry and express themselves emotionally—and these are not necessarily instinctive functions. On the other hand, girls are often discouraged from developing mechanical skills and from being "too smart" or independent. And they are taught to get their way through subtle manipulation rather than direct competition.

Boys, on the other hand, many be instinctively aggressive or "active"—but they are also encouraged by socialization to develop their competitive edge and not to form nurturing characteristics. Instead, they are given tools and sports equipment. Their competitive efforts are rewarded, and they are taught to be "tough" and rational rather than overtly loving, caring, or "weak." They learn to judge themselves and others according to physical size, athletic ability, or other ways of standing out from the "pack."

In the process of this socialization, boys and girls become men and women with very different sex-role scripts. Some of these scripts are quite appropriate. Many are not.

What defines the appropriate male or female role is quite arbitrary when you think about it, and it differs from culture to culture. In some primitive cultures, for instance, women do all the heavy labor. In others, men deck themselves out with glamorous clothes. Quite the reverse of what we expect.

Now, the result of this "culturization" process is very interesting. Each sex ends up deficient in some personality characteristics that are strongly developed in the other sex. Each sex then looks to the other to supply the "missing" functions—often with devastating consequences.

For instance, women typically grow up better able to form intimate relationships than men. A man, therefore, may search for a caring, nurturing partner to make up this deficiency, but then be incapable of providing warmth and caring in return. Or a woman who has been raised to be responsive and dependent may look for a "strong, silent type" to take care of her, then become clingy and unable to provide emotional support to him. This inability to supply mutual fulfillment is a major cause of marital discord.

Furthermore, by overemphasizing sex-role differences in our culture, especially at the emotional level, we create personality "gaps" that limit people's potential to become *whole* human beings. Many are left feeling "incomplete" or "deficient." Some even feel "immature" because only a part of them has been allowed to develop. They have been coerced to develop certain life-scripts that are based on *myths* about the differences between the sexes, not on the real differences.

This is a vital point. There *are* real differences in the basic makeup of males and females. And I believe these differences should be acknowledged and even celebrated, because they represent complementary aspects of human nature. On the other hand, many distinctions are purely arbitrary—and potentially limiting to human growth.

Science has yet to state definitively which characteristics are innate and which are culturally imposed. So there is no way I can categorically say, for instance, whether little boys play with tools and girls play with dolls (or vice versa) because of some innate tendency or because of parental modeling. But I do know that many so-called "masculine" or "feminine" traits are distortions of basic masculinity and femininity. And these distortions get in the way of allowing men and women to be whole persons.

We pay dearly for these distortions in terms of broken marriages, distorted ideas about life, and unsatisfactory male-female relationships. This may even be a factor in shaping same-sex relationship preferences.

Now what does all this have to do with divorce? Our culture already does a lot of harm in shaping different life-scripts for boys and girls and in widening the emotional gap between them. Divorce widens this gap further. It does so in several ways:

- Fathers usually abandon their sons after divorce, and thus leave their sons without an adequate model. Occasional visits do not make up for this deficiency.
- The pain of the divorce accentuates the cultural pressure for boys to suppress their emotions while girls can give expression to them. This trains the sexes in different modes of emotional expression.
- Boys, abandoned to the sole care of their mothers and sisters, often reject the modeling of females and exaggerate their male characteristics, in the process becoming stoic and unfeeling.
- Girls, bereft of a male mentor, are denied exposure on an intimate basis to masculine characteristics. This shapes them even more in a feminine direction, leaving them confused about the "masculine mystique."
- The custodial parent's dislike of the absent parent is likely to interfere with the child's ability to identify with him or her. It is hard for a boy to emulate his father, for instance, when the mother constantly berates him.
- When parents abandon their responsibility in shaping children, the children are more at the mercy of cultural stereotypes as promoted in schools, the media, and so on.

In summary, divorce upsets the delicate shaping process that ideally should help both boys and girls develop security in their own gender role while reflecting the best qualities from *both* the sexes. Divorce accentuates the development of unbalanced life-scripts that can be harmful to both sexes in the long run.

TYPICAL MALE ACOD LIFE-SCRIPTS

Several negative life-scripts are typical of males (although females sometimes develop them as well) and are worsened through divorce.

"BE COOL—DON'T ALLOW ANY FEELINGS"

Feelings are sources of terror for many males. The male hero of our culture is "cool," independent, self-contained, solitary, and aggressive—almost robotlike. When overcome by feelings, he is greatly embarrassed and discomforted. Men believe—perhaps correctly—that to show spontaneous emotion like anger or to break down in tears will tarnish their image and prevent them from achieving leadership positions. So men strive to become autonomous and independent, always in control of their feelings. The only emotional release they allow themselves is through sports—even if only as a shouting spectator. This powerful life-script is handed down from father to son, generation to generation. It is now deeply entrenched in our culture.

Men strive to become autonomous and independent, always in control of their feelings. The only emotional release they allow themselves is through sports. This powerful life-script is handed down from father to son, generation to generation.

I can identify more with this script than any other. It came to me primarily through my father, who was an anesthetized stoic. He never cried, and he never jumped for joy. He hardly ever said something hurtful but he never told you he loved you, either; you were supposed to know everything he felt through mental telepathy. He was also programmed to repress and deny any emotion.

The divorce of my parents came and went—and my father showed little outward emotion. He had been taught, just as he had taught me, that boys were strong, always logical, never controlled by feelings. "Boys who cling to their parents are an embarrassment; you must cut off all apron strings as early as possible!" was his philosophy. The result? I learned never to admit to feeling any pain. In fact, when I broke my toe during athletics one day, I never told anyone. I was in excruciating pain for several days, but I never winced. The life-script I had been taught was "don't feel." And this meant not only holding feelings in; it meant not even experiencing them, if possible.

By the time my parents divorced, my "be cool" life-script was already well-established, and I saw that experience as just another pain to be suppressed. How could I allow myself to feel this pain when my father was modeling stoic denial? The emotional disruption was there, of course; I just wouldn't let it out and deal with it. I was sad, but I wouldn't allow myself to grieve. I was angry, but I could only turn the anger back on myself. Clearly, the experience of divorce feeds this "no feelings" script in many boys.

Men who are out of touch with their feelings because of this life-script may later turn to drugs or alcohol as a way of coping with their pain—or they may resort to other "safe" emotional outlets such as sports. They also become intolerant of those who are open with their feelings. I clearly recall my father berating men who expressed feelings: "He's got no guts" was his favorite expression. In the face of such an example, it's easy to grow up believing that any man who shows any weakness (perhaps by being overtly emotional) is less than normal. Under such pressure, how can a child learn to express feelings in a healthy manner?

One of my great joys as a psychotherapist has been to help men such as myself discover the sheer joy of being able to feel their feelings openly. The therapeutic value of crying, for instance, has long been neglected in our culture. It was only late in my adult years that I learned to cry unashamedly, and I very much regret that I did not learn to shed tears as a child. Tears are necessary to psychological, physical, *and* spiritual health. Emotional tears are unique to human beings and, I believe, are uniquely intended to restore mind and body to sanity, relieve stress, and restore balance in our lives. My grandmother, in her wisdom, would often prescribe a "good cry" whenever I felt hurt. I wish I had listened to her when I was a child. And I wish all men in our culture could come to understand the positive power of rewriting their "don't feel" life-scripts and learning both to feel and to express their honest emotions.

"DON'T GET TIED DOWN"

"Don't make commitments" is a life motto for many a male ACOD. This means that commitments of a personal nature should be avoided, so many of these men make heroic efforts to avoid being "tied down." This effort may involve many aspects of life—such as renting instead of buying or moving from job to job. But by far the most common result of this life-script is avoidance of commitment to relationships. These men typically put off marriage as long as possible—or avoid it altogether. The decision to live together without marriage is often a consequence of this life-script. So are quick divorces. The sheer disposability of marriage breeds a faulty attitude toward commitment.

It's easy to see how such a life-script develops. A child sees the unhappiness in his parents' marriage. He knows firsthand how even the most romantic of lovers can end up hating each other. In addition, he has probably picked up the "don't get tied down" message from the culture around him—the way we socialize boys tends to encourage this script. So he designs his script around the theme of "staying free." The primary appeal of the script is its apparent *safety*. If you never commit yourself to anyone, you never get hurt.

One young man I was counseling told me that he didn't really love his fiancée. "But it doesn't matter, you see, because if the marriage doesn't work out, we'll just get a quick divorce," he explained. Such a cavalier attitude toward serious commitment will all but guarantee that the marriage won't work out. Marriage cannot survive without commitment.

When I explored this young man's attitudes in more depth we discovered that "not getting hurt" was a big priority for him. As a child of divorced parents, he swore very early in his life never to allow anyone to hurt him like his father had hurt his mother. So he maintains his distance. He detaches himself and avoids caring too much. The risks of abandoning himself in love are too scary. He fears he will lose control and be trapped.

How does one overcome a deep fear of commitment like this? I will outline some strategies later in the chapter. But at this point I want to stress that this life-script, like other life-scripts, is not best overcome by ignoring it—by just taking a deep breath and plunging into commitments! Deep-seated fears of commitment cannot just be brushed aside; they need careful analysis and deliberate healing. Relationships must be allowed to develop slowly so that trust can develop, and professional help may be required as well to get at the underlying cause of the fear and rewrite the life-script. A premature act of commitment invariably backfires, causing panic and creating an even greater fear.

One middle-aged man with whom I worked had already failed in two previous marriages and was now dating a younger woman who wanted to marry him. He balked; he couldn't trust himself or his feelings. Every time they set a date, he would panic and break off the engagement.

"Don't make commitments"
is a life motto for many a male ACOD.

One Sunday evening, however, he finally decided, against my advice, to go ahead and set a final date. The next morning when I arrived at my office, I found him sitting on the doorstep, shaking uncontrollably. I invited his fiancée to join our next session so that we could strategize how best to work around her beloved's fear of commitment. We slowed the courtship down, and they both spent time talking through their expectations and their fears. I'm pleased to say that finally they did marry, and eight years later they are still happily together.

TYPICAL FEMALE ACOD LIFE-SCRIPTS

Some life-scripts are more typical of women than men. Here are some examples:

"POOR LITTLE ME"

This is a script identified by Claude Steiner.[2] In this script, a woman spends her life acting like a victim and looking for a rescuer. While Steiner sees the origin for this script in parents who do everything for their "helpless" little girl, I see a variation of this script in ACOD women. It originates in girls who are abandoned by one parent and whose remaining parent (often a father) feeling overly guilty, gives them everything they desire.

These little girls tend to be consumed by self-pity. Cinderella and Little Orphan Annie become favorite mythical heroines. They tend to be weak physically and to demand that their needs be catered to.

"Poor little me" eventually grows up and spends a lot of time complaining about how awful things are. And in her relationships—especially marriage—she looks for a "rescuer" to take care of her and to cater to her needs just like her parents and other adults did.

The "poor little me" syndrome can be reinforced in children by sympathetic aunts, uncles, grandparents, or other adults as well as by parents. Erroneously believing that showering pity (as opposed to understanding) on the "poor little children" will make the children feel better, they unwittingly reinforce the child's sense of being a victim. Statements like, "You poor thing, how will you ever get over this?" or "How can anyone do this to you?" simply teach children that they can do nothing about their pain.

"Poor little me" eventually grows up and spends a lot of time complaining about how awful things are. She has learned that she can get sympathy more easily if she tells people about her troubles. She keeps proving that she is a victim by setting herself up for failure. And in her relationships—especially marriage—she looks for a "rescuer" to take care of her and to cater to her needs just like her parents and other adults did.

A "poor little me" life-script can emerge in any situation where one feels victimized and self-pity is encouraged. The remedy, then, lies in *not reinforcing this feeling of self-pity*. In part, this means learning to recognize the victim scenario for what it is. It also may mean taking practical steps to learn to care for yourself—taking classes, learning new skills, building a history of success.

"I'VE GOT TO SAVE THE WORLD"

"I feel best when I'm rescuing," a young woman told me recently. Hers is the classic "messiah complex" script that programs its followers to be people-rescuers. It is a common script not only among the children of divorce but also in alcoholic homes.

In fact, the ACOA (Adult Children of Alcoholics) movement has had a lot to say about this life-script. They call it "codependency" and tie the phenomenon almost exclusively to the person's association with an alcoholic or addict. In other words, the ACOA becomes enmeshed in the chaotic life of a parent or spouse who is addicted. When the parent or spouse is drunk, the codependent washes him or her and puts him or her to bed. When the addict or drunk behaves badly, the codependent makes excuses for him or her. Over time, codependents become depressed, lose their identity and independence, and increasingly let their whole life become wrapped up in the addict's problems.

But it is not only the alcoholic or addicted home that stifles the development of a child's independence. The intense fighting; the projection of blame; the screaming, insecurity, and general emotional upheaval of a dysfunctional family can create just as much conflict. Many children of divorce, like children of alcoholics, end up "rescuing" a mother or father.

Every member of such a conflict-ridden family has the potential to assume the *rescuer role*, but children are especially vulnerable. When mother is emotionally abused and retreats to the bedroom to cry, children rush in to comfort, placate, plead, and cry with her. When an angry father is about to come home from work, children shake and fear his arrival just as much as they do a father who comes home drunk.

Many children of divorce, like children of alcoholics, end up "rescuing" a mother or father.

Children easily become tied to the chaotic, self-centered, unpredictable behaviors of their parents. They feel shame, guilt, frustration, and fear. And because they are desperate to establish some kind of order in their lives, they take upon themselves the role of rescuers—the "saviors" of the family. They develop the fantasy that somehow they can fix things. And they carry this fantasy into adulthood. Again and again, they put themselves in situations where they must act out their "rescue" script. They may marry someone with chronic problems. They become "caretakers to the world," surrounding themselves with needy, dependent, or self-destructive people. They may even continue to rescue their parent or parents.

Ironically, instead of giving rescuers the control they crave, the "messiah complex" robs them of their autonomy. The more you rescue others, the more powerless you feel. ACOD females tend to feel powerless. Socialization reinforces the nurturing image and pushes them to the nurturing role. They learn not to think for themselves, enjoy themselves, cry for themselves, or determine their own life plan. The script does it all for them.

Helping others can be healthy, but feeling the compulsive need to "fix" other people's problems clearly is not!

Now there is a caution I must sound here. I am not saying that selfless love is unhealthy. Real generosity is clearly a virtue, and reaching out to help others can bring joy and contentment like no other experience. Sacrificial love is essential to restoring the balance of selfishness in our broken world. I fear that many men and women are being labeled as "codependent" simply because they are fulfilling Jesus' commandment to love others as we love ourselves.

But it is important that we distinguish the positive, loving, helping experience from the destructive rescuing game that I call the "messiah complex." Helping others can be healthy, but feeling the compulsive need to "fix" other people's problems clearly is not!

What creates this rescue script? Usually it is some form of a vicious triangle in the home. For example, father may be the persecutor, mother the victim, and kids the rescuers.[3] The children rescue mother whenever father attempts to physically or emotionally abuse her, while she passively submits. As the children grow up they internalize this rescuer's script.

Or sometimes the process backfires and the children become the persecutors—by refusing to work, doing badly in school, abusing drugs, or getting arrested. (There are many ways you can punish your folks for messing up your life!) One of the parents then becomes the rescuer, teaching the children how to play this role.

How does one break such a script? With resolve and determination, plus these specific principles:

1. Understand when rescuing is sick. For instance, if you consistently sacrifice your own needs to others—your form of "helping" is unhealthy. If your motives for helping involve control—if, for instance, you help others so as to be "one up" on them—your "helping" is sick. If you constantly refuse your own rights so as to please others or because you fear their rejection—your "helping" is sick. And if you find yourself consistently angry or resentful of the people you are helping, your "helping" almost certainly is sick. Endless sacrifice is the true Messiah's role, not yours. You must have limits and learn when to say no.

2. Understand that when you stop playing the rescue game, you help the "rescuees" as well as yourself. Truly selfless love is *tough;* it desires the well-being of the other person. Quite often, that means saying "do it yourself" to someone instead of doing it for him or her.

3. Avoid people who tend to push your "rescue buttons." It's a fact: Chronic "rescuers" and chronic "victims" attract one another like moths to a candle. In order to get a handle on your rescuer tendencies, you may need to keep your distance from those people you just can't refuse.

4. Take steps to take control of your own life. Move the power back to yourself. You will be held accountable for how you control your own life, not how you rescued others.

"I HATE MEN"

This is the saddest life-script I know that can develop in a divorced childhood—and you don't have to dig too deeply for the cause. The most significant male in a girl's life is her father, and when a father plays the role of "villain" in the house, his daughter will be unavoidably affected. The father's "villainy" may take the form of angry outbursts, mistreatment of the mother, even cold silence or criticism. As the divorce proceeds, it may be expressed through custody battles, settlement disputes, and the sabotaging of family happiness. The more erratic and uncontrolled the father's behavior, the more frightened his daughter becomes. When the father is finally out of the way and the girl feels a little safer, this fear turns to *hatred*.

Now, this hatred may well be unconscious. After all, we are supposed to love our parents; the idea that one hates one's own father may be intolerable. So the girl represses the hatred, pushing it down into her unconscious mind. Unfortunately, pushing such feelings under doesn't make them go away. The hatred continues to do its damage and eventually becomes generalized to all men. And the girl's mother, in her pain, may reinforce this generalization over and over again.

The "dialogue" of this life-script consists of many variations on one theme. "They" cannot be trusted. "They" are all brutes. "They" are cold and unfeeling, dangerous and treacherous, "only out for one thing"—in short, "they" are better avoided. And this hatred of men may find many different expressions in adult life. Sometimes the female will turn solely to other women for intimacy (sexual or otherwise). She may avoid marriage altogether or she may marry badly—choosing a mate who reinforces her own unconscious script. Sometimes "male-bashing" becomes a lifelong passion. Men are attacked, criticized, put down, or avoided. *All* men will pay for the hate felt for only one man.

But again, this hatred for men is not always overt or conscious. Most times it is more subtle, and does not even emerge in everyday life. But whenever a male behaves abusively or aggressively, hatred and fear raise their ugly heads.

Man hating can be a particular problem when a female ACOD with this life-script becomes a mother. This is what happened to Paula. Her father's violence and abuse had made her childhood a misery. Then, when she was twelve, her parents had divorced. And she had seen the breakup not as the end of the world, but the beginning of a new freedom from his erratic anger—or so she thought.

But gradually her fear of her father began to change. At first she had blamed herself for her feelings. Perhaps she didn't understand her father. Maybe she provoked him when he was tired or she didn't get out of his way fast enough. Then she began to realize his behavior was *his* fault, not hers. Fear turned to hate—but she didn't know that this hate was festering beneath the surface of her mind. She avoided her father as much as possible and never sent him gifts at Christmas or on birthdays, but she didn't really know why. She refused, at first, even to talk about him in therapy.

The real problem, she said, was with her husband and her two boys, aged seven and nine. She was extremely irritable with the children—unreasonably so. She lashed out excessively and sometimes violently. She just could not control herself when they misbehaved. Even her husband "caught it" a lot of the time, and couldn't understand her excessive rage. She would pull away, refusing to talk or even sleep in the same room with him. She loved her husband, and she knew their relationship was deteriorating, so she sought help.

As Paula and I talked, her rage toward her father slowly came to the surface. She began to realize that her boisterous two sons resembled *her* father, not her husband, and that this frightened her. Men in general frightened her, in fact, and she had become aggressive toward them. She was supercritical of all males. Her life-script was that of a "male-hater," and she was living her life according to its dictates.

Why had Paula married at all? "Why not?" was her reply when I asked why she got married. Like so many women with such a life-script, she didn't know it was controlling her. She was naturally drawn to be fulfilled sexually. She wanted to be a mother and raise a family. But the forced intimacy of family life eventually took its toll and brought out the worst in her.

Just knowing the reasons for her behavior was the starting point for Paula's healing, as it is for all of us. We must force our hidden scripts into the open and face them courageously. I'll have more to say about this healing process in the next section.

"RESCRIPTING" YOUR LIFE

I have described but a few life-scripts that have their origin in childhood divorce—and there are many more we could examine if space permitted. They include:

- "Playing sick,"
- "I'll get you for that,"
- "Tell me everything's going to be all right,"
- "Why do I say one thing and do another?" and
- "I've got to please everyone."

Much of this book, in fact, is involved with identifying and changing the "programmed dispositions" that are shaped by our divorce experiences. The few I have described, however, should help you in the process of uncovering some of the hidden "stage directions" that are controlling your behavior.

While I have already given a few suggestions for changing specific life-scripts, let me now summarize some general principles for rewriting your life-scripts.

The real value of owning up to your life-scripts and accurately labeling them is that, once you have done so, you can give yourself permission to change.

STEP #1: IDENTIFY YOUR OWN SET OF SCRIPTS

We all have life-scripts. Some are healthy, some sick. If you have experienced childhood trauma or have been forced to make premature life decisions, you are more likely to have scripts that are unhealthy. ACODs particularly tend toward self-defeating scripts, whether conscious or unconscious.

If you want to move toward healing, therefore, you must work at exposing your scripts—getting them into the open and labeling them for what they are. If you don't have someone to help you do this, then I strongly urge you to engage the help of a professional counselor. Life is too short and precious to be wasted. Don't fritter away precious days, let alone precious years of your life, being controlled by life-scripts that *can* be changed.

The real value of owning up to your life-scripts and accurately labeling them is that, once you have done so, you can give yourself permission to change. You will also have a much clearer idea about what to change.

STEP #2: STRATEGIZE WAYS
TO CHALLENGE THESE SCRIPTS

By "challenging" I really mean stopping and thinking about what you are doing and then trying to come up with creative alternatives. Be reflective. Be analytical. Study your actions. Ask yourself: "Why am I acting this way? What do I hope to achieve? Where will it end for me?" And then ask, "What can I do differently?"

Again, talking the situation over with someone else or writing out your thoughts can be very helpful. You can't solve problems when you keep them locked up in your mind. "Externalizing" our thoughts by talking or writing them out helps us see them more clearly and then develop the motivation to act on them.

STEP #3: KEEP YOUR FOCUS ON THE ESSENTIALS OF LIFE

Life becomes burdensome when we lose track of its essentials—and following preordained life-scripts easily causes us to do this.

What are life's essentials for you? Contentment? Peace? Happiness? Responsible living? Fulfillment through a meaningful existence? Freedom from debilitating anxiety? Spiritual maturity? These are what most thinking people would list as the "essentials" of life. Focus on achieving these. Deliberately give them priority over other agendas—including the promptings of your negative life-scripts.

One of the values of growing older (and hopefully more "mature") is that you do focus more on achieving life's essentials. You make choices guided more by what is important than by what is convenient or conventional. When someone disagrees with you over some minor issue, you are able to respond out of an understanding of the "larger" picture. You check your impulsiveness by asking yourself, "Is it really necessary to react in anger here?" or "Will a greater purpose be served if I just ignore the provocation?"

Maturity helps you to be more objective. And you don't have to wait until you are old before you act maturely! By focusing on the essentials of life, you *can choose to break your life-script.*

Life becomes burdensome when we lose track of its essentials—and following preordained life-scripts easily causes us to do this.

STEP #4: WRITE HEALTHIER LIFE-SCRIPTS

Most proponents of script theory say that life-scripts are firmly established by the age of fourteen.[4] I believe their foundation is laid much earlier. Nevertheless, life-scripts *can* be rewritten. At any time later in life you can, with determination and some wise strategy, change old patterns and create new ones. It's not as hard as you might imagine; in my work I see it happen all the time.

But I want to sound a word of warning here. Too many people confuse a healthy life-script with a "success" script. Success scripts are *not* always good scripts, especially if they are the only script a person follows. A person who programs himself or herself to be rich or famous by focusing only on getting ahead and pursuing advancement at all costs may end up unhappy and broken. To avoid such disaster, success scripts must be balanced by other, more basic, life plans.

As you work to develop your healthy life-script, try to be guided by the following criteria:

1. It must be noncompetitive. Scripts that force you to win over others will jeopardize your long-term happiness. Unfortunately our culture encourages unhealthy competition; it's up to you to find a better balance. One can engage in *any* occupation *without* being competitive by simply being content to be the best person you can be. You really don't have to win over others. If someone else is better than you—so be it! The same is true for relationships. Don't set up power struggles or "I can do anything better than you" games. Be yourself—but be the best self you can be. This *always* creates a healthier life-script.

2. It must be nonjudgmental, both of yourself and others. If your life plan fosters constant self-criticism, you will not be happy, because you will constantly find something to be displeased about. Contrary to popular opinion, self-criticism is not an adequate motivator for change. In fact, change is more likely if you stop condemning yourself. So work to develop an attitude of tolerance and to accept the reality of who you are.

3. It must be forgiving. A healthy life-script must have plenty of forgiveness built into it—and again, a large dose of this forgiveness must be for yourself. The happiest people I know are those who know how to forgive themselves as well as others and to practice this forgiveness *daily*. I have to keep reminding myself that the Bible sets a deadline for solving *every* personal grievance—sundown. "Do not let the sun go down on your wrath" (Ephesians 4:26). This instruction is not easy, but I believe it is wise counsel.

Practically every destructive life-script has an element of resentment in it, some rage that is being repressed. Like a cancer, such buried emotion eats away at your wholeness. Building forgiveness into your life plan helps act as an antidote to destructive resentment.

TEACHING CHILDREN HEALTHY SCRIPTS

Life-scripts are easily passed from generation to generation. You derived your own life-scripts, in part, from your parents' attitudes and beliefs. And your own life-scripts, in turn, are likely to shape those of your children. For this reason, an understanding of life-scripts can go a long way toward helping you become a better parent. Let me close this chapter, then, with some brief thoughts about helping your own children develop healthy life-scripts. There are ten essential rules:

1. Do your utmost to minimize severe conflict in the family and to avoid any form of abuse. This doesn't mean neglecting discipline.

Children need clear guidelines, definite boundaries, and reasonable consequences that are communicated *before* any misbehavior and consistently applied after the behavior. But abuse—either physical or emotional—is both unnecessary and harmful. If your children don't obey you, then *you* are doing something wrong. I urge you to rethink your methods and, if necessary, to seek help.

2. Help your children to be honest about their feelings. Teach them to talk about their emotions—and be ready to listen. Model a "feeling vocabulary" to them. For boys, especially, consciously avoid creating a "macho" life-script that forbids the feelings of weakness. You do this by demonstrating honesty about your own feelings. Obviously, if "being cool" or repressing emotion is part of your own life-script, you will need to work on this in order to help your children. Your love for your children can therefore be a powerful motivation for your own healing.

Children remember what you say and often internalize your words as part of their life-script. So concentrate on praise instead of criticism.

---

3. Be careful what you call your kids. Children remember what you say and often internalize your words as part of their life-script. So concentrate on praise instead of criticism. Discipline wrong behavior, but work hard not to criticize a child for merely being himself or herself. Labels like "dumb" or "stupid" easily become self-fulfilling prophecies. Instead, try to use affirming labels like "genius," "precious," and "you're the greatest." Your praise should be honest and accurate, of course; indiscriminate praise quickly loses its power. But in my experience, any praise is better than no praise at all. I have yet to meet a juvenile delinquent whose Dad called him "awesome." But I've met many who were called "stupid"!

4. Do not allow your children to dominate your life. They need to learn that others have rights, feelings, and needs. There are times, especially as they grow older, when their needs must come second. So don't hesitate to block out some space for yourself:

- "Please stay out of my clothes closet."
- "My purse is off-limits."
- "In the future, I am not available for taxi service without prior notice."
- "I don't want you to use that word in my presence."
- "I need some time for myself; please don't disturb me unless it is an emergency."

Showing respect for yourself will teach your children to respect themselves as well as others.

5. Remember that anger and hostility are natural emotions. Children have every right to feel angry and to *talk* about it when they are old enough. They *don't* have a right, however, to act out their anger through hitting, hurtful words, or other destructive behavior. Anger will be quickly diffused if you accept it and give your children the opportunity to talk it out, while firmly setting limits on acting out.

6. Do not give your child everything his or her little heart desires. It is sometimes very tempting for adults who have had an unhappy childhood to try to "make it up" by spoiling their own children. This can be very destructive. Children who have their every whim satisfied learn impatience and impulsiveness. Part of growing up is learning how to delay gratification and wait for life's rewards.

7. Allow each child to be himself or herself. Don't crush a child's spirit, and don't force him or her to conform to the mold you have designed. Each child is unique. Find and foster that uniqueness.

8. Never withdraw love to punish your child. You do this when you become cold, distant, or even silently angry at your child. You may even say, "I don't love you," but most times a child just senses your withdrawal of love. I know that this tactic can be a powerful attention-getter. Children pay attention when they sense you've pulled back from them. But such measures wreak havoc in a child's psyche. Love should be a constant that is unaffected by discipline.

9. Constantly remind yourself that your child is a gift from God, the richest of all blessings. He or she is on loan to you for a few brief years and must then be let free. Your job as a parent is to equip your child to live a healthy life.

10. Live an honest, spiritual, and committed life yourself. Don't expect your children to become what you are not. Make prayer a part of your time spent with your children and show them that you believe in them because God believes in them. When you do this, your children will be more likely to reward you by living a wholesome life and coming to love you for it.

Now, there is no guarantee that this rule—or any of the others— will automatically work. No matter how much care you take in parenting, there is always the chance that your children will disappoint you. Other forces—like genes, unsavory peers, or unfortunate encounters with life traumas—may be more powerful than your parenting. Even parents who do all the right things can raise a child who goes off the rails.

Nevertheless, your example is the best possible way to provide your children with the foundation they need. The rest is up to them. But the overwhelming odds are that, as you work to develop healthy life-scripts and as you teach these to your children, your whole family will discover more wholesome and fulfilling ways to live.

Personal Inventory

7

How Self-Conscious Are You?

We all have degrees of self-consciousness—fears about how we are being evaluated by others. Too much self-consciousness can inhibit you from being your true self. It can also be a major cause of shame, since we feel shame when we are too preoccupied with how others perceive us.

Using the following scale, rate yourself on each of the items and enter your score in the column.

    0 = I rarely or never feel this way.
    1 = Some of the time I feel this way.
    2 = Often, or most of the time, I feel this way.

SCORE

_____   1. When I meet new people, I am overcome with shyness.

_____   2. After an encounter with someone, I continue to fantasize about what happened and wish I could have acted differently.

_____   3. I look at reflections of myself (in mirrors, windows, etc.) to check up on how I look.

_____   4. When I am with someone, I try to figure out what they are thinking.

_____ 5. I feel that people always notice me first in a crowd.

_____ 6. I can feel people staring at me, even at a distance.

_____ 7. Whenever I am in public, I feel that people follow me with their eyes.

_____ 8. I am always trying to figure out what people really mean by what they say.

_____ 9. I worry about whether I am making a good impression on those around me.

_____ 10. I try to plan ahead what sort of impression I want to make on someone.

_____ 11. I am quick to notice the mood of someone with whom I am talking.

_____ 12. I don't like large groups because they make me nervous.

_____ TOTAL SCORE

INTERPRETING PERSONAL INVENTORY SEVEN

Range *Interpretation*

0–5 This score is within normal range. Self-consciousness is probably not a problem for you.

6–10 Your level of self-consciousness may be beginning to cause personal problems.

11–15 You have an above-average feeling of self-consciousness.

16–24 Your degree of self-consciousness may be serious enough to be incapacitating; it warrants immediate therapeutic attention.

Part Three

Continuing Your Recovery

IT IS VERY EASY TO GET BOGGED DOWN in the beginning phase of recovery as an ACOD. Progress may be too slow. Emotions may be too overpowering. Self-discoveries may be too painful. You may sometimes feel that you just don't have the strength or will to carry on. There'll be no evidence of progress, and you'll be tempted to throw in the towel and surrender to your past.

If that happens, let me urge you: Don't give up! The darkest moments of the night usually come just before the new day begins!

I see this truth often while working in therapy with depressed patients. They often reach the point of deepest despair just as recovery is really beginning. Partly it's because this is when they finally reach the end of themselves, abandon their own limited resources, and reach out for God's help. Partly it's because they intuitively know that healing is on its way and they don't have to hang on too tightly.

At the beginning of part 2, I emphasized the importance of *beginning* your recovery, and I asked you to record your decision. Now in this part, I want to examine several important aspects of your ongoing life as an ACOD: how you can overcome helplessness and self-pity, how being an ACOD affects your life as a parent, and finally, how you can break the "divorce cycle" of ACODs getting their own divorces.

Finally, I will summarize the major points of the book (and some I've not covered) in a chapter I've called "Success Strategies for the ACOD." In a sense, these might more accurately be call "survival strategies"—and at times you may feel that all you are doing is managing to survive. Nevertheless, your ongoing life as an ACOD can become much more than just getting by. With God's help, you can be well on your way toward glorious, all-encompassing victory.

CHAPTER 8

Getting On with Your Life

DIVORCE IS NOT A ONE-TIME crisis, but an ongoing trauma. Its disastrous consequences can reverberate for years. Children are raised, educated, and launched into adulthood from a base that is troubled and shaky—and the outcome of their upbringing is difficult to predict. When they finally marry and have children, the drama continues, as loyalties are divided among grandparents and ACODs struggle with their painful legacy of anger and mistrust.

No matter what their intentions, in other words, and even under the "best" conditions, divorcing parents wreak ongoing havoc in their children's lives. That's a sad fact—one that you as an adult child of divorce must face squarely and understand. And yet, the time must finally come when you stop digging around in your past and look to the future. You have to accept what is history and take responsibility for playing the game of life with whatever cards you hold in your hand.

The danger for you and your fellow ACODs is that you will remain "fixated" where you were as children. You risk perpetuating the same patterns, the same reactions, the same depressive feelings, helplessness, and defeatism that you experienced in those hopeless days, months, or years surrounding the divorce.

But this need not be so! Every crisis, every tragedy holds within it the possibility of healing. Something new can be built on the foundation of what has been destroyed. This is the genius of the human spirit—*it is indeed resilient.* And with God in your life, providing both hope and strength, the healing and rebuilding are speeded up. You have "bounce-back" potential in every ounce of your being. And God can release this power!

So *now* is the time to put it all behind you. Together we have identified the areas of damage that you have suffered and have begun the healing process. Now resolve to see it through—you *can* make it—as you get on with your life.

You have "bounce-back" potential in every ounce of your being. God can release this power!

OBSTACLES TO GETTING ON WITH YOUR LIFE

Jim and Sarah had been childhood sweethearts. They had grown up in the same neighborhood, gone to the same schools, known the same neighbors. Now they were married and living in their childhood neighborhood. They had everything going for them. Deeply in love, well-matched and compatible, they were determined to make life together work well. Their three young sons were their pride and joy.

But there was a cloud over their marital bliss. Jim felt "stuck." He just wasn't moving ahead—in his job, in his personal feelings, in his spiritual life. It was as though some heavy weight was holding him down. He saw himself as a phony, the world's greatest hypocrite, because he had everything to live for and felt the way he did. He began to fear that Sarah and especially the boys would be hurt by his failure to move ahead with his life.

What was wrong? Several things, really. But mainly Jim was increasingly having flashbacks to his parents' bitter divorce battle. He had been almost fourteen, an only child, when they split up. The breakup was a total surprise, stunning all their family and friends. There had been no overt conflict, no apparent incompatibility, no identifiable crisis. They, too, had been childhood sweethearts and had always believed that they were "meant" for each other. But an affair with a secretary had sent Jim's father into a classic midlife crisis, and when the dust had settled, the marriage was over.

Jim had never really gotten over the divorce. He had idealized his father. Then, after the breakup, his anger at his father had been overwhelmingly intense. Jim had not felt this anger immediately after the divorce. It had come upon him slowly, especially as he observed his father's postdivorce behavior—his neglect, and sometimes his emotional abuse, of Jim's mother.

Jim had grown up. He had married, had children—had appeared to move on with his life. But as we explored Jim's "blocked" feelings, it became obvious that Jim was still "fixated" on his divorce experience. Emotionally, he had not moved beyond the pain that had been triggered in his life at age fourteen.

In particular, Jim had never quite gotten over the destruction of his idol. He had never quite figured out how a father could go from being perfect one moment to being a total scoundrel the next. Jim was obsessed with finding out what had caused his father's downfall, and he was haunted by the idea that he might have been responsible—that somehow his not being a perfect kid had soured his father on family life. And now he feared that he in turn would be the cause of his own beautiful family's downfall. "Am I like my father?" he repeatedly agonized.

What causes someone like Jim to "get stuck"—to fixate on an earlier life point instead of moving on to maturity? There are many possible answers, but I want to explore three of the most common. All of these involve both *beliefs* and *actions:*

- a failure to make the right "adjustments,"
- a tendency to expect God to do all the work for you, and
- a form of self-blame that believes that all personal suffering is a form of punishment from God.

FAILURE TO MAKE THE RIGHT ADJUSTMENTS

The concept of *adjustment* is essential to all emotional healing—but is especially important for ACODs. In order to heal, you must know how to *make changes.* If you don't adjust or adapt to changing circumstances, you will inevitably get pushed out of shape.

Inherent in the concept of adjustment is the idea that something must *shift* a little. If I am standing barefoot on a thorn and it is hurting me, *I need to move* before I can stop the hurting. I must change to a different position. If I don't change or adapt, the stress intensifies dramatically.

In order to heal, you must know how to make changes.
If you don't adjust or adapt to changing circumstances,
you will inevitably get pushed out of shape.

Let me illustrate. In many years as a psychologist I have worked with a number of single persons who resent their single status. They did not choose to be unmarried; the unavailability of a suitable partner forced them to remain single.

Occasionally, taking practical action (such as a move to another city to find a different pool of "prospects") will be successful, and one of these single people will find someone to marry. More often, however, such search strategies just don't work. It eventually becomes clear that for many of these people, singleness will probably be a fact of life.

At that point, the single person has a choice: either to *adjust* to the prospect of the single life or to continue being unhappy. Failure to make the appropriate adjustment in attitudes and expectations can create intensified stress and eventually leads to a group of emotional problems we call "adjustment disorders." Perhaps we should call them "maladjustment disorders." They occur when we fail to adjust by making appropriate allowances for a difficult or unchangeable life situation. And usually they involve becoming emotionally fixated at the point where the adjustment failed.

Psychologically, then, people can get stuck in the same place and stay there for a long time without making changes. This perpetuates their unhappiness. Rather than make necessary changes in their lives, they spend all their energy searching for other explanations for their misery, trying to find someone or something else to blame. And as long as they do this, they will be unable to move on.

Can I put it more directly? If you are hurting because of some early life trauma—particularly your parents' divorce—don't expect your world to change. It's you who must do the changing.

I can't begin to tell you how often I sit with patients who are in emotional turmoil and are unable to adjust because of what someone else has done. Either life has dealt them a great unhappiness, or they cannot get something they desire very deeply. But they refuse to adjust to these limitations.

For instance, Sue is an attractive thirty-four-year-old woman who is struggling with chronic resentment and frustration. When she first came to see me, I was puzzled that someone as beautiful as she (and I don't just mean looks) could remain single, and finally she told me why. She is deeply in love with a man she had met on her twenty-first birthday—but he has never been in love with her. She continued to love him for thirteen years, refusing to give up hope. She saw him occasionally, and these meetings only intensified Sue's desire to be with him on a permanent basis. In the intervening periods he was engaged several times, and each time he broke off the relationship. All the time, she continued to love him and to reject all other suitors.

Finally, the man Sue loved did marry, leaving her bitter and depressed. At no time did he promise her anything—or even give her reason to keep up her hopes. Yet she remains stuck on him and incapable of adjusting to life without him.

If you are hurting because of some early life trauma— particularly your parents' divorce—don't expect your world to change. It's you who must do the changing.

What can Sue do to be healed? Obviously the man she loves won't have her—and now he's "taken." To somehow force him into a marriage with her would be a disaster. She has only one choice—to accept that she can't have him, adjust to that reality, and move on. And so must we all—especially adult children of divorce.

Adjustment is a slow process, of course. Sometimes it involves much grief and not a little depression. It's a fact of life that we cannot have everything we want, that bad things happen to us, that we experience pain and disappointment. But if we can avoid becoming fixated on our negative experiences, we will eventually be able to put our pain behind us and move on to whatever future God has in store for us.

EXPECTING GOD TO DO ALL THE WORK FOR YOU

Some people get "stuck" in their lives because they expect God to do the moving on for them. Even people who aren't particularly religious get hung up on this expectation! "God" means different things to different people. For many nonbelievers, "god" is some supernatural force, some fairy godmother who makes things right without any strings attached. And they persist in the irrational belief that if they wait long enough, somehow "God" will work everything to their advantage.

Deeply religious people also get trapped by this idea. "All things will work out fine if you just leave them alone," they believe, misquoting Romans 8:28. So they sit back, take no responsibility for their troubles, and expect God to fix their lives for them. When he doesn't, they rail and rant at him (either consciously or unconsciously): "If God won't give me what I want, what good is he? Who needs him?" This pouting response is spoken (or felt) as a challenge, just like a disappointed child trying to coax a parent into giving him his heart's desire.

But God doesn't respond to such peevish manipulations. Miracles are not dispensed to appease our disappointments. God expects us to tackle life with deliberate intention. Whatever our circumstances, and no matter what our misery, God loves us too much to do what only we can do for ourselves.

So many times I have encountered parents who are eager to see their children do well in school. They coax, cajole, threaten, and even battle their kids into working hard. And then they do their homework for them! I know one father who spends every evening doing his teenaged daughter's homework while she watches her favorite television program. She is failing at school, and he can't understand why.

Is God like this? Absolutely not! God *can* do anything—but he chooses not to, just as any wise parent would refuse to do everything for a child.

However, there are some things God *wants* to do for us, if we let him. He wants to help us make better decisions. He longs to teach us better self-discipline. He desires to be close to us in our troubles. He feels our pain and is right by our side when we are afflicted. He doesn't want to be bribed by pseudo-holiness. He doesn't need to be coaxed by the right words or by lengthy prayers to renew our hope and patience. He doesn't wait until we've pleaded and begged ourselves to the end of our wits before he brings comfort. He is ready and willing to give us *all* that we need in order to do the work of healing—but this healing requires us to take the first step of obedience or to make some change in our lives.

There are people out there who have put their lives on hold, waiting for a miracle from God. How sad! God *does* do miracles in our lives—but he expects us to do our part. How else are we going to grow?

God is ready and willing to give us all that we need to do the work of healing—but this healing requires us to take the first step of obedience or to make some change in our lives.

BLAMING GOD FOR PUNISHING YOU

It is quite common for ACODs to see all their unhappiness as some sort of punishment from God. How does this come about? Very interestingly, as I will show from my own history.

My parents fought a lot. Ever since I can remember, our home was in conflict. On rare occasions, happiness would drift over us like a cloud. But then, just as quickly, it would be blown away by some misunderstanding or unintentional comment.

This alternating pattern of conflict and peace, in my young mind, must have had a cause. And where did I look for this cause? Within myself. Like all young children, I assumed that I was the center of the universe. And so, in my very young mind I began to imagine that my parents' unhappiness had its origin in *me*. When I had done something wrong, I assumed, God punished me by making my parents quarrel. When I was good, God made our home happy.

Such an assumption is quite common in children, for several possible reasons:

- We are very susceptible to blame as children.
- We don't understand the real causes of life's unhappiness.
- We get blamed a lot, anyway, either overtly—by statements made by our parents when they are angry with us—or covertly—through body language and implication.
- We are still trying to figure out the cause and effect of many life issues. As children, we are generally taught that everything has a cause. If we burn a finger, "it's because you put it on the hot stove." So it's quite natural for children to look for a cause for family unhappiness. If we can't understand the real cause, or if we are often in trouble with those who are unhappy, it's very easy to blame ourselves for what is going on.

Naturally, once I made the assumption that God was punishing me by making my parents quarrel, I distorted a lot of my perceptions to fit it. Whenever my parents quarreled, I could easily find something in myself to blame—a little lie, a cookie taken without permission, or (as I grew older) some sexual thought or fantasy. A child's life is full of microscopic sins that a troubled mind can exaggerate. And the connection between my wrongdoing and my parents' unhappiness was easily established by empirical evidence. I would do something wrong—and my parents would fight. It looked simple. And so I reasoned that if I tried to be very good they would be loving. It didn't always work—but I forced the facts to fit the feelings.

Gradually I came to internalize the idea that our unhappiness was my fault and that somehow God was punishing me for my sins. Even today, mature as I am (and I hope that I have achieved a modicum of maturity), I occasionally catch myself blaming God for some bad thing and thinking that he is punishing me for something I've done wrong. I've stopped doing it in the little things, such as when the children catch a minor illness. But I still get hung up on the "big" things. Whenever a major problem arises, I instinctively wonder if God is punishing me by allowing it. And this starts an extensive moral inventory. What have I done to deserve this? Why is God punishing me? It may be several days before I pull myself up short and remind myself that I cannot place the blame for every catastrophe on him.

Why do we so quickly assume that God must be punishing us if some catastrophe befalls us or those we love?

Why do we so quickly assume that God must be punishing us if some catastrophe befalls us or those we love? Partly it is because of the faulty teaching we have received about the nature of God. We have been told that he is harsh and demanding, eager to punish the smallest infraction. (But what puzzles me here is how people can think that God would hurt *someone else*—even an innocent child—to teach *them* a lesson. Yet I frequently encounter parents, living with a tragedy such as the death of their child, who punish themselves by believing that their sins, big or small, brought this calamity upon them.)

Partly we believe that our unhappiness is due to God's punishment because we have been taught that God is like a parent—and our own parents left a lot to be desired. And partly we believe it because our overall sense of guilt is out of control.

Guilt is a major control mechanism in our culture. As a result, many sensitive people feel guilty about almost everything. Parents teach vulnerable children how to feel guilty. We don't realize when we do it, but we do it all the time. We want them to feel bad whenever they bother us, hoping that this will stop their behavior. It doesn't. They just grow up feeling guilty. In conflict-ridden homes, this tendency is exaggerated. It is very common, therefore, for ACODs to grow up blaming themselves for things which are clearly not their fault.

Such intense guilt feelings have no basis in our Christian faith— although many Christians have them. A major tenet of Christianity is that we are living in a day of grace. To believe that your unhappiness is due to God's punishment makes a mockery of the gospel. If he has already passed judgment, then how can he be extending his hand of grace to you? This is the classic "double bind" that many Christians fail to grasp.

The idea that God may be punishing you for the sins of your parents is just as ridiculous. This idea is a lot more common than you might suppose in ACODs. Why would God punish you for someone else's sin? What sort of God would he be if his standards of justice were no better than the average human's?

Far from being the cause of our unhappiness, God longs to be the cure of it—but how can he if we run from him and blame him for what has happened to us?

This is not to say that the *consequences* of our parents' sins or behaviors may not be passed on to us. Babies born to crack addicts or AIDS-infected mothers, for example, may suffer brain damage or die at a very young age. But these terrible afflictions are the natural results of certain human behaviors, not expressions of God's judgment and punishment. The unfortunate reality is that sin does far more damage than we realize or can control. When we act in hurtful ways, not only do we reap what we sow, but others suffer as well. Drunken drivers kill or maim people every day. But once again, being killed or maimed is not God's punishment. God will hold us accountable for our own actions, not punish us for the actions of others.

Whatever your suffering, you can be sure of one thing: *Your pain is the consequence of natural factors, not of divine retribution.* Life is not always fair—we all know that. Harold Kushner says it so well: "The wrong people get sick and the wrong people get robbed and the wrong people get killed in wars and accidents."[1] Divorce, like illness and robbery and wars and accidents, is a tragedy—a terrible consequence of human choice.

Attributing your divorce-related pain to God's punishment is simply faulty thinking. So is thinking—as so many sermons claim—that God gave you an extra-heavy cross to bear because he knows you have the strength to carry it. God no more wants to hurt you for anything than you would want to hurt the child you love. We blame God for too many bad things! If only the strong are called to carry the heaviest burdens, then why would any of us want to be strong?

The saddest thing about believing our pain is God's punishment is that we cut ourselves off from God as our source of strength. Far from being the *cause* of our unhappiness, God longs to be the *cure* of it—but how can he if we run for him and blame him for what has happened to us? In the final chapter we will explore in more depth how a right attitude toward God and his grace can help us in our healing.

MAJOR LIFE ISSUES FOR THE ACOD

There are several arenas of life where ACODs easily get "stuck"—and where healing and growth can make a tremendous difference. I want to discuss the three of them here:

- Coming to terms with commitment and intimacy,
- Repairing distorted notions of romantic love, and
- Learning to resolve conflict.

COMING TO TERMS WITH COMMITMENT AND INTIMACY

At several points thus far I have touched on how childhood divorce can damage the ability to establish and maintain relationships. Children of divorce tend both to fear and distort relationships. But much of this fear and distortion is unconscious, and many ACODs fail to realize just how serious this problem is in their lives.

Dr. Judith Wallerstein, an expert on the impact of divorce on children, tells of meeting with a girl named Dolores.[2] Dolores was a youngster who at the time of her parents' divorce lived in a Chicago duplex. Her father was away a lot. Her mother worked sixty hours a week. And Dolores was starved for affection. Soon after graduation from high school, she moved out to live with a man who put her on a pedestal, but she left after three months. Soon she had many boyfriends. Each of these relationships lasted only a few months—"and then I moved on," she explained.

Dolores particularly liked older men. "They're not as sticky-sweet, and they treat you like a queen." (Just like a dad!)

Dr. Wallerstein goes on to report on a whole group of young women she has studied who behave much like Dolores in relationships. They are attracted to older men, who they say treat them better and don't offer emotional complications such as jealousy, infidelity, and "falling in love." But the relationships don't last. Like Dolores, these women resist committing themselves to a long-term relationship. Instead, they move on as soon as things get intimate.

Is the same thing true of males? Dr. Wallerstein reports that ten years after her study of "divorced children," half of the boys she had talked to—now aged nineteen to twenty-nine—were still unhappy and lonely. Few, if any, had developed lasting relationships with women. Even sadder, these young men had *little conscious recognition* of how divorce had affected their ability to relate deeply to others. They were blind to their emotional constrictedness and their poor relationship skills.

Of course, relational constrictedness is not confined to the children of divorce. People from intact homes sometimes display similar relationship disturbances. Still, there is much about the divorce situation that can disturb good relationships. Conflict, fear, hatred, and bad parental modeling can pile up the obstacles to meeting and settling down in marriage with another person.

Two words, especially, tend to strike fear deep in the heart of an ACOD. One is a "C" word: *commitment*—especially commitment to marriage.

How do the children of divorce typically avoid commitment? One common way is to just live together, delaying marriage. Another is to float from relationship to relationship—or just not to date at all. The only consistent theme I see is the ease with which ACODs run from commitment.

How does this "allergy" to commitment begin? Growing up in chaos makes it easy to fear or distrust commitment. For an ACOD, entering into a lasting and meaningful relationship may mean peeling away layers of conflicting feelings, insecurities, threats of abandonment, distrust of love, and fear of being known for who they really are. In addition, they lack models for healthy, long-term relationships. Children who grow up in families where there is a strong commitment to make the marriage work, where parents stick together no matter how bad their circumstances and find ways to work through their problems, are inherently better equipped to build solid relationships themselves. Children who do not have this background almost invariably find commitment more difficult.

Two words, especially, tend to strike fear deep in the heart of an ACOD. One is "C" word: commitment—especially commitment to marriage. The "I" word—intimacy—also frightens them, although they may desperately want it.

But the "C" word is not the only relationship challenge for adult children of divorce. The "I" word—*intimacy*—also frightens them, although they may desperately want it.

Every human being longs for intimacy. I suspect that this longing is instinctive. We want to be close to another, warmly embraced and sustained by togetherness and familiarity. But we cannot be close to another without risking being discovered for who we really are. And to a child of divorce, raised in an atmosphere of blame, secrecy, and distrust, that possibility can be truly terrifying.

Most ACODs have much about themselves that they are afraid of revealing. They fear that people won't like this "concealed self," so they set up barriers to its being discovered. Anxiety rises dramatically when someone else (and in many cases even we ourselves) gets too close to their "secret self."

Again, divorce is not the only culprit in making people fear intimacy. Our highly mobile culture, with its emphasis on appearance rather than substance, does not foster long-term intimate relationships. And overcrowding in cities forces many people to relate superficially just to maintain some privacy.

As a result, real, personal intimacy has become so rare that most people use the word only to describe sexual or erotic closeness. And sexual intimacy, although it may involve emotional transparency as well, can also become a hormone-controlled substitute for true intimacy. One can always retreat quickly to emotional privacy as soon as the excitement is over.

Real, personal intimacy is a rarity today. And I cannot help but wonder whether the high incidence of divorce has something to do with it. The greater the number of children whose lives have been disrupted by divorce, the greater the number of adults who will have difficulty in finding a satisfying intimacy. This has *major* implications for the future of marriage in our society. We have an overdeveloped, sexualized hunger for intimacy and underdeveloped skills for building it.

Now, a very strong connection exists between commitment and intimacy. Commitment opens the door to intimacy. In fact, it is commitment that makes true intimacy possible. A look at the basic characteristics of true intimacy makes this connection clear:

- *Intimacy takes time to develop.* There is *no* such thing as instant closeness. It is sustained through frightening discoveries by a covenant of commitment: "I'm with you through thick and thin, good and bad, acceptable and unacceptable discoveries. Whatever happens, I'll be here."
- *Intimacy is never self-serving.* Its object is to give, rather than to receive. And inherent in the idea of commitment is the decision to give.
- *Intimacy is essentially warm and affirming.* How can this warmth develop outside of commitment?
- *Intimacy demands truthfulness,* the honesty that springs from the security of knowing that the other person (friend, parent, or spouse) will be there *after* the honesty.
- *Intimacy is shared memory.* How can one build a history with another if there is no continuity? All truly intimate relationships have a history, and commitment builds this history.
- *Intimacy always involves accountability.* One holds oneself accountable for keeping confidences and never using the intimate knowledge of another to hurt or betray. The act of commitment opens the way for trust.

What does all this mean for you as an adult child of divorce? First, there is a strong possibility that you may have relationship problems you are not aware of and that need healing. Second, it means that you cannot begin to heal your relationship problems without opening yourself to commitment and taking the plunge into intimacy. But this may not be easy. Chances are you have been running from commitment, intimacy, or both, for a long time. Being shut off from others may feel "normal" to you, and reaching out to others may feel "extreme" or "dangerous." You may have no idea where to begin in strengthening your intimate relationships.

You cannot begin to heal your relationship problems
without opening yourself to commitment and taking the
plunge into intimacy.

Here are a few key questions that may help you determine whether intimacy and commitment really are problems for you. Your answers to these questions should point you to relationship problems that may need attention:

- Do you tend to sabotage closeness with other people? Under what circumstances does this tend to happen?
- Are there particular people with whom you find it hard to be open and honest?
- Have you developed a fierce independence (often seen in ACODs) in order to survive? Does this independence distance you from people?
- Do you find it hard to trust those in authority? Perhaps you fear their discovery of your true self and the misuse of knowledge about your intimate secrets.
- Are you excessively jealous? Do you find it hard to share someone you love with others? Are you always fearing that they will abandon you?

Problems of intimacy don't lend themselves to easy, quick-fix solutions. They need to be explored in a safe, nonreactive environment.

You may find it very helpful, in fact, to explore your approach to relationships in what pastoral theologian Thomas Oden calls the "surrogate intimacy" of therapy.[3] By "surrogate" he doesn't mean phony, artificial, or unreal; he's just acknowledging that therapy is a special substitute way of exploring the possibilities of closeness.

But therapy is not the only place where you can learn to relate more intimately to others. Involvement in a support group, a Bible study group, or even a church or community committee can also provide you with opportunities to explore more intimate relationships. These kinds of small groups provide closeness so that you can come to know other people more personally.

If you are not aware of such groups in your area, why not start one yourself? Almost anyone can be a catalyst and invite three or four others to join together—perhaps for a meal such as breakfast or lunch. I have found that people are generally starving for such contact. The group can have a specific focus such as prayer or Bible study, or members can simply meet to share their lives. (For such a group to be effective, members must pledge absolute confidentiality.) From this starting point, you and the others in your group can begin to move toward larger life relationships with the confidence that increased self-understanding provides.

REPAIRING DISTORTED NOTIONS OF ROMANTIC LOVE

Children of divorce often arrive at adulthood with a skewed notion of what romantic love is all about. And since our culture considers romantic love an absolute necessity for courtship and marriage (not many cultures emphasize it as much), ACODs need to come to terms with and heal their distorted concepts.

Two extremes of distortion are common among adult children of divorce:

1. Children of divorce may develop a fear of romantic love. In this first distortion of love, the child has learned to associate romantic love with emotional pain. I have already discussed this with reference to how girls are affected by divorce, but it deserves some further expansion here with respect to both sexes.

Many divorce situations teach girls to react to men with anger, dislike, and distrust.[4] These girls observe how love has turned sour for their parents; they may conclude that romantic love cannot be trusted. They may anticipate that all men, like their fathers, will ultimately abandon them. They come to associate so much pain with romantic love that they cannot imagine that one can exist without the other. No wonder they withdraw from anyone who is attractive to them or who offers them affection!

Boys also observe this pain, but their reaction tends to be different—perhaps because they tend to idealize romantic love less than girls do, perhaps because they identify themselves more with their fathers, perhaps because they are more likely to repress their emotions. Boys are just constructed differently than girls! Whatever the reason, a male's fear of romantic love tends to involve giving more than receiving. Male children of divorce tend to distrust themselves, fearing they will be unable to sustain their love for long.

Since our culture considers romantic love an absolute necessity for courtship and marriage, ACODs need to come to terms with and heal their distorted concepts.

Over time, males also learn to separate romance (which they fear) from their sexual urges (which are biologically determined and therefore more fundamental and acceptable) and thus end up with a "split" between these two very important components of passionate relationships. Men tend not to associate sex with love as much as girls do; they can take sex without love and often prefer it that way. This, of course, affects how men view the dating game. They can't understand why many women refuse sexual advances even when there is no love and commitment.

This disparity in viewpoint over love's role can be an even greater problem in marriage, especially when it has become distorted by fears and misconceptions. Many men have no difficulty showing disrespect to a wife one moment and expecting her to be sexually responsive the next. When she refuses, they are baffled by the rebuff. "Why can't a woman be more like a man?" *My Fair Lady's*

Henry Higgins was not the first, and will not be the last, man to ask this question.

Many factors probably cause this "splitting" of love and sex by males, but I consider childhood divorce, with all the associated disfiguring of the face of love, to be a major factor. We learn our sexuality from our parents. If they don't model a healthy connection between love and sex, we just don't learn it!

2. Children of divorce may develop a neurotic need for romantic love. I know I'm treading on holy ground when I even hint that there may be something wrong with our culture-wide quest for romantic love! A whole industry of novels, movies, and soap operas has developed around the exploitation of this thing we call "romance." In our Western world, to be "in love" is the only socially accepted reason for getting married.

And I agree, up to a point, that romantic love should be the basis for marriage. Romantic passion helps bond a man and woman together and therefore gives a relationship a "jump start." But falling head over heels "in love" is not an absolute prerequisite for a successful marriage. My wife has a very good friend from another culture who was promised in marriage when she was born. She first met her future husband on her wedding day. And yet the two of them have come to love each other deeply; they have built an extremely happy marriage. A risky beginning? Of course. But does our cultural obsession with romantic love necessarily produce better results?

Why is it that the blissful state of preoccupation so many of us think of as love so quickly disappears after the marital knot is tied? Why is it that the special elation we call romantic love cannot be sustained for a lifetime with one partner?

The answer is very simple: what we call "romantic love" is not true love. For many it is nothing more than the projection of numerous distorted and unmet needs (they can even be called "cravings") on another. But even if it is not distorted, romantic love in itself is inadequate as a basis for long-term marriage. It is only a *beginning* for love—an infant that must ultimately come to maturity. If we don't understand this, we will abandon our marriages prematurely.

Now, let me hasten to add that there is nothing inherently wrong with romance. It can be beautiful, wholesome, and enriching—everything the poets describe. It can even be useful, providing the little bit of craziness we all need to get up the courage to date someone. Without the intense pleasure it provides, we might not ever pursue long-term commitment. But unless it develops and matures, romantic love will not last forever. It just doesn't have the staying power to sustain a relationship—inside or outside of marriage.

My wife and I have been married for thirty-six years, and we feel more love toward each other now than we did at the beginning. But our love, which started out as an intense (and wonderful) romanticism, has matured through the years into something even more wonderful. And that's all I'm really trying to say. Romantic love is only the beginning. It must move on to better things.

Romance can be beautiful, wholesome, and enriching—everything the poets describe. But unless it develops and matures, romantic love just doesn't have the staying power to sustain a relationship.

Why is romantic love, when left in its incomplete and infantile stage, a problem? There are several possible reasons. First, romantic love can be neurotic and selfish. Its appeal lies primarily in how good it makes you feel. Second, romantic love can be extremely intense—as addicting as a narcotic—leading you to neglect other aspects of your life. In addition, because it is so pleasant and absorbing, romance can easily be used as a form of escape from other problems, including relationship problems. Finally, romantic love, by its very nature, is temporary. It comes and goes in a long-term relationship, and it may disappear entirely unless bolstered by a more mature form of love.

Why are adult children of divorce especially likely to develop problems with romantic love? Underlying all forms of romantic love are several common themes that may raise particular problems for you as an ACOD:

- *Romantic love often involves a distorted vision of the loved one.* When you are "in love" with another person, you tend to idealize him or her and to deny or overlook his or her deficiencies—shortcomings that are obvious to others. This idealization is the first thing to go when you "fall out of love" again. Children of divorce, who often are disillusioned with their own parents, tend to transfer their idealization to others and thus become much more likely to experience intensified romantic needs.
- *Loneliness intensifies the craving for romantic involvement.* A bad childhood or unhappy upbringing can create emotional loneliness that makes you susceptible to romantic cravings.
- *The more your love needs have been unfulfilled as a child, the greater the prospect that you will fall prey to repeated romantic involvements.* Because you have no model for lasting love, you tend to move from one relationship to another as soon as romance cools.

Now, while romantic love, in itself, is nothing more than infatuation with an idealized other, in our culture it is generally accepted to be the starting point for romance and marriage. What must occur for this love to mature into true love?

- *The loved person must become fully known to the lover.* In other words, you *cannot* be in love (real love) with a total stranger. The best you can hope for is romantic love or infatuation. Intimacy is essential to true love.
- *True love must be allowed to develop over time.* It is only with time and a deep commitment to make marriage work that you can begin to substitute the neurotic romantic love with true love.
- *Idealization must be resolved sooner or later—and preferably before marriage.* In other words, you have to come to know the other person for whom he or she really is and still love that person. As long as you continue idealizing the object of your affections, you may be perpetuating the unhealthy aspects of romantic love. Romantic love may be blind, but true love has 20/20 vision!

What does this all mean for the adult child of divorce? It means that to continue your healing you must *take a chance on love*. This is a most important task for every ACOD. But you must be willing to go beyond romantic love. Don't settle for infatuation. Don't stop at romance. Beware of the tendency toward idealization and of addictive romantic flings.

Romantic love may be blind,
but true love has 20/20 vision!

Remember that if you were significantly deprived of love as a child, you can easily be seduced into a craving for the wrong sort of love. And recognize that distortions of romantic love can easily flow into other forms of love also. Be alert to your "all or nothing" attitudes regarding your love relationships, and make the development of mature attitudes about love a priority.

Despite any disillusionment you may have suffered, despite your fears and anxieties about whether you can build a healthy love relationship, real love is a possibility for you. As an adult child of divorce, you must continue to grow. *You must believe* that you can both love and be loved in a mature way.

In my own life, I have tried hard to turn my early disappointment with and fear of love into opportunities for growth and enlightenment—especially in my marriage, but also in other relationships (such as with my daughters). I've tried to learn from my father's insensitivity and my mother's excessive need for emotional security.

I often remind myself that their failure in love was *their* failure; it doesn't have to be mine. Their model was wrong because it was built upon the expectation that romantic love will last forever. When it didn't, they became disenchanted with each other. My model works because I saw romantic love as only a beginning, not the whole journey. Now that I am well on the way in my journey of love, my romantic feelings toward my wife have matured and grown. They are even more satisfying now than they were at the beginning.

LEARNING TO RESOLVE CONFLICT

The last important life issue I want to discuss here is that of *conflict*. This important subject ties in very closely with the previous two sections because conflict is almost inevitable in close and loving relationships.

ACODs often lack adequate models for resolving conflict in healthy ways. This carries over to their marriages, parenting, and even into their jobs. They tend to panic when faced with opposition. They become insecure and fear that the relationship in which the conflict occurs is at stake every time there is a disagreement or someone becomes angry at them.

The source of most ACODs' inadequacy in dealing with conflict is their own parents' scanty knowledge of how to resolve strife.

The source of most ACODs' inadequacy in dealing with conflict is their own parents' scanty knowledge of how to resolve strife. After all, if the parents had been skilled at resolving conflict, the divorce probably would not have occurred in the first place!

The children of divorce are bound to be trapped by many angry clashes. Not only are they caught in the crossfire, they often become scapegoats for their parents' frustration. They are captive prey—too small to fight back or stand up for themselves and unable to run away from the battle. An intense fear of conflict thus develops.

I vividly recall the tightness in my chest, the rumbling in my stomach, the sweat on my palms, and the urge to flee whenever anger erupted in our home. Your memories may be similar. You prayed incessantly for an end to the hostilities. You avoided every confrontation. It was better not to talk about something disagreeable than to have it backfire in your face.

All of these feelings may well have carried over into your adult life. You may run away from conflict because you never developed healthy strategies for handling it. You may inhibit your own anger and bottle up your rage because you don't know what to do with it. Then, when you finally do explode, you may overreact, causing more harm than good.

Other patterns for dealing with conflict can also emerge. (We've seen some of them before.):

- *Denial.* You may simply convince yourself that the conflict doesn't exist—or that it has nothing to do with you.
- *Escape.* You may avoid coming home or facing conflict-ridden relationships. You may also shrink from clearing the air or confronting the issues.
- *Scapegoating.* You may take out your anger by punishing innocent bystanders—spouse, children, friends. They are "safer" to attack than the real enemy.
- *Threats.* You may resort to "scare tactics"—veiled threats, overt threats, accusations, insinuations, critical comments, and even physical intimidation as a way of handling conflict.

Why do we find conflict so difficult to handle? There are many possibilities. We are afraid to expose our vulnerability and reveal our weaknesses. We shrink from discovering our childish fixations. We fear rejection. We fear losing. We don't think we have the weapons or defenses to stand our ground.

No doubt you can think up a dozen more reasons why you avoid conflict, but there is one that underlies them all: *We have problems handling conflict because we lack courage.* Divorce in our childhood taught us to be afraid. As a result, we may be deficient in assertiveness. And a considerate, loving, and sacrificial form of assertiveness is both appropriate and necessary for health. Without it, we compound our problems because we cannot face our conflicts directly.

Most people can benefit from training in conflict management, and I suspect this is especially true for ACODs. We need to learn how to talk our feelings out, to listen to the other side of the story, to identify the major conflict issues, to be willing to speak our minds. But above all, we need to learn courage. Courage to be ourselves. Courage to be strong when we have to stand up to anger and conflict. Courage to keep silent when appropriate and to speak up when necessary.

To overcome my own fear of conflict, I have found it helpful to tackle small examples first and to "practice" being more assertive in matters that are not really important. For instance, I have gradually conquered my reluctance to return items I've purchased but don't want, and I've learned to ask more questions before agreeing to do someone a favor.

Mastery of assertiveness in little matters builds confidence in tackling larger, more conflict-ridden issues. A pastor I am counseling recently told me he that had confronted a chronically tardy associate. Talking out that issue had cleared the air and begun the healing of an increasingly conflict-ridden relationship. When I asked my client what had given him the courage to confront his colleague, he replied: "You keep pushing me to be honest in other areas of my life; I just felt I could manage this one as well."

Developing assertiveness can help you build courage, but it doesn't mean you will never be afraid. Don't lose heart when you can't seem to create courage within yourself. In such times, God has promised be your source of strength. Again and again we are told in the Bible to "be courageous" (2 Chronicles 19:11; 32:7; Ezra 10:4). And this command to be courageous is always accompanied by a reminder that God is with us.

No doubt you can think up a dozen more reasons why you avoid conflict, but there is one that underlies them all: We have problems handling conflict because we lack courage. Divorce in our childhood taught us to be afraid.

A perfect illustration of this can be found in Deuteronomy 31. Moses is leading the people of Israel through the wilderness to the Promised Land. Every man and woman is told what is expected of him or her as they go forward and claim the new territory. And Moses' discourse ends with this promise: "Be strong and of good courage, do not fear nor be afraid of them; for the Lord your God, he is the one who goes with you, he will not leave you nor forsake you" (v. 6).

The idea that God could "go with" the Israelites was unique to their understanding of him. The heathens' gods were immovable, fixed objects, kept in temples. They were cut from large chunks of stone that couldn't be budged. But Israel's God was able to go wherever the people went. Into battle. Into life.

You can take courage, therefore, as you face your conflicts and move on with your life. God is with you—and he wants only the best for you. With such a courageous companion, you have no need to be afraid.

Personal Inventory

8

Are You Depression-Prone?

Depression is a common emotion among adult children of divorce, although it is not always easily recognizable—it may masquerade as lethargy, lack of ambition, disinterest in sex, or irritability, as well as sadness. One of the reasons it is important to treat depressions is that they quickly erode self-esteem, thus exacerbating an ACOD's difficulty in taking care of himself or herself. This short test will give you a quick measure of your present mood state. Answer the following questions as carefully as possible by using the following scale and entering your score in the column to the right.

0 = I rarely or never feel this way.
1 = I sometimes feel this way.
2 = Most of the time I feel this way.

SCORE

_____ 1. I have difficulty falling asleep, or I wake up in the early hours of the morning.

_____ 2. I feel very sad or I want to cry.

_____ 3. I hate socializing and prefer to do things by myself.

_____ 4. I have "gut problems"—stomachaches, diarrhea, or other discomfort in the digestive tract.

_____ 5. Life doesn't seem worth living.

_____ 6. I have difficulty getting up enough energy to get things started or to take care of regular responsibilities.

_____ 7. I do not have a lot of interest in hobbies, activities, work, or activities that others find interesting.

_____ 8. I wish something would happen to end my life easily and painlessly—like not waking up in the morning.

_____ 9. My dreams are mostly unpleasant and even frightening.

_____ 10. Loneliness is a real problem for me.

_____ 11. It is very hard for me to feel cheered up about anything.

_____ 12. I feel quite hopeless and pessimistic about how life will turn out for me.

_____ 13. I have difficulty concentrating and my thinking is slow.

_____ 14. When I compare myself with others, I feel worthless.

_____ 15. Even if I tried, I couldn't really make myself find pleasure in anything.

_____ TOTAL SCORE

INTERPRETING PERSONAL INVENTORY EIGHT

Depression is a very complex emotion. It can range from mild—a simple and temporary feeling of sadness and lethargy—to severe—an inability to work or fulfill normal obligations. Since many forms of depression involve changes in body chemistry, a trained professional should be retained to diagnose and treat depression. However, this self-test may be helpful in alerting you to a potential problem. I urge you to seek immediate professional help if you are concerned about your score or if you feel depressed for more than a week, no matter what your score.

Range   *Interpretation*

0–5   This score is normal. Although you experience normal variations in mood, it is unlikely that you have a problem with depression.

6–10   You occasionally experience depression, but it may not be a problem for you. You have probably discovered how to get over your low mood quickly.

11–15   You are acknowledging some depressive tendencies. You may want to review how you feel with someone trained to work with depression.

16–20   Your level of depression is quite high and warrants attention.

20 or More You are experiencing a very significant depression and should seek professional help right away.

CHAPTER 9

Building Your Own Happy Family

WHEN MICHELLE FIRST TOLD me her history, I felt that I was talking to someone from my own family. Her life story seemed to parallel my own so closely that I had to remind myself to keep my personal reactions out of the picture. It's not that easy to be an objective psychotherapist when your patient's problems are so similar to your own!

Michelle had been married for eight years when she first saw me. She had intentionally avoided having children, fearing that she wouldn't be a good mother. Now, even being a "good wife" was becoming a problem for her. Her husband, she related, was a saint—patient, tolerant, supportive, and loving. She, on the other hand, was jealous, suspicious, and overly sensitive. He tried everything to make their marriage a happy one. To her dismay, she found herself doing everything possible to sabotage it. At least, that is what she told me, and I had no reason to doubt her. The sort of sabotage she described—always finding fault with her husband and rejecting his kindness—is a very common form of unconscious sabotage in marriage.

Where was the similarity between myself and Michelle? We had both grown up with a mother who was a master of marital sabotage.

Now, I'm not blaming my mother. She did the best she could in a very unhappy situation. Emotional survival was her primary focus. If she were alive today, I'm sure she could more than adequately justify the way she defended her emotions. And the same was probably true of Michelle's mother.

227

An only child, Michelle could remember her childhood vividly. She could not remember a time when her parents were not quarreling constantly. Then, when Michelle was about six years of age, her mother had realized that the marriage wasn't going to work out and had begun pulling away from her husband. She set clear limits on his sexual privileges. To get ammunition for a separation, she became suspicious—even jealous at times. (Jealousy often has nothing to do with love, but is triggered by a fear of being humiliated or being betrayed.) Furthermore, she went on the attack, criticizing constantly and using every putdown in the book. She did it to protect and distance herself—even, I suppose, to try to kill the little love she may still have felt for her husband.

How you adjust to your parents' divorce will largely determine what sort of marriage partner and parent you make—and may even effect the outcome of your marriage.

Whatever the justification, the resulting family dynamics were damaging for Michelle, as mine were for me. Dysfunctional relating is something one learns. You don't catch it like a disease. There's no direct gene involved (although some genetically determined personality traits may be involved). It's infectious only by modeling. And Michelle's mother was a highly effective model of how to protect yourself through subtle sabotage—and destroy your relationship in the meantime.

Michelle and I have laughed, cried, and shared much about our similar experiences. And she is doing much better now in her marriage. I predict she is well on the road to recovery.

There is no doubt in my mind that the impact of divorce and the conflicts surrounding it carry over to the ACOD's own marriage. I see this fact in the stories of people like Michelle, and I have felt it in my own story as well. How you adjust to the consequences of your parents' divorce will largely determine what sort of marriage partner and parent you make—and may even effect the outcome of your marriage.

It is true that the traditional concept of "marriage and family" seems to be changing. The soaring divorce rate, reports of widespread child abuse, proliferating accounts of violence between spouses, and increasing numbers of illegitimate births have led some authorities to assume that family stability is declining.[1] And a number of "alternate living arrangements"—unwed couples, married couples who choose not to have children, women bearing and raising children without men, homosexual relationships, and many others—have shaken society's assumptions about what is "normal" in family living. These changes have profoundly affected the development of children and will, in turn, influence how these children function in their own future families.

Nevertheless, while alternative family structures may perhaps be better than no family structures at all, I still believe it is hard to improve on the time-tested pattern of mother, father, and children living together in one home. Health begets health. And I am convinced that a healthy, intact family is the best preparation anyone can have for a happy and successful life—including marriage and parenthood.

There is no better place than a functional home to prepare children for relationships. Conversely, there is no better way to teach children dysfunctional ways of behaving in relationships than a conflict-ridden or divorced home.

But that is not to say that you are doomed to an unhappy family life if your parents divorced! Even if you have missed out on a healthy, functional family as a child, you have the opportunity to build one now. But in order to do so, you must understand a little bit about how your childhood divorce is likely to affect your family life. And then you must make some intentional choices to reverse the trend toward trouble.

HEALTHY—AND UNHEALTHY FAMILIES

Building a successful marriage and family never has and never will be easy. It is *hard work,* to put it bluntly, even when you have been dealt a perfect hand—and many ACODs have the deck stacked against them!

---

*Even if you have missed out on a healthy, functional family
as a child, you have the opportunity to build one now.*

Many significant studies have been conducted to identify the basic ingredients for building a strong marriage and family. Perhaps the most impressive study was one conducted by Herbert Otto of the University of Georgia. After studying many families in depth over a long period of time, he concluded that healthy families displayed twelve identifiable "strengths."[2] Replication studies (in which the previous study is repeated by someone else to see if there are similar results) have consistently supported Otto's findings.

What were the strengths Otto discovered? Here they are listed in descending order of importance.

Twelve Strengths of Healthy Families

1. A shared faith, religious and moral values.
2. Love, consideration, and understanding.
3. Common interests, goals, and purposes.
4. Love and happiness of children.
5. Working and playing together.
6. Sharing specific recreational activities.
7. Being in accord on discipline.
8. Respect for individuality of family members.
9. Shared sense of humor.
10. Enjoyment of companionship.
11. Good health.
12. Desire for learning and education.

Just examining this list will show clearly how few of these strengths are modeled or taught in a conflictive family. The divorcing family is often described by twelve different traits.

Twelve Weaknesses of Conflicted Families

1. Divided over faith, religious and moral issues.
2. Devoid of love, consideration, and understanding.
3. Diverse in interests, goals, and activities.
4. Destructive toward its children.
5. Separate in its work and its play.
6. Lacking in shared recreational activities.
7. In disagreement over discipline.
8. Demeaning and disrespectful of one another.
9. Humorless or sarcastic.
10. Distant, not enjoying each other's companionship.
11. Wracked by stress-related illness or even physical abuse.
12. Caught up in its own problems and incapable of reaching out.

With these deficiencies as a background, the ACOD has a lot of damage to undo and many new behaviors to learn in order to become an effective marriage partner and parent.

CHOOSING YOUR PARTNER

"A perfect wife is any woman with a perfect husband!" True? Just as true as "a perfect husband is any man with a perfect wife." In other words, since marriage is inevitably the union of two imperfect people, there is no such thing as a perfect marriage. But that does not mean that one person is just as good as another when it comes to marriage!

There are some unions of persons so unsuited for each other that a miracle would be needed to make the marriage work. Now, I'm prepared to accept miracles. But humanly speaking, the greatest risk to any marriage lies in a poor choice of mates. And a sound decision about whom to marry is one of the most important factors in developing and maintaining a healthy marriage relationship.

There is no such thing as a perfect marriage. But that does not mean that one person is just as good as another when it comes to marriage!

I am not just referring to matters of "compatibility." I happen to believe that *all* marital partners are basically incompatible—this is a given in marriage. Partners come from different backgrounds, with diverse sets of values. They have different genes, different histories, different expectations. They may *think* they are compatible when in the throes of romantic love, but in the course of time they inevitably discover just how different they really are.

Then there is the most fundamental incompatibility of all: our gender. A man marries a woman. And can anything be more opposite than male and female? This is one factor that makes marriage both beautiful and problematic. Simply because of gender, married people start life with a fundamentally different set of interests, actions, feelings, and genes.

And so I repeat: Incompatibility is a given. It has to be factored into our marital adjustment. This is what makes marriage so beautiful. We learn to understand each other and our differences, and we come to accept and even value these differences. Out of this understanding, *real love* emerges.

Areas of Incompatibility

1. Different religious backgrounds.
2. Large age differences.
3. Significant differences in education.
4. Differences in fundamental values.
5. Differences in the level of trust (jealousy).
6. Differing reactions to life crises.
7. Underlying rage.
8. Differences in general tolerance for stress.

But how far apart can a couple be and still make marriage work? How much incompatibility is too much? When is the gulf of differences so great that, humanly speaking, no meeting of the minds can occur?

Clearly there is a limit to how much incompatibility a marriage can stand. And this limit is often exceeded when someone from a divorced childhood chooses a potential partner for the wrong reasons, or when certain elements from that person's childhood divorce influence his or her choice.

I happen to believe that all marital partners are basically incompatible—this is the given in marriage.

Any of these areas of incompatibility can be overcome, of course, but overcoming them will require a lot of time and energy. Watching out for such possible trouble spots ahead of time can save you a lot of grief in the long run—as can understanding the ways that your childhood divorce could affect your choice of marital partners:

- *Your divorce experience may force you to choose the most available partner at short notice just to get out of your conflict-ridden home.* ACODs have been known to marry too young—or marry whoever was at hand—just to escape an unhappy home life.
- *It may cause you to marry someone who is exactly the opposite of your mother or father because you fear anyone similar.* You then discover that the person is so "opposite" that you cannot live with him or her.
- *It may cause you to select someone overly passive so as to "play it safe,"* only to find you cannot live with such passivity.
- *It may cause you to look for a substitute father or mother,* and then discover you have a parent as a partner, not a spouse.
- *It may blind you to your tendency to idealize any available partner.* Your "eyes" are only restored to see the real person when it is too late.

- *It may cause you to be overly critical of yourself and to believe you will never get anyone better.* So you take the plunge and discover you have settled for someone very inferior.
- *You may come to fear conflict so much that you choose someone who is incapable of matching you in strength.* In due course you will outgrow this person and be left feeling lonely and empty.

What can you do about this influence on your choice of partners? First, you need to increase your awareness of how factors from your conflicted childhood can influence your selection of a partner. You need to find a way of clarifying what is *really* influencing your choices. And then you need to take some practical steps to prevent a mistake.

To begin with, there are some time-honored safeguards that should be seriously considered:

1. Take time to get to know the person you are marrying. This means you should avoid whirlwind courtships or premature sexual relationships. (Early sex can easily become a form of "substitute intimacy" that actually keeps you from getting to know one another as persons.) It takes time to get to know someone, and the best time to do this is *before* you're married. After a failed first marriage, especially, you should resist rushing into a second marriage. There are no hard and fast rules on how long a courtship is "adequate," but I generally consider twelve months to be the *minimum*. This is little enough time to give to dating, considering you will live with your partner the rest of your life. I realize that a long courtship can place tremendous sexual pressures on a couple. But if you value building a long-term marriage, you will put this pressure in proper perspective.

2. Don't marry too young. There is no "ideal" age for marriage, but I tend to counsel against couples' getting married when they are still in their late teens or early twenties. There is abundant research evidence to indicate that adolescent marriages have the highest divorce rate.[3] This may not have been true in times past, when extended families provided financial security and less education was required to make a living in the world. But times have changed. Our complex and economically demanding society can be a deathtrap for very young marriages. There are exceptions, of course, but I believe that people who take the time to establish themselves as persons have a better chance when it comes to marriage.

You need to increase your awareness of how factors from your conflicted childhood can influence your selection of a partner. And then you need to take some practical steps to prevent a mistake.

Unfortunately, some parents are guilty of bringing undue pressure to bear on their children, especially on their daughters, to marry early. I see this happening particularly in very religious homes or close-knit communities. It's a hangover from a previous era when a girl was pushed into marriage as soon after college (or even high school) as possible. *Many* divorces can later be traced to this premature pressure from parents—usually to relieve their own anxieties. Children marry to please their parents—and girls usually marry a boy pushed on them by overly concerned parents.

As a professor and administrator in a seminary, I have seen similar dynamics at work in potential ministers. Many show up at seminary for the same reason people may arrive in marriage: They are pushed by well-meaning parents. It takes them a few years to figure out what they really want to do, but the outcome is often a rejection of the ministry. Unfortunately, the same thing often happens with "pushed" marriages.

It is possible, of course, to put off getting married for the wrong reasons. There are those who fear commitment and delay marriage because they "need time to mature." Not only do such "late bloomers" risk infertility and other childbearing problems, they also risk not marrying at all, since the fear of commitment tends to loom larger, not grow smaller, as more and more time has been invested in the single life. In addition, the emotional reservations that cause a person to delay marriage can carry over into the marriage itself and cause problems. I suppose this "delayed marriage" phenomenon is becoming the more common problem today, and I have addressed it in an earlier chapter.

3. Never get married without premarital counseling. Good counseling will either force you to abandon a bad match or will help you lay a foundation for a solid marriage. If I had my way, *every* engaged couple would be required to undergo six months of mandatory weekly counseling before they would be allowed to marry!

4. If you've been married before, make sure your counseling focuses not only on premarital issues, but also on identifying dysfunctional patterns from your previous marriage. We human beings tend to repeat our mistakes again and again. A failed marriage, therefore, should be viewed as an important training ground—an invaluable source of information about what is likely to go wrong. Make an effort to learn from your mistakes and God will bless your choices.

---

*A clearer understanding of your own personality
will help you to make better partner choices because you
will have better understanding of where
"clashes" are likely to happen.*

None of these precautions, of course, guarantee a good marriage. It is certainly possible, for instance, to marry at age thirty, after a long courtship and premarital counseling—and still fail at marriage. But following the basic rules of time and forethought do increase your chances of making a wise choice. In addition, taking the time to clarify the childhood influences on your choice of a partner can be extremely helpful. Here are some suggestions for examining your background:

1. Talk over your thoughts and share your emotional life with someone else. You will not solve your questions by keeping them in your own head. You need to share them with an understanding listener who can help you sort out the pieces.

2. Examine all your previous dating relationships (or previous marriage). Do you see a consistent pattern? Do you tend to date the same kind of person? If so, why? Do you have expectations for a partner that are unusual or extraordinary?

3. Make a list of all the dysfunctional patterns you have observed in your family of origin. For example, was your family:

- always fighting or yelling?
- seldom trusting of each other?
- rarely confrontative about their hurts—tending to hold grudges instead?
- excessively competitive?
- afraid of feelings, even feelings of love?
- rarely supportive or comforting?
- mostly critical and blaming?
- manipulative of each other?

Now compare this list with your present relationships. Do you tend to repeat these patterns? How and when does this happen? By increasing your awareness of these patterns, you increase your ability to make better choices and reverse these patterns.

4. Make a list of the "holes" in your own personality. Where are your weak or vulnerable points? A clearer understanding of your own personality will help you to make better partner choices because you will have better understanding of where "clashes" are likely to happen.

For instance:

- Are you a poor listener? If you are, someone who needs a good listener will be frustrated with you.
- Are you a very dependent person? An independent spouse will drive you crazy.
- Are you a very independent person? You are likely to disappoint a spouse who desires extreme closeness.

5. Work to change any aspects of your personality that you don't like. It's important to realize that behavior really can change some aspects of your personality—even though who you basically are cannot be changed. In other words, acting like the person you would like to be really can help you become who you want to be.

Even if you are basically shy and introverted, for example, you can begin to *behave* in a friendly manner toward others. You won't change your basic introversion, but who says an introvert can't be friendly? Push yourself to greet others. Talk to them. Set aside your natural shyness and reach out. Slowly, very slowly, this new behavior will start to reinforce your friendliness. People will start to like you. You will start to like people. Although I am shy by nature, I have made an effort over the years to reach out to others, and I have gradually become more sociable.

If growing up in a dysfunctional family teaches you anything, it teaches you how to "fight dirty." You develop an arsenal of offensive and defensive weapons that can be very effective in hurting the other person—but also in hurting your relationship.

Eventually—and it doesn't matter if it takes a long time—you can begin to change those aspects of your personality that you would like to change. But you should realize that not everything can or should be changed. Self-acceptance—contentment with who you basically are—must accompany your attempts to change your undesirable traits.

LEARNING TO "FIGHT FAIR"

Being a child of divorce influences not only the partner you choose but also how you behave as a marriage partner. I want to cover this aspect of being an ACOD by discussing aspects of dealing with conflict. Conflicts in a marriage are inevitable, but the tactics you use in fighting can do a lot to determine the ongoing health of your marriage. And if growing up in a dysfunctional family teaches you anything, it teaches you how to "fight dirty." You develop an arsenal of offensive and defensive weapons that can be very effective in hurting the other person—but also in hurting your relationship.

In every conflict there is an attacker and a defender—although both partners may end up playing both roles in the course of the "battle." Let's look at how a background of divorce can influence both your "attack strategies" and your "defense tactics"—and at how you can modify your methods of dealing with conflict in the interest of a healthy and lasting marriage.

STYLES OF ATTACK

I can illustrate a common "offensive strategy" very well with a personal story. My wife, Kathleen, and I had a very romantic courtship. We were engaged to be married for nearly three years, due mainly to my need to finish my studies. We finally settled down three hundred fifty miles away from our hometown, where I got my first job. So we got two basic "rules" for healthy marriage right: 1.) allow time during courtship to get to know one another, and 2.) establish some autonomy from your families of origin. (In our case, the autonomy was geographically enforced, though it doesn't have to be.)

But in other ways we were bound for trouble right from the start. I was the product of a divorced family. My wife came from a dysfunctional home where her father was an alcoholic. So we brought some interesting styles of relating into our marriage.

Very early in our marriage, I discovered that I could effectively attack my young wife by saying, in the heat of argument, "Oh, you are just like your mother!" Now, I don't know why this is never taken as a compliment. It always seems to create the most violent of reactions. Anywhere you go in the world it is the same sensitive button. To be "like your mother" (even if she is a saint) is to imply that you are not your own person but are behaving as if you have no character of your own. If mother has a few quirks, then this adds insult to injury.

But this was only the beginning. My wife quickly learned to retaliate with "Well, you need to know just how much you are like your father," and would then proceed to describe the similarities in fair detail. Now if you think that being like your mother is the ultimate insult, wait until you are accused of being like your father! Almost everyone I know takes such a comparison as the worst kind of put-down.

Not long ago, I mentioned this style of attack to a group of pastors and their spouses. I discovered that everyone present had experienced it in their marriages—and hated it! I then asked them if their mothers or fathers were really that bad. No, they were not. Apparently it was the comparison that was irritating to these people, not the quality of the parents themselves.

In my case, however, it was much more than just the comparison that set me off. I did not like the way my father behaved in our family, so I deeply resented being compared to him. And, of course, the similarities were there. Genetic transmission will always guarantee both physical and psychological similarities—including some that we do not like at all.

This pattern of attack became very destructive in our marriage, but we finally developed a strategy that killed it in a matter of days. Whenever we got into a heated argument, I would turn to Kathleen and say, "Well, now, what about my father? Tell me again how much like him I am." This was our way of diffusing the tension. She would do the same to me: "Tell me how much I am like my mother." We would begin to laugh, and the argument would soon wind down.

Once we learned to take the initiative in this way, several things happened:

- We showed that we were no longer afraid to be compared with our parents.
- This robbed the accusation of its painful power.
- It also removed its usefulness as a weapon.
- The element of humor injected a bit of sanity into an argument.

We quickly stopped using this attacking style. And we have taught this technique for stopping it to scores of couples with similar results.

Comparing each other to your parents is not the only harmful style of attack, of course. There are other attacking styles that are also destructive, including:

1. Using anger to intimidate the other. Out-of-control anger, expressed by shouting or even by implied or overt violence, is a very common weapon in unfair fighting.

2. Using insulting and abusive language to frighten the other.
Certain four-letter words can be violent in their effects, especially in
homes where they are seldom used.

3. Dragging up old hurts or failures from the past to remind the
partner of his or her frailty.

4. Excessive blaming. ACODs are exposed as children to a lot of
blaming and general faultfinding and learn how to use it very effectively.

5. Picking fights at inappropriate moments specifically to
heighten the embarrassment of the other. The classic dinner conversation is typical. The guests are respected friends—perhaps a
boss or a pastor. You wait for the right moment, then slam-dunk
your comment home: "Honey, don't you think you've had enough?
You know how much weight you've put on lately."

6. Withdrawal, silence, and sulking. Some people develop this
whole bag of tricks to perfection. And although this is mostly used
as a defensive strategy, it can also be a subtle but deadly attack
weapon. You are afraid of being hurt or being at a disadvantage. You
fear humiliation. So what is your strategy? You pull away. You withdraw into your shell and maintain a position of distance. And this
hurts or frightens your spouse, forcing him or her into a defensive
posture. Your partner is demolished, because there is no way effectively to fight withdrawal and silence.

How does one stop these unfair methods of combat in marriage?
The most effective method is to make a point of stopping and
reflecting—either at the time of the battle or afterward. Sometimes,
of course, you may be acting out of deep hurt and not really be
aware of what you are doing. But talking to your spouse during a
time of quiet discussion (not during an argument) can give you
insight on the tactics you are using. So can talking to a counselor.

Video feedback can be a powerful modifier of behavior and is
being used increasingly by therapists. Couples report that every
time they get into an argument, they have flashbacks of seeing
themselves on the TV screen. They don't like what they saw—so
they quickly change to new behaviors.

In these days of compact camcorders, I don't see why this technique cannot be used at home to provide feedback on how you handle conflict. Try setting up a camera on a tripod and taping one of

your typical, but less serious, fights. You can then play back the tape in a calmer moment to ponder your attacking styles. (You would need to plan this ahead of time of course—and you should never do it without your partner's permission.)

Very deep conflicts and very vicious attacking styles cannot be modified by such simple techniques and may need extensive therapy to eradicate. If a marriage is worth saving—and I believe every marriage is precious and deserving of effort—then there is value in taking the time to address the deeper issues in therapy together. However, do not underrate the power of simple common sense and accurate self-awareness to mobilize a will to change. If you know *what* you are doing wrong, you can do a lot to change your behavior. After all, formal psychotherapy is only a recent invention. With God's help, people have managed to find solutions to their relationship problems for many centuries.

Even when you know why you do something, you still have the task of changing your behavior.

This may be an appropriate point for me to comment on a common misconception that has always bothered me as a therapist: the idea that change cannot happen until we know exactly what is wrong and why it happened.

I'm sorry to say that even the most astute psychotherapist can only come up with a *plausible* explanation for your behavior, not necessarily the absolute truth. Many behaviors have their origins in an obscure past, and there is no way in the world that you will be able to reconstruct your history with complete accuracy. Memory distorts everything—facts, motives, and circumstances. A satisfactory explanation of the "why" of your behavior may help to motivate a desire to change, but that's about all it does. The exploration of early childhood events may help uncover repressed memories and even illuminate or expose obscure behavior patterns. But even when you know *why* you do something, you still have the task of changing your behavior.

For instance, you may have a bad temper and the habit of expressing it physically; you like to punch, shout, scratch, bite, or pull hair. You delve into your past and discover that this is exactly how your father (or mother) behaved toward you. So you conclude that you learned this behavior from your parents. What now? Knowing where your bad temper came from doesn't necessarily change it. You might feel a little better knowing that there is someone to blame for it—but you still have to stop acting like a bully.

There are times, in fact, when pursuing the "why" of your behavior may even get in the way of your changing it. You can waste a lot of time and money searching for explanations when you should be getting on with your transformation. So by all means, search for reasons—but don't wait until you've found all the "answers" to begin changing. The act of the will is fully as important as understanding in bringing about change.

Of course, while willpower can do a lot to help us avoid "paralysis of analysis" (the tendency to put off making a change until you understand *why*), even the strongest willpower has its limits. Many have experienced failure after failure, even though they are strong in their wills and clear about what they need to change. And this is where God comes into the picture. It is precisely because our wills are limited that he gives us power and grace.

To put it more clearly, God can and will help us do what we can't do for ourselves, if we will invite him to participate. All it takes is a prayer of invitation—then trust that God will carry through with his promises.

This may sound too good to be true, but I have seen it work again and again. I have seen countless numbers of people ask for God's help in their difficult situations and then marvel at how God has empowered and helped them. "Our extremity is God's opportunity." That may like a cliché, but how better can it be said? It's true.

STYLES OF DEFENSE

In the course of our childhood divorce experiences, we learn not only how to attack; we also learn how to defend ourselves from real or imagined attacks. Sometimes the "best offense" is indeed a "good defense"—or so we unconsciously believe. Unhealthy defensive strategies can be just as damaging to a relationship as any attack. Some of us are masters of the *blitzkrieg;* others of the fortified castle. Either way, we can destroy our partners—and our relationships—if we aren't careful.

There are two "styles of defense" I would like to discuss because they commonly have their origin in the divorce experience:

1. Withdrawing emotional support. The most frequently used defensive strategy in marriage is the withdrawal of emotional support. This very common and destructive strategy operates in practically every predivorce marriage—which, of course, is where the ACOD learns it.

Marriage usually begins in an atmosphere of emotional support. The partner is praised, valued, respected, and even worshiped. Then something happens and the magic vanishes. Here's a typical scenario: Say, for example, that a wife becomes displeased with certain of her husband's behaviors or, more commonly, she is not getting her way. At first she may try attacking her partner, but this only makes her husband angry and her less likely to get what she wants. So her strategy then shifts to the defensive: withdrawal. As soon as there is a grievance, she may:

- stop praising her husband,
- refuse to sleep in the same room with him,
- withdraw sexual privileges,
- communicate tersely with grunts and nods.

Naturally this form of punishment is met with a similar defense. The husband may:

- leave the house,
- stay out late,
- refuse to do normal chores,
- forget to purchase requested goods… and so on.

The possibilities for such scenarios are endless. With some ingenuity—and some modeling from a conflict-ridden childhood—a creative partner can come up with a fascinating battery of weapons and defenses. Some couples develop quite a reputation among their acquaintances for the ingenuity of their emotional destructiveness. They even boast to friends and relatives about their escapades, as if there were some virtue in destroying another's emotional security. And they seem to be blind to the impact of such behavior on their offspring.

Unhealthy defensive strategies can be just as damaging to a relationship as any attack. Some of us are masters of the blitzkrieg; others of the fortified castle. Either way, we can destroy our partners—and our relationships— if we aren't careful.

I believe that any form of punishment that involves the withdrawal of emotional support is "dirty pool" and should be placed off limits in marital warfare. This defensive behavior is simply too destructive—to children in the home as well as to the spouses; it should be avoided at all costs.

Another variation of withdrawal is much slower and more insidious. The partner who is not getting his or her way slowly begins to display and even feel boredom and indifference. The spouse may not even be aware of the development because it happens so slowly. The "little things" like kisses at the front door are the first to go. Gradually, sex becomes perfunctory. Birthdays or anniversaries are forgotten—and those acts of neglect are followed by a thousand acts of carelessness. It is always low-key neglect, nothing ever stands out or draws enough attention to itself to merit an argument. Most affairs take place at this low ebb of a marital relationship—when one spouse is convinced that the relationship is no longer satisfying.

The emergence of this boredom is an unconscious way of protecting oneself against pain or against not getting one's way. It is a defensive strategy that allows disappointments to go untreated. One stops putting in the effort to repair the "little holes" in the relationship. Soon these little holes begin to erode and become big ones.

246 / Adult Children of Divorce

This kind of defensive strategy is based upon acts of omission, not commission—the marriage deteriorates into stalemate not because of a deliberate act of destruction, but because you are doing nothing to take care of or repair it. You may be too hurt or feel too vulnerable to want to spend the time and energy to cultivate the marriage relationship. So you settle for indifference.

I have always seen marriage as analogous to a garden. It can be either a beautiful garden or a shamble of ugly weeds. And what is the difference? The beautiful garden has a gardener who cares for and tends the plants, watering and fertilizing and removing the weeds. An ugly garden just grows by itself. It needs no tending. But it grows nothing worthwhile, either, and eventually it loses its identity as a garden. Indifference to the marital relationship is like failing to weed and water a garden. Over time, both garden and marriage can lose their ability to give happiness.

Indifference in the marital relationship is like failing to weed and water a garden. Over time, both garden and marriage can lose their ability to give happiness.

How does one counter this indifference—especially when it has developed as a defensive strategy against hurt? There is a simple but effective antidote: Do in marriage what you would do in courtship. Reinstate emotional support. Address the underlying causes of hurt. Then, working on the "actions beget feelings" theory, try to turn your complaints into compliments, your attacks into affection. Give time to the relationship. Have regular "dates" when you can get away from the kids and chores and be alone. This gives reassurance to the one feeling defensive. One can fall "in love" again with the same beautiful person you were in love with before if you will give it a chance—along with some time and attention.

I once heard a story of a psychologist whose wife was complaining because she sensed that their marriage was going stale. Her husband had retreated into indifference because he feared she no longer loved him.

She asked her husband, "How much time do you spend with a patient?"

"Fifty minutes."

"Then I would at least like to have the equivalent of one session per day with you, too!"

He got the point. He saw that she really did want to love him more. That night they spent time alone together on a special "date"—their first in many, many years. They continued to set aside such time on a regular basis, and their marriage improved immensely.

2. Hiding behind masks. Increasingly I am hearing marital partners complain that their spouses live behind "masks"—they resist revealing who they really are. In exploring these complaints, I have discovered that the "hidden" partners almost invariably are adult children of divorce who, upon further prodding, will confess that they don't really have a clear sense of who they are themselves. They also feel that they live behind masks—playing the roles of husband, father, employee, or whatever, without any deep sense of personal identity—but they have no idea how to come out from behind these masks.

In an earlier chapter, I discussed the ways in which the ACOD denies his or her "self" and how this neglect of self can impair self-esteem. In your divorcing home, you may not only have been self-critical and self-neglecting, but also have been putting up a "good front" to the world outside. You may have been pushed into playing a family role you were not prepared to take. As a result, you may have begun to "act a part"—the brave little kid, the mother's helper, the clown, or even the troublemaker.

As this "mask building" proceeds, there may be a gradual parting of the ways between who you are on the inside and who you are on the outside. You become "incongruent," and after a while you lose touch with who you are on the inside. You become a stranger to your true self. And as a result, you begin to fake who you are, to live up to the image you believe others have of you.

How does this become a defense? Very easily. Whenever you feel threatened or you can't get your way, you step behind your mask. It becomes a "shield" to protect you from your hurts. The mask causes you to be dishonest about your feelings and act as "he" or "she" would act. When you are angry and someone calls you on it, you deny feeling angry. When you are sad about some loss, you put on the "hero's smile" and behave as if nothing is missing from your life.

Intimacy becomes a real problem in such a circumstance. It is almost impossible to be close to someone else from behind a mask. This is what the spouse complains about: "I can't get close to him (her). I feel like I'm living with a suit of clothes or 'paper doll.'" To be fully exposed in one's innermost being is the most threatening of all fears. You protect your secret feelings at all costs.

And if you are a Christian, you may have learned to wear the "good witness" mask, to hide behind a facade of "upright living" rather than letting your real self show. Sadly, this tendency feeds the mass denial that is so prevalent in Christian circles. No one must know we hurt. No one must see us struggle. We must hide our weaknesses and display our strengths. Sadly, I believe, such an unreal exterior can do more to prevent the real sharing of the gospel than any number of "questionable" activities.

For ACODs, as for so many others who have been traumatized in childhood, one of the most difficult tasks of maturity is learning how to be honestly human. There are many reasons why this is important. When we are honestly ourselves, we become healthier. We can enjoy relationships a whole lot more. We can devote the energy we have used in hiding to other, more positive pursuits.

For ACODs, as for so many others who have been traumatized in childhood, one of the most difficult tasks of maturity is learning how to be honestly human.

I believe we all long to know who we really are, to become full and complete people who don't feel the need to hide behind masks. In the deepest part of our being we yearn to become *real* to ourselves and others. Those of us who were forced to deny our true feelings as children and who lacked an environment of authenticity, unconditional love, and models of genuineness may have more difficulty coming out from behind our masks than others. But even the smallest of steps can reward us with a rich harvest of happiness.

What are some of these "small steps"?

- *Commit yourself to being as honest as you can about your feelings*—but remember, honesty doesn't mean you have to be inconsiderate of the feelings of others.
- *If possible, talk out your feelings with the one causing them.* But be careful to claim your feelings as your own; don't blame others for them.
- *Give up on your "people pleasing" efforts.* Stop acting in certain ways just because you want to make others happy. Don't try to *displease* them; just don't let their potential reaction dictate your behavior.
- *Choose a few "low risk" situations in which to experiment in being yourself honestly.* In conversation, for instance, if you find yourself disagreeing with someone—say so. Do it gracefully, without anger. Learn that you can disagree without being disagreeable. Slowly you will discover that you can express your opinions honestly without the world's turning against you.
- *Learn to say no.* When someone asks you to do them a favor and you would genuinely like to refuse—go ahead and say no. You may find this extremely difficult, but go ahead and try it in minor situations. To be yourself honestly, you must be able to say no honestly—and to say it quite often.
- *Be bountiful with kindnesses and compliments.* Make a point of affirming your family, friends, and work acquaintances. Doing this will help you be freer in expressing your true self. It will also help to create an environment that encourages you to be more honest.

In my book *Unlocking the Mystery of Your Emotions,*[4] I use Margery Williams' beautiful story, *The Velveteen Rabbit,* to illustrate the struggle we all have to become fully human. Her simple fable makes it clear that we can become "real" only as we learn to give ourselves in relationships, painful though that may be. In the words of Margery Williams' skin horse, who advises the velveteen rabbit in what "being Real" means:

It takes a long time [to become Real].... Generally, by the time you are Real, most of the hair has been loved off, and your eyes drop out and you get loose in the joints and very shabby. But these things don't matter at all, because once you are Real you can't be ugly, except to people who don't understand.[5]

"DOING THINGS RIGHT" IN MARRIAGE

It is very easy to get bogged down in identifying the problems associated with being an adult who has experienced the trauma of childhood divorce. But building a healthy marriage is not just a process of avoiding negatives; it must also involve learning positives. We need to consider some specific actions that can build a good marriage.

These positive marriage behaviors can also be invaluable to healing a marriage that is not going well. Perhaps you have already made a marriage commitment that was based upon the unhealthy influences of your childhood. You already may be united in a relationship that is giving you trouble or causing unhappiness. Is the solution to throw this marriage away and start all over again? Not by any means. If you are already committed in marriage, then your first obligation is to try to make it work for you. Running away when things get tough will just perpetuate your problems.

Building a healthy marriage is not just a process of avoiding negatives; it must also involve learning positives. We need to consider some specific actions that can build a good marriage.

Unfortunately, *every* relationship has its dark valleys. If we quit every time things look bleak and foreboding, none of us would make a success of marriage. The key to building a strong marriage is to push forward through the dark valleys and come out the other side with renewed commitment and new relationship skills. Each valley conquered builds strength of character and a more solid foundation for your marriage.

Without writing a complete manual for building a happy marriage here, allow me to emphasize a few important issues that are typically not addressed in marital handbooks. I will attempt to apply these principles specifically to the ACOD situation.

GET YOUR "MODEL" OF MARRIAGE STRAIGHT

Most couples enter marriage with a particular "model" in mind—a set of ideas about which partner will take what role in the relationship, how power will be shared, who will make what decisions, and so on. For most couples, however, the model is something like this:

Our marriage is like a brand new car. It has never been driven before. We will be the first to drive it. While it is new and shiny, it will give us a lot of joy. In the process of time, however, it will get dings in the doors. The carpets will show wear and tear, and kids will throw up on the back seat. As it gets older, the engine may begin to falter and may even die. If this happens, then we'll try to rebuild the car and restore it to its former newness. If we can't, then one of us may even consider throwing it away and changing to a new car!

A good model of marriage? I don't think so. It assumes that marriage starts out perfect, with the relationship functioning at its best—just like a brand new car. It feels good, runs good, even smells good, but in the process of time it deteriorates. The couple, then, tries to recreate the newness and, failing to do this, throws the marriage away and finds a new car.

Many ACODs, out of their disillusionment with their own parents' marriage, approach their own matrimony with a great deal of idealization. They want their union to work out. They may even swear never to repeat their parents' mistakes. But their idealized view of marriage doesn't necessarily help them, because they sometimes expect the marriage not only to be like a new car, but a luxury one at that. When it doesn't turn out like they expected—and few marriages do—disillusionment quickly sets in, and that disillusionment can ultimately destroy the relationship.

The "new car" model of marriage easily becomes a self-fulfilling prophecy. Couples expect the "car" to become old and decrepit and eventually to be beyond repair—and unconsciously they let this happen. Then they are either ready to "trade it in" and to abandon the marriage or to live stoically with a "junker" of a marriage.

I prefer a different model for marriage. It goes like this:

> When we get married, we are given a box of parts. It contains all the pieces we need to build a beautiful car—gears, wires, pipes, wheels, even a hood ornament. We don't exactly have a good set of plans for it, but we have some idea of what shape and form it should take. In the process of time, we figure out how the axles connect to the chassis, how the transmission goes together, where to put the brakes. *Gradually* we build something that begins to run well, and one day it may even smell good!

After many years of marriage, I am convinced that a beautiful marriage is not something that springs into being of its own accord, nor does it grow automatically. Marriage does *not* start out perfect; it is simply a collection of well-chosen possibilities. It is up to us to figure out *how* it goes together and to work at connecting its components. In this model, then, the mind-set is one of *building, creating, fashioning, and constructing*. We know it started as just a box of parts, so we don't feel disappointed when things don't go together so well. Instead, when problems arise, we are motivated to modify the parts until it runs well.

Many couples I have worked with in therapy have found that changing their model of marriage to a more realistic one has freed them from a lot of guilt. They stop blaming themselves for the way their "car" has deteriorated. And then they are ready to get started on the "do it yourself" work.

MAKE YOUR COMMITMENT NOW

Almost everybody believes in marriage vows when we make them: "In sickness and in health... until death do us part." But the high divorce rate obviously proves that we don't keep them. Something changes. In the course of time, our commitment weakens and dies.

Part of the reason for this is that we believe at *different levels*. I may believe that a vow or promise I am making is genuine and from my heart. But the vow, at the time I make it, is made against the background of *other* beliefs. There is a context for every promise. I may promise to come and rescue you from being stranded on the highway because I do want to help—and because nothing else in my life is as important at the moment. But if, after I hang up the phone, my wife falls and breaks an arm, my promise to you will have to take second place.

Marriage does not start out perfect; it is simply a collection of well-chosen possibilities. It is up to us to figure out how it goes together and to work at connecting its components.

A dear friend and colleague of mine, Dr. Lewis Smedes, has written a marvelous book called *Caring and Commitment,* which clarifies this idea of commitments made in context. He points out, first, that this would be a terrible world if we made promises we didn't keep. Every relationship, especially the deepest ones, is held together by the transparent bonds we call commitment. Every profession of love is a statement of promise. Every conception of a child is a pledge to be a good parent. Our world is held together by our commitments to be honest, to be good friends, to do our jobs well, to take care of others, to be faithful to what we believe, and to do what we promise. And it is only a meaningful commitment when it has a "no matter what" quality to it.

But are all commitments forever? The answer is no. Dr. Smedes puts it this way: "I wonder what life would be like if we were stuck forever to every commitment we ever made. Absolutely stuck!"[6] Some commitments are bad. The member of a teenage gang who has promised to honor and obey his leader, even when it means shooting the sister of a rival gang member, has made a bad promise—a vow that *must* be broken. One cannot keep such promises and create a good life.

Where the rubber hits the road for us here, of course, is the question of whether a marriage should—or can—be a "forever" commitment. Is the promise we make at the matrimonial altar for a lifetime? Is it even possible to fulfill a promise to stay with one person forever? Many people, obviously, think not. But my understanding of God's will is that *marriage can and should be a lifetime commitment.* And my experience with countless couples in therapy convinces me that making marriage a forever vow is the first step to restoring healthy marriages.

Yes, I know there will be some exceptions—cases of physical abuse, abandonment. Almost anyone can think of a "yes, but." If you will be honest, however, you will see that these extreme examples simply don't apply to most situations. And they can easily become excuses for devaluing the importance of lifelong commitment in marriage.

Where the rubber hits the road for us here, of course, is the question of whether a marriage should—or can—be a "forever" commitment.

I really think that the primary reason the divorce rate has become so high is that most people, including many devout Christians, have developed a "low" view of the marriage vow. Couples give up hope too quickly. Little problems become catastrophes from which one or the other wants to run. Few people want to stay with the struggle any more. Few want to stay committed when the road gets rough. And those who grow up in divorced homes are especially likely to have this "ditch it if it gets too hard" attitude.

I would like to see us restore a "high" view of marriage in our society. I would like "forever" commitments to once more be the norm. But in order for this to happen, we need to keep in mind the idea of "context."

We must remember that like every commitment, a promise to be married for life to one partner takes place in a *context*—for good or bad. I would wish that we could all make a "perfect" or unconditional commitment at the time of marriage, but this isn't always possible. Even in my own marriage I went through a period when I convinced myself that my vow was "conditional." If my wife doesn't give me what I want, then why should I stay?

It then dawned on me that most of us really need to think about the importance of remaking (or at least reaffirming) our vows when we are more mature, when we can make them against a context of really understanding what it means to say, "This is for life!"

Commitment has emerged as a very key component in "love research" at several major universities including Dr. Sternberg's work at Yale. The other two components are *passion* and *intimacy,* and together they form the so-called "love triangle." The more "balanced" these components are in a relationship, the healthier the relationship will be. However, commitment seems to be the foundational element in long-lasting love relationships. Without a "base" of commitment, the love triangle is incapable of lasting very long. But a solid base of commitment can keep a marriage viable during periods when passion or intimacy are at a low ebb.

Sometimes commitment is low at the beginning of a marriage and grows with time. While commitment is not, in itself, a feeling, it often depends on feelings of passion, attraction, and closeness. In other words, it is common for couples to feel committed when they "feel in love," and not to feel committed when the love isn't "felt."

This is most unfortunate. Commitment ought to transcend feelings. It should be a choice, an act of the will, a decision, whether or not the right passion is there. This is why marriage is in such serious trouble in our age. We have come to believe that commitment depends on whether or not we have the right romantic feelings. Love must mature beyond this so that when the road of matrimony gets rough, one doesn't quit. God calls us to make commitments in marriage that will see us through the troubled parts of the journey.

Most of us really need to think about the importance of remaking (or at least reaffirming) our vows when we are more mature, when we can make them against a context of really understanding what it means to say, "This is for life!"

I didn't really make my true commitment until I was well into my marriage. Being a child of divorce, I had grown up feeling that marriage was a "tentative" affair. You stayed married if the relationship was pulsing and throbbing with excitement, and you separated if the thrills subsided. I held a very low view of marriage.

Because I knew how devastating the divorce had been on us kids,

I had paid lip service to commitment. "I don't ever want to get divorced," I told myself. "I want to stick it through to the end." But deep down, my real feeling was, "If things don't work out, I will split."

The time came when—even though we had three beautiful girls, a home of our own, and prospects for a happy life—either my wife or I would threaten separation every time we had a disagreement. "I want a divorce." "I don't want to put up with this anymore." "I want out." We took turns threatening each other with dissolving our marriage. And while these threats probably served some emotional purpose and gave us a feeling of not being trapped, the day came when I realized that they were destructive in themselves because they undermined our commitment. They implied that we were conditionally committed to each other.

So I called for a quiet discussion—just my wife and I—and made the following speech:

> I know that we threaten separation as a way of scaring and even punishing each other, but I don't think it honors our marriage or glorifies God. From this moment on, I am making a commitment to you for the rest of my life. I will never ever use divorce as a threat again. I will stay with you until I die—no matter what happens or how bad the circumstances. I would like you to stop threatening divorce to me. Let us pledge to each other absolute loyalty.

My wife cried. I cried. And from that day on, we *never* once spoke of separation; our staying together "till death do us part" is an unquestioned given. And from that day on, our marriage took a turn for the better. When we *knew* that we were in it "for better or worse," we began to handle our problems more directly. The damaging influence of my parents' divorce was finally broken, and I was free to build my own happy marriage.

USE YOUR GOD-GIVEN RESOURCES TO BUILD YOUR MARRIAGE

Every marriage has a rich supply of resources that can help to build happiness. These resources do *not* have to cost money. And they are available to all of us if we will simply make use of them.

1. The resource of love. Very few people in our culture get married just for physical security or to have a roof over their head or food in their stomach. Most marry for love, for intimacy, and for companionship. Love is a marriage's greatest resource. But love can only thrive in an atmosphere of acceptance and caring. To maintain love in a marriage, one must *be* loving.

I recently counseled with a man in his late forties who had come to see me because he no longer "felt love" toward his wife. He didn't want to separate, mainly because he felt that "God would be displeased" with this action. As we talked it appeared that the real reason was that he and all his friends went to the same church and he feared that they would ostracize him if he left his wife. Yet his lack of love bothered him.

Behavior precedes feelings. If we behave in the right way,
feelings associated with this behavior will
almost certainly follow.

So I sat him down and explained that love was not just a feeling. I pointed him to 1 Corinthians 13, which spells out that *love is behavior.* Love is what we *do,* not what we feel. And yet, when you act in a loving way to someone, something does happen to your feelings. I then challenged this man to begin acting toward his wife *as if* he loved her, then to wait and see what happened to the way he felt.

He did exactly what I recommended. Within the month, he began to report a dramatic change in his feelings. He started holding his wife's hand in public. He caressed her hair. He kissed her cheeks. He stroked her back. He did everything that young lovers do. And as he did this, his feelings for her returned.

This happened because of a very powerful psychological law at work: *Behavior precedes feelings.* If we behave in the right way, the feelings associated with this behavior will almost certainly follow. Invariably they are just dormant, waiting to receive fresh life.

2. There is also the resource of time. Spending time together has been found, in study after study, to be a critical factor in marital happiness.[7] Of course, it is not just the time itself, but *how* that time is spent, that makes the difference.

Most couples today face many competing demands for their time. Work demands. Children's projects. Church activities. But *nothing* is as important to a marriage as a couple's spending time together—alone. Some couples set aside regular time for a "date." Others work together on a hobby or on planning activities and vacations. There are *many* ways couples can spend time together. If you are out of the habit, however, you may need to make this an intentional priority in order for it to happen.

3. The resource of mutual encouragement and support. ACODs are notoriously deficient in this area. They withhold encouragement, or may even tend toward being discouraging, because of what has been modeled to them during their childhoods. The withholding of encouragement and even outright criticism is a major punitive tool in many dysfunctional families.

One of our most important struggles as adult children of divorce is setting ourselves free to be our own persons. Those we love also deserve the same privilege.

To be an encourager is a little risky because you risk being rejected when the other person doesn't accept your encouragement. But the risk is worthwhile because the more the partners appreciate and support each other, the closer together they grow.

What is especially important here is to give your partner unconditional permission to be himself or herself. Many spouses feel violated by their partners' insistence that they be a certain type of person or that they conform to expectations that are not their own. Some husbands want their wives to be "just like mother." Some wives expect their husbands to be "just like father." The opposite is also true. I have often heard an ACOD husband, for example, complain, "My wife is just like my mother—even though they are not blood related—and I hate it."

We limit our partners' growth when we impose our blueprints

upon their lives. We restrict our partners' potential to become fully what God wants them to become when we press them into molds of our making.

Encouraging your partner, therefore, means letting him or her go free—without limitations. One of our most important struggles as adult children of divorce is setting ourselves free to be our own persons. Those we love also deserve the same privilege. Letting them be themselves is the essence of encouragement.

THE ACOD AS A PARENT

In closing this chapter on ACODs and marriage, let me touch on the topic of ACODs as parents. I will have more to say on this topic in the next chapter.

Nearly twenty years ago, I read a report by an English educational psychologist entitled "Divorce Begins in the Nursery."[8] In a speech to the Royal Society of Health Sex Education, he stated that "high marriage risks can already be spotted in our primary [elementary] schools." He goes on to describe how certain traits in children could make them ideal candidates for divorce as adults. He pleaded with parents and teachers to be alert to children who are uncooperative and isolated, who spoil the games of others, who have intense feelings of inferiority, and who boast excessively. He believed that these children could be taught to be better marriage partners if they were helped to be healthier children.

I believe this observant psychologist has a point. And I believe the obverse is also true: children who have been raised in divorced homes may have a more difficult time being effective parents. There are several possible reasons for this.

- You may be too strict, fearing that your kids may "go off the rails."
- You may be too lenient, feeling guilty about every act of discipline.
- You may want to please your children too much as a way of appeasing your own childhood pain.

- Not having been parented well yourself, you may lack an adequate model for parenting.
- You may be so afraid of making mistakes or of being like your parents that you are frozen into inaction.

Having said that, let me urge you to relax! No parent is perfect. If you know anyone whose children are beautifully well-adjusted, totally obedient, reliable to a fault, always courteous, respectful, considerate, and brilliant in school to boot, I suggest that you send that parent's name to the Smithsonian Institution for display! Such a parent would be a unique treasure. Unfortunately, I don't believe that parent exists.

If you feel hassled, if you sometimes wish you weren't a parent, if you occasionally feel tempted either to commit murder or leave home permanently, then join the club called "The Average Parent."

If you feel hassled, if you sometimes wish you weren't a parent, if you occasionally feel tempted either to commit murder or leave home permanently; and if exhaustion, annoyance, and worry are familiar companions... then join the club called "The Average Parent." There is no application form, no dues, no annual renewal. And you can count on being a member until your kids grow up and leave home!

Seriously, parenting *is* hard work. All parents must continually walk a narrow line between being too permissive and too strict. Excessive permissiveness produces disturbed kids. Excessive strictness produces disturbed kids. In the middle lies health, happiness, and harmony. But it's hard for any parent to manage that balance. For ACODs it may be additionally difficult.

REVIEWING YOUR PARENTING PAST

How can ACODs improve their parenting skills? Since many of your possible parenting problems began in your childhood, I would begin by examining some of the unhelpful parent-child patterns you may have learned at home. For example:

1. You may have been used as a "bridge" between your conflicted parents. One study shows that 75 percent of the children of divorce are used to bridge gaps between former spouses.[9] They are forced to transport messages, to mediate disagreements, to spy, to act as "buffers." These tactics are tantamount to child abuse. They invariably cause feelings of insecurity, betrayal, guilt, divided loyalties—and these feelings usually carry over into adulthood.

2. You may have felt "robbed" of your childhood. Many children feel that they were physically and psychologically overburdened in their childhood and thus denied the chance to have a "normal" childhood. Their privacy was invaded, their development thwarted, their dominant feelings were loneliness, isolation, vulnerability, and anger. It is very common for children of divorce to long to leave home as soon as possible.

3. You may have felt like a "substitute" spouse for one or both of your parents. Children of divorce are often used as conversational partners or escorts. Instead of spending time with friends their own age, they are expected to spend most of their time with their parents. And they often feel overtaxed by this responsibility.

4. You probably experienced scapegoating in your parent-child interactions. Blame is a major component in most conflicted homes, and children often feel the brunt of it. They learn that scapegoating and accusations are a way of life.

BREAKING NEGATIVE PARENTING PROBLEMS

Once you recognize patterns from your own childhood, you can devise strategies for breaking them. Here are some suggestions that have helped many adults from conflicted homes break the pattern of negative parenting:

1. Face the fact that you have a strong chance of following your parents' example. Regardless of how you feel about your parents, you will probably end up parenting the way they did unless you take decisive steps to counter that tendency.

2. Set up a system of accountability to alert you when you exhibit these unhealthy parenting behaviors. Much of your negative parenting will be instinctive and unconscious. For this reason you need to devise ways of being aware of what you're doing. Talk openly with your family both about your past and your intentions to break free from it. Then ask your spouse or children to tell you when you are repeating behavior from your past. This system of accountability will quickly shape you toward healthy parenting habits and will make you a better marriage partner as well.

Much of your negative parenting will be instinctive and unconscious. For this reason you need to devise ways of being aware of what you're doing.

Allow me to illustrate. Suppose that as a child you were severely criticized every time you did something that displeased your mother or father. They called you "stupid" and told you that you would never amount to anything. Now, you have a son who has just turned thirteen. You become frustrated when he doesn't try hard enough at school. And the words just slip out: "You really are stupid, you know. Can't you do any better? I don't think you're going to make it in life." These words are intended to motivate your son to try harder. But they only demoralize him and make him feel like a failure—just like you felt as a child.

This is exactly what happened in a family I counseled. And this is the accountability system we set up to change this destructive pattern. I asked the mother to talk to her son and explain that her father used to talk to her this way. "Ask him to help you break this habit," I told her, "by alerting you whenever you speak this way to him."

They devised a "hand signal" that the son would use to tell his mother when he felt she was putting him down. And their new system eventually became a game with them. Mom would begin her tirades, and the son would raise his hand and give the sign. In just a short while, the son learned not to take the putdowns personally, and mother stopped her criticisms. Eventually, the son began to put out more effort, and his grades improved.

3. Draw up a "good parenting" plan. Once you have made the decision to break the negative parenting patterns you learned as a child, you will benefit by making a study of *positive* parenting patterns you want to adopt. Here is a sample list of characteristics found in good parents:

- They are consistent in their discipline and provide firm guidelines.
- They always keep their promises.
- They are unconditionally loving.
- They operate with a strategy of warmth.
- They communicate their expectations clearly.
- They don't blame their spouses or ex-spouses for their children's behavior.
- They are not afraid to be the boss.
- They accept that there are times when their children will hate them, and they don't allow this fact to intimidate them.
- They allow children to talk about feelings and encourage development of a "feeling vocabulary," but they don't allow the children to hit or act out anger in other ways.
- They allow children to be themselves and don't expect them to act like little adults.
- They work at being happy themselves.
- They model a deep spiritual commitment.

A long list? Not really. Every one of these principles is easy to implement if you set your mind to it. And the last is perhaps the most important. I am convinced that parents owe their children some religious training. I don't mean the sort that fills them with fear and guilt. I mean exposure to a belief system that provides comfort, strength, and forgiveness for being an imperfect human being. Children need the emotional support that religion can give. And there is no greater caring to be found anywhere than in a church— no matter how imperfect that church may be.

Peace is not the product of turmoil and rebellion, but of root-edness and spiritual security. And that is the gift you give your children when you commit yourself to spiritual growth and teach them to do the same.

A strong spiritual foundation will also help your child be happy in later life. Happiness is not to be found in a moral wilderness, where so many children are forced to wander, but in a life of integrity and purpose. Peace is not the product of turmoil and rebellion, but of rootedness and spiritual security. And that is the gift you give your children when you commit yourself to spiritual growth and teach them to do the same.

CHAPTER 10

Breaking the
Divorce Cycle

"**H**OW DOES BEING AN ACOD affect my chances of staying married? Am I doomed to repeat my parents' marital mistakes?" These questions haunt many adult children of divorce. And it was tearing twenty-three-year-old Andrew apart.

"My girlfriend's parents say that anyone whose parents are divorced has a much higher risk for getting divorced himself," he wailed. "There's no way she's going to marry me now that my folks are splitting up!"

Andrew's parents had just decided to divorce. Actually, his father had done the deciding. He announced one day that he was "in love" with another woman and wanted to marry her. Andrew's mother had been devastated by the announcement. She had assumed—correctly—that the marriage was reasonably good, but she had been totally unaware that even men with satisfactory marriages are vulnerable to affairs at certain times in their lives.

"How does being an ACOD affect my chances of staying married? Am I doomed to repeat my parents' marital mistakes?"

I had tried hard to help save that couple's marriage. Knowing that some affairs fizzle out if you give them time, I had tried to reduce the wife's need to act precipitously. But she felt so humiliated that she had just wanted to get the divorce over with quickly. Despite our time in counseling, they chose to go their separate ways.

Since I couldn't prevent the parents from splitting up, I decided to do what I could to help their son. So I asked Andrew and his fiancée to come talk to me. I explained that despite their recent troubles, his parents had basically built a good marriage. They had laid a solid foundation of effective communication, patience, and loving behavior in the home. There had been a few serious conflicts over the years, but the father's recent affair had been a most unfortunate and unpremeditated action. It had occurred at a low point in his professional career, as it often does in a midlife crisis, and it had little to do with the more typical dysfunctions that precipitate divorce.

In addition, I pointed out, Andrew was twenty-three years old when the separation occurred. He had already left home, and he was beyond the stage where the divorce would have any permanent effect. It was sad, of course, that their children would never know two sets of grandparents in intact homes. But this particular divorce was no reason for these young people to abandon their marriage plans.

Andrew and his girlfriend did marry. To my knowledge they have a very happy marriage—the more so because they know how easily something can happen to upset their marital bliss. They are especially careful to avoid the many pitfalls to successful marriage and to intentionally develop their relationship.

FROM GENERATION TO GENERATION

In Andrew's case, the fear that his parents' divorce would somehow "rub off" and seriously threaten his own marriage was basically unfounded. But sadly, this is not true for most children of divorce.

The vast majority of divorces are not brought on by chance events or unforeseen twists of fate; they are the consequence of years of conflict. Dysfunctional patterns have had plenty of opportunity to be rehearsed and acted out. Family problems have become chronic, and hurt is inflicted almost daily. How can this not influence a child?

A popular term for such a dysfunctional family system is "toxic";

its dynamics often end up poisoning the mind and the emotions of everyone involved. To use another metaphor, someone has described such a family system as a multicar pileup on the freeway[1]—one car piles into another until there is a mountain of broken vehicles.

"Toxicity" also tends to be transferred from one generation to another. The rules, behaviors, reactions, attitudes, and accumulated feelings get handed down, unwittingly, from parents to children, who then become parents and hand them on to their children. Their inheritance becomes a hurtful legacy of dysfunction—and often divorce as well.

"Toxicity" tends to be transferred from one generation to another. The rules, behaviors, reactions, attitudes, and accumulated feelings get handed down, unwittingly, from parents to children, who then become parents and hand them on to their children.

This phenomenon, known technically as the "intergenerational transmission of divorce," has been given a lot of research attention this past decade.[2] Just how "heritable" is divorce? Does the absence of satisfactory role models in unhappy or broken homes statistically decrease the chances for a happy marriage in the offspring?

The research clearly indicates that there is at least a "modest" effect. One study reported, for instance, that when neither set of parents was divorced, there was only a 15 percent chance that a couple would divorce. This figure rose to 38 percent if both sets of parents were divorced.[3]

There are several conceivable explanations for these figures. Recent research favors the idea that divorce is "contagious" because children of divorce share other factors with their divorced parents that could contribute to divorce—including social class, educational level, and age at marriage.[4] I am convinced the connection goes beyond these factors and includes the mimicking of personality styles and learned patterns of relating in dysfunctional families.

Obviously, a child's actual experience of divorce will depend on many factors—including the degree of support from other family members, the number of lifestyle changes that are required, and even the relative quickness or slowness of the proceedings. Most important, parental conflict can be just as damaging to children as divorce itself. Unfortunately, little research has been done to isolate these contributing factors and to study the extent to which they affect the child in later life.

How many children of divorce actually do get divorced themselves? We don't really know. The divorce rate is so high in our Western world that it would be almost impossible to single out the childhood divorce factor entirely from these statistics.

Dr. Judith Wallerstein, in her epic long-term study of the effects of divorce, was able to compile statistics on the children of sixty middle-class families that she has been following since 1971. She reports that the girls in her study tended to abandon their unhappy home situation by marrying early (before age twenty) and by marrying the first man who came along[5]—and that all but one of these young women eventually divorced. But this result may be as much a function of marrying too young as it is a result of divorce per se. It would be a mistake to take her evidence as conclusive proof that divorce begets divorce in the life of an ACOD.

DOES DIVORCE HAVE TO RUN IN FAMILIES?

It's true that we don't have clear, unequivocal statistics about the "contagiousness" of divorce. As I stated in the first chapter, the best I can offer is the cumulative wisdom of my own experience both as a child of divorce and as a clinician, as well as the wisdom of the many others who have written on this topic.

I am convinced, from experience and research, that the combination of family dysfunction and the disruptions caused by divorce is indeed likely to affect the way ACODs approach their own marriages. In this sense, their childhood experiences clearly increase their chances of marital failure.

What are some of the ways your own divorce experience may predispose you to divorce?

1. Childhood divorce may cause you to be less trusting of human relationships and to look upon them as unstable and unreliable.[6] ACODs often tend to feel insecure with their spouses because they expect rejection and abandonment. This causes them either to become clinging and jealous or to withdraw emotionally in order to protect themselves.

2. You may have learned unhealthy ways of managing conflict. Some ACODs, who have observed how harmful their own parents' fighting was, try not to fight at all in their own marriages. They repress their anger until it breaks out in the form of physical sickness or explodes inappropriately. Other ACODs model their conflict resolution after their parents'; their marriages are characterized by fighting and even physical violence.

Since divorce is a familiar occurrence in an ACOD's life, it may seem like the logical solution to marital difficulties.

---

3. You may be quicker to see divorce as an option. Since divorce is a familiar occurrence in an ACOD's life, it may seem like the logical solution to marital difficulties. And this may be true even if the divorced parents themselves argue against a divorce for their child. (This is a little like alcoholic parents trying to persuade their child to sober up. Their motives may be good, but their attempts at persuasion are an exercise in futility!) Studies have shown, in fact, that the more divorce there is in a family's history, the greater is the likelihood that younger married couples will resort to it.[7]

But don't read my remarks on the "heritability of divorce" too pessimistically. My intention is not to prescribe doom to every child of divorce, but to highlight the pitfalls so that they can be avoided.

After all, I have succeeded in building a very strong and loving marriage despite my family background, so I know that divorce doesn't have to run in families. If you can open your eyes to the dysfunctional patterns you have inherited and intentionally work at changing them, you *can* learn from your parents' mistakes and break the divorce cycle. In the remainder of this chapter I hope to show some ways you can do just that.

PARENTAL FACTORS THAT PERPETUATE DIVORCE

Let's look, first of all, at some of the ways your exposure to the mistakes of your parents makes you especially vulnerable to divorce in your adult life. If you are going to break the cycle of divorce, you will have to make a determined effort to overcome the influences that *parental attitudes, parental behaviors,* and *parental injunctions* have had on your life.

PARENTAL ATTITUDES

There are several important attitudes that divorcing parents transmit to their children. I have already touched on some of these in other contexts, but let me pull them together here for completeness:

To enter into marriage with the idea that one partner must be a "perfect fit" with another is to simply set yourself up for disillusionment.

---

1. Belief that marriages must be "compatible" in order to work. The most common excuse I hear from couples who intend to separate is that they are "incompatible." When you push them to explain what they mean by this, they say that their personalities clash, that they have different values, or that their backgrounds are so different that they cannot agree on anything. The attitude that they pass along to their children, therefore, is that incompatibility is an insurmountable barrier. According to this way of thinking, opposites may attract, but opposites just can't live together.

I believe this a myth because incompatibility is the rule, not the exception, in marriage. No one enters marriage without a monumental set of differences in terms of ideas, habits, and attitudes. In fact, as I have already said, the male/female mix in itself is a major source of incompatibility.

In my experience, what couples mean when they say they want to separate because they are incompatible is that they no longer want to work at overcoming their differences. They have lost the will to make their marriage work.

I am convinced that children of divorce must reject this myth of compatibility outright if they want their own marriages to be successful. To enter into marriage with the idea that one partner must be a "perfect fit" with another is simply to set yourself up for disillusionment.

If you have assimilated a disillusioned attitude about marriage, you must do your best to confront your assumptions and get them out in the open. And then you must challenge your disillusionment with all the intelligence you can muster.

---

2. Disillusionment. Disappointment and resentment are common elements in the emotional fallout of a divorce. Say, for example, that a wife has been abandoned by her husband, who "no longer loves" her and who has moved in with someone else. After a lengthy power struggle over custody, she has gained the right to keep the children with her. But she soon discovers that raising the children by herself, while trying to work and build a new life for herself, is more than any human was designed to bear. As a result, she becomes bitter and disillusioned, convinced that marriage is a curse and that all men are evil.

Or perhaps it is the husband who is abandoned. The wife has found her "true love" and gone to live with him in paradise. She put up some token resistance at the custody hearing, but was relieved when the children were dumped on her ex. The poor, disillusioned husband now begins to teach his sons how terrible women are: "You can't trust them. They'll betray you at the drop of a hat!"

Another couple finally gives up after years of attempts to resolve their conflicts. They're weary. They're depressed. They just can't handle their lives anymore. "It's no use," they tell their children. "People change. It's just not realistic to expect two people to live their whole lives together. Things just don't work out."

As a result of any of these scenarios, the children grow up disillusioned about marriage, and their disillusionment can easily become a self-fulfilling prophecy. They may date and marry, but in the back of their minds there is the assumption that the marriage just won't work out: "It's just a matter of time before he/she leaves me. So I had better be the one to go. It's better to reject than be rejected."

If you have assimilated a disillusioned attitude about marriage, you must do your best to confront your assumptions and get them out in the open. And then you must challenge your disillusionment with all the intelligence you can muster. Collect "happy marriage" stories. Search your ideas about marriage for "holes" and fantasies. Get professional help, if necessary. And ask God for healing and hope as you go about rethinking your ideas and conquering disillusionment.

3. Dislike of children. The children of divorce have usually been deeply hurt by their parents' specific acts of commission and omission. Often, however, they are hurt even more deeply by absorbing an attitude that children are inherently bad. "All children eventually turn on you." "They just take and take; they think only of themselves."

Parents who feel overloaded and angry can easily communicate an attitude of dislike to their children. This seems paradoxical, but it happens. The abused becomes the abuser. The one who was hurt becomes the hurter. Having suffered yourself becomes an excuse to cause suffering to others.

While I see this phenomenon more frequently in lower socioeconomic groups, it also occurs in upper-class circles. These children then become adults with a bad attitude toward children. In extreme form, this attitude may be acted out in the form of physical abuse.

A learned dislike of children can hurt a marriage in several ways:

- It can lead to physical or emotional abuse and a general unhappy atmosphere.

- It can cause conflicts between the parents as the healthy parent tries to intervene and stop the abuser.
- It prevents the bonding of the family.
- It may cause the ACOD to abandon the family because he or she "just couldn't cut it" as a parent.

Divorce is often just one step away as well, and the children of this divorce tend to perpetuate the cycle when their turn at marriage and parenthood arrives.

Deep-seated attitudes like this are not easy to eradicate. I would be misleading you to suggest that they can be overcome in a series of simple steps. If your experience of divorce has given you a bad attitude toward children, understanding the problem may be a starting point. But therapy will probably be needed in order to explore the deeper attitudes that drive your behavior. However, it is not so important that you uncover the origins of your attitude to children as it is to expose *what* these attitudes are and to develop strategies for changing them.

Even if you are only faintly aware of a dislike for children, you should not proceed to become a parent until you have done some therapeutic work on your problem. Don't give in to social or peer pressure if you would really prefer not to have children. Gone are the days when being childless was a stigma. Parenting is a wonderful experience. But if you don't have the right attitude, parenting can also cause a lot of grief for you, your spouse, and your children.

PARENTAL BEHAVIORS

Marriage is the most intimate of all relationships. No other affiliation demands as much of the people who enter into it, and no other joint venture can match it for the pressures it imposes on the human frame. To develop harmony in wishes, plans, activities, likes and dislikes—even to live together in the same house—takes enormous skill and willingness to adjust. You literally trade in some of your autonomy for the sake of togetherness. How much independence you give up depends on circumstances. But some of it (not too much) must be traded for the sake of a healthy relationship.

Now here's the rub. If harmony—or at least cooperation—does

not emerge, the relationship may become a battleground. One or both of the partners may be racked with distress. And the behaviors that emerge as a result can be the most destructive that the human mind can devise. Unfortunately, these behaviors become part of a model that children learn and may later put into play themselves.

What are some of the negative behaviors you as an ACOD may have learned from your parents?

1. How to Scream. When partners are evenly matched and endowed with good lungs and healthy vocal cords, sheer noise can fuel any fight. The successful screamer learns to do it loud enough for the neighbors to hear. Worse still, the screamer learns to turn on the decibels in public places—so that the partner and the children fear going to restaurants or stores.

A home filled with shouting arguments can condition the most horrible of fears in children. They can become extremely sensitive to anything loud and become particularly anxious whenever anyone raises his or her voice.

Those who scream their battles often think the noise level is quite "innocent." One husband, justifying his tendency to yell, told me that "it was better than beating my wife and kids." I was flabbergasted and told him so. The fact that screaming is only noise doesn't make it any less harmful. The bruises may not be on the outside, but they are just as real on the inside. In fact, many children have told me they would rather be beaten than to be yelled or screamed at day after day. Many spouses feel the same way.

I am not just talking about noise levels here. In some cultures, noise is considered normal. Families are warm and expressive, and there may even be a lot of yelling. But when I say screaming can be harmful, I am speaking of angry, critical, and often vicious screaming—the kind done by people who either don't know how to handle their problems effectively or have lost the will to do so.

2. How to Use Cruel Words. Not only can we learn the habit of screaming and pass it on to our children; we can also learn to use words in cruel and hurtful ways.

Most parents, at some time or another, say something derogatory to their spouse or children. In a healthy family situation, these cutting words will be balanced with positive comments. The other person usually dismisses the comment because he or she knows it is said in anger. But frequent attacks on a child or spouse's appearance, competence, intelligence, or value as a person clearly ranks as verbal abuse—and it is clearly harmful.

Some parents who use cruel labels never shout; they criticize with cool detachment. This can pack their words with even more venom.

Barbara's father could be like this. He was a quiet, even shy, person. But when he had too much drink, he would begin to pick on Barbara. He would tease her excessively, call her by insulting nicknames, or respond sarcastically to some story she had told. And then he would criticize the way she looked: "You're too fat." "Why don't you dress pretty?" "Can't you do your hair another way?" In fact, so many of his verbal barbs focused on her appearance that Barbara began to suspect he was attracted to her physically. Although she was almost seventeen, she would tremble when she heard him walk past her room at night.

Today, at twenty-six, Barbara remains deeply scarred by her gentle father's cruel words. "I hate him," she once told me. "He's as much of a brute as my friend's father, who used to beat her all the time. And he still makes fun of me. He never misses a chance to put me down in his quiet, calm way."

Barbara quickly learned, through therapy, to confront her father directly and to express her deep feelings of fear and hate for the way he treated her. At first her father reacted in anger and refused even to talk to her. But very slowly he began to realize what he was doing and to change his behavior.

Today, Barbara's father treats her with respect, but her problems are not over. Barbara is now faced with how her father's cruel words shaped her own style of relating to those she loves. Several times she has found herself treating her five-year-old son much as her father treated her. She has a long haul ahead in learning to overcome this legacy from her childhood.

PARENTAL INJUNCTIONS

Many children of divorce are also influenced by the many "injunctions" with which their parents indoctrinate them. The more dysfunctional and neurotic a parent, the more likely he or she is to use and impose injunctions.

What is an injunction? It is like the "curse" often pronounced in fairy and folk tales. It is a *command* given by a parent to an innocent and unthinking child—an order to behave and to think in a certain way. It is not always spoken, but sometimes implied by attitude or tone of voice. The effect of the injunction, which may be quite arbitrary, is to inhibit the child's freedom. Disturbed parents create, use, and impose injunctions with great emphasis. They don't always have to spell it out. Children are sensitive enough that they get the message even when it's not spoken.

Parental injunctions are nearly always negatives:

- Don't sing in the house.
- Don't laugh loudly.
- Don't eat too many sweets.
- Don't go out after dark.
- Don't tell your father what I told you.
- Don't sit sloppily.

Some of them come from deep within a parent's own troubled self:

- Don't smile.
- Don't show anger.
- Don't do anything that makes you unhappy.
- Don't even think; just do what I say.
- Don't be assertive.
- Don't enjoy sex.
- Don't be a tomboy.

In addition, parents from religious backgrounds often come up with their own set of injunctions:

- Don't forget that God sees everything you do and will punish you.

- Don't sit there doing nothing; God doesn't like us to be idle.
- Don't give me any lip; remember, God says you must honor your parents.

Of course, some injunctions are necessary to a child's well-being. Children do need to be told, in no uncertain terms:

- Don't touch the electrical socket.
- Don't run into the street.
- Don't take other people's belongings.

Neurotic parents, however, magnify the neurotic injunctions; they multiply the "don'ts" without adequate reason or explanation. In very troubled homes, they become even more serious:

- Don't be successful.
- Don't stand out in a crowd.
- Don't be important.
- Don't feel your feelings.
- Don't be happy.

Many ACODs report that their mental lists of parental injunctions play in their minds like broken records or continuous-loop tapes. And then, in turn, they begin to impose these commands on their spouses and children.

Many ACODs report that their mental lists of parental injunctions play in their minds like broken records or continuous-loop tapes. They can hear their mother's or father's voice telling them over and over again that they mustn't do something. And then, in turn, they begin to impose these commands on their spouses and children.

The antidote for neurotic injunctions or commands is to "give yourself permission" to do the things your parents said you mustn't. You allow yourself to counter the injunction by recognizing that it is not necessary for health, happiness, or safety and then deliberately telling yourself that it is all right to do whatever it is you choose to do.

As you can imagine, the underlying purpose of neurotic parental injunctions is to create guilt feelings when they are violated. They are an unhealthy form of control. To free yourself from that control, you must break their power to make you feel evil when you violate them.

I recall a well-to-do businessman who had grown up in a rather austere Christian home. Although both of his parents professed a deep, personal faith, they fought like cats and dogs. Injunctions were multitudinous in their home. "Don't play with your food." "Don't ever get angry in this house" (a strangely paradoxical command, because the parents got angry all the time). "Don't waste money."

This last injunction became a very powerful controller of the man's adult behavior. Years later, long after his parents had divorced, the words "Don't waste money" would ring in his head. Every time he went to a restaurant, he could hear his mother's voice saying, "Don't waste money. You could be at home cooking your own meal. Why do you spend money unnecessarily?"

He became so obsessive about this injunction and so riddled with false guilt over it that he could not give his own children any gifts. He fought constantly with his wife, who he felt was overcontrolling him like his mother had.

My therapeutic strategy was to help this man identify as many of his injunctions as possible and to separate the "good" from the "bad." Together, we made a two-columned list and assigned each injunction to one column or the other.

It was "good," we agreed, that he felt responsible for his children. It was "bad" that he felt guilty for eating a simple meal in a restaurant. It was "good" not to lie or steal. It was "bad" to withhold all treats from his children.

Once the list was completed, we developed a series of "permissions" in the form of self-statements—one for each "bad" injunction he had listed—that he could repeat to himself whenever he was bothered by an injunction:

- "I give myself permission to be successful."
- "I give myself permission to feel my feelings."

- "I give myself permission to eat in this restaurant."
- "I give myself permission to be happy."

My client grasped the idea behind these statements very quickly. They were designed to reinforce the idea that *he* was in control of his thoughts and behavior. He could choose to do whatever he wanted.

Over the ensuing months, this man worked hard at using his permission statements. He gave himself permission to receive compliments from others. He gave himself permission to be honest with his friends. Gradually he was able to break away from his parents' neurotic injunctions. He stabilized his life, stopped the deterioration of his marriage, and now has a very happy family.

"Giving yourself permission" is a very useful mental strategy that can reverse many "don't" commands and resolve the intense guilt feelings that follow their violation. Be aware, however, that as you defeat some injunctions, others may move to the surface. The strategy must be a progressive one, therefore: Conquer one injunction, then tackle the next.

You may find it helpful to spend a week or two thinking about and writing down every injunction you ever learned from your parents (or anyone else) and to keep this list before you as you go about your daily chores. Examine your list regularly. Choose the ones you want to retain and work at dumping the rest!

PERSONALITY FACTORS THAT PERPETUATE DIVORCE

Personality is a major cause of marital problems. Couples can find themselves in trouble when their conflict is deeply rooted in or inextricably linked to the neurotic personality patterns of one or both partners. Contrary to popular opinion, I do not believe that personality, once formed, cannot be changed. Change may be slow in coming, but change *is* possible.

Personality is shaped by two forces: genes *and* environment. And it's not really possible to determine which is dominant; the mix of heredity and upbringing differs for each individual. But unless we are adopted, both factors are determined by our parents. We cannot choose our genetic makeup, nor can we entirely control our environment. The development of our personalities, therefore, is very much at the mercy of our parents. From the moment of conception, our parents begin to shape us, and their influence continues through childhood and adolescence.

Desirably, parents should raise children in an atmosphere of secure love and tenderness. Unhappy and conflict-ridden parents have difficulty providing such an environment; in their own misery they may create a "toxic" household—one full of threat, rejection, hostility, and anxiety. These influences, combined with genetic predisposition, shape not only the child's personality but how he or she will interact with the world.

I have already touched on how "holes" develop in personality. But what characteristics of the ACOD's personality are likely to perpetuate the divorce cycle?

Contrary to popular opinion, I do not believe that personality, once formed, cannot be changed. Change may be slow in coming, but change is possible.

As long as twenty-five years ago, in England, a close connection was drawn between being raised in a broken home and both psychiatric illness and personality disorders.[8] More recent studies have found similar effects.[9] A greater incidence of attempted suicide, delinquency, illness, accidents, psychiatric problems, and emotional disorders are to be found among "divorced" children. Psychologist John Guidubaldi of Kent State University, in perhaps the largest national study yet done on the impact of divorce on schoolchildren, found that divorced children generally ranked lower than their classmates in academic achievement, communication, social interaction, happiness, and health.[10]

But what does this prove? It certainly doesn't separate the genetic factors from environmental ones. Surely this is a "chicken and egg" dilemma. No list of statistics will convince some people of the damaging effects of divorce on children.

Whatever the specific contributions of divorce to shaping personality, I think it is safe to say that children of divorce are overburdened by life's pressures. The need to make rapid and difficult adjustments, coupled with the parents' decreased availability to care for the child's emotional needs, certainly disturbs his or her development. This disturbance, added to certain genetic predisposition, can lay the ground for severe personality distortion.

What personality problems can emerge in ACODs? I have seen practically the whole gamut, as spelled out in the Diagnostic and Statistical Manual of the American Psychiatric Association. Without being too technical, allow me to discuss just two personality disturbances that can influence the perpetuation of divorce:

ANGRY PERSONALITY

This personality type is usually characterized by an inability to control anger, whether the anger is "active" (throwing things, screaming) or "passive" (sarcasm, pouting). This lack of control is both learned (from observing our parents) and experienced (from the pressure of overwhelming internal conflicts). When no parent is available to set limits on this anger (usually the father does this), a child may grow up to be an angry young man or woman.

Interestingly enough, many angry people don't recognize their own anger, especially when it takes the form of "passive" anger. People who play "mind games," sulk, withdraw, or take a generally negative attitude are often deeply but unconsciously angry. This is particularly true for ACODs, who are shaped by circumstances to suppress rage.

There are many sources of anger that the children of a conflictive family have to cope with:

- They are exposed to many frustrating experiences, blocked goals, and disillusional dreams. Frustration leads naturally to anger.
- They are constantly torn between the parents.
- They feel abandoned and fearful. Fear is a powerful trigger for anger.

- They resent being "different" from their peers.
- Postdivorce conflicts over custody and support increase their sense of rejection, creating more fear and anger.
- Misunderstandings with or resentment of stepparents may intensify fear and anger.
- The children themselves may become the target of a lot of direct hostility from their parents.

The list could go on and on. In fact, I can think of no life-event with greater potential to create anger and rage than being caught in a severely conflict-ridden or divorcing family.

Now, there are several things you can do with your anger, according to most psychologists. You can give vent to it—ranting, raving, throwing things. Or, if this is not acceptable to you, you can choose to *repress* or *suppress* your anger.

The two terms are not synonymous. Repression refers to an *unconscious* process in which you literally push the anger out of consciousness. Suppression is a conscious process; you just refuse to think about your grievances. The first tries to erase the anger; the second tries to ignore it. Both are unhealthy.

Repression is bad for you because it invalidates one of anger's primary healthy functions. One of the purposes of anger, in addition to preparing you for "fight or flight," is to *alert* you to a grievance. Carol Tavris, in her excellent book called *Anger: The Misunderstood Emotion,* makes this point very well.[11] She stresses that *anger is a signal;* it alerts you to when you've been violated. Like a smoke alarm, it warns you of a possible "fire" in your personal rights. Anger must be heeded, therefore, at least until its "message" can be heard. This is why therapists always push for anger to be acknowledged and brought into the open. When we suppress our anger, we don't heed the message, which is why suppression is usually (though not always) unhealthy. Own up to your anger, and you are usually on the road to healing.

But how do you handle anger once you've become conscious of it? Is your only choice between forgetting it (suppression) and throwing plates (venting)? No. You can choose a healthy compromise that lies somewhere between the two.

I don't believe that all anger has to be expressed just because it's there. Sometimes we are angry at the wrong person. Sometimes we are angry for the wrong reason. Just being angry doesn't give us any special privileges. Once you have owned up to your anger and discovered *who* or *what* is causing it, you then need to ask, "What is a positive way of handling this anger?" Most people with angry personalities never stop to ask that question.

All anger must lead us to some action, even if that action is a choice to *do nothing*. The emotion of anger is telling us that there has been a violation. It expects us to do something about it. *If we don't*, the anger will demand payment of a penalty in terms of some physical or emotional damage.

I don't have the space to expand here on either a healthy psy-

---

Once you have owned up to your anger and discovered who or what is causing it, you then need to ask, "What is a positive way of handling this anger?" Most people with angry personalities never stop to ask that question.

---

chology or a theology of anger. (A complete treatment can be found in my book, *Unlocking the Mystery of Your Emotions*.[12]) For our purposes here, let me just say that God did not design us for perpetual anger. Our anger response should always be a *temporary* response, not a pattern of personality. We should always work to get closure on and dispose of our anger *as soon as possible*.

As I have mentioned before, the best advice I can think of concerning anger can be found in the Bible (Ephesians 4:26): get rid of each day's anger before the sun sets. This is *great psychological wisdom*. If you don't handle your anger and be done with it, you greatly increase your chances of suffering from ulcers, high blood pressure, heart disease, immune-deficiency disorders, or a host of other problems. Unresolved anger is a devastating source of stress—a cancer that eats away at our personalities. It puts the body and mind into a perpetual "alert" status and robs us of both spiritual and psychological peace. It also becomes a time-bomb waiting to blow a relationship to smithereens. Anger that is not handled in a healthy way can quickly destroy a marriage.

But what can an ACOD do about years of accumulated hurts that feed a perpetual fire of rage? How can you create a future worth living when your mind is racked with resentment? I've already given the answer several times in this book. The most effective antidote to anger is the power to *forgive*. We cannot go back and change our painful pasts. We cannot undo the hurts done nor the neglect we suffered as children. We cannot remake our parents or remake history. *But with God's help, we can forgive.* And learning to forgive can set us truly free from even the most deeply entrenched anger.

DENIAL AS A PERSONALITY PROBLEM

Denial is the most primitive of all our psychological defense mechanisms. People use it to protect themselves from feeling emotional pain, especially anxiety. We protect ourselves from sleepless nights, heart palpitations, and incapacitating fears by blotting out awareness that there is anything to feel pain about.

Denial is not really a conscious process. You don't just decide, "I'm not going to let this thing bother me." Rather, you block awareness without realizing you are doing it. You look the other way. You refuse to face reality. And you often have no idea that you are doing this.

Denial is the most primitive of all our psychological defense mechanisms. One uses it to protect oneself from feeling emotional pain, especially anxiety.

A background of divorce is ideal for creating the conditions that lead to denial—and a parent or parents who are into denial can increase the likelihood of its developing. Silence and noncommunication are also great aids to learning denial. The less you know, the easier it is to avoid what is going on. Many divorcing parents feed denial, therefore, by keeping their children in the dark about what is going on in the family. They may think they are protecting their child. But they may be preventing short-term pain at the expense of developing a lifelong personality handicap.

The denial mechanism is a very powerful one. It can be useful, in that it helps us to tolerate very traumatic events. It is useful, then, only in real emergencies. Human beings are capable of blocking out great tragedies and blinding themselves to severe pain. But in the lesser issues of life, denial can cause as much harm as it prevents. Sooner or later, however, reality catches up—and the results can be as devastating as the original occurrence. Most serious psychosomatic disorders, for example, have their roots in denial.

Children learn denial through the divorce experience in several ways:

- They are told to ignore their feelings: "Be brave," "Put on a smiling face." "Don't cry." This fosters the suppression of emotional pain through denial.
- The anxiety of separation from a parent may be so intense that children convince themselves it is a "good thing"—just to avoid the pain.
- Children may retreat into a fantasy world where everything is perfect and harmony is fully restored. Every time anxiety raises its head, the child uses fantasy to relieve it.
- A very traumatic event, such as the parent's packing and leaving or a child's being put in the care of a foster parent, can be temporarily erased from memory. It is never really forgotten, however—just denied.

Denial operates to perpetuate the divorce cycle in several ways. The ACOD who learned denial as a child continues to avoid reality in his or her own marriage. He or she refuses to confront reality, avoids resolving conflicts, and runs away from anxiety—often leading the spouse to handle difficulties singlehandedly. Communication suffers. Problems mount up. And resentment builds.

In addition, paradoxically, those who use denial excessively tend to become overly reactive to all troubles. They become irrationally angry, invoke the denial mechanism by refusing to deal with the source of their anger, then settle back as if nothing happened. The next time anger strikes, their reaction may be even more intense.

Paradoxically, those who use denial excessively tend to become overly reactive to all troubles.

Denial easily becomes downright dishonesty. The lies are not intentional, but the facts are distorted nevertheless. One distorts history, as part of the denial, so that it doesn't cause anxiety in the present. For instance, one may "reconstruct" some past incident so that it no longer feels bad. A mother's rejection may be excused by making up stories about "how hard her childhood was," or a father's emotional coldness may be explained away as "working so hard" to support the family. The denial can lead to full-blown lies about the ACOD's "wonderful" childhood or complete fabrications of past events. Fact and fantasy may become inextricably fused.

Denial builds a false optimism. People who are in denial tend to look at all problems as if they don't exist or that they will quickly solve themselves. I know one woman who embarked on a thousand-mile journey in a rundown car that could hardly go around the block. When her car finally gave up the ghost just a hundred miles into her journey, she was amazed. I asked her, "Didn't you realize that the car was in such bad shape?" "Yes," she replied, "but I thought that if I just got started, everything would be all right."

The truth is, this woman had made denial a basic part of her personality; she consistently refused to face reality. Unfortunately, her husband eventually ran out of patience with her denial and left her.

Once denial becomes entrenched as an aspect of personality, it has become deeply rooted. It cannot be healed by simple self-help, because *the denial itself operates to deny the denial.* Sound confusing? It really isn't. When you have denied painful stimuli all your life, it is quite easy to deny that you are refusing to face reality. Long-term psychotherapy is the treatment of choice for this difficulty.

If you suspect that someone you know suffers from this problem, realize that confronting the denial head-on will only increase the need for the defense. Take your time, gently suggest that there is a problem, and encourage the person to seek professional help.

In addition, if someone close to you—or more than one person—suggests that you are retreating from reality in some way, pay attention. The other person may be wrong. But if he or she is right, the very nature of denial means you will be unable to perceive the problem in yourself. Your denial may be sabotaging your chances for happiness. Seeking help for this elusive problem may be the only way you can stop the divorce cycle in your own life.

Your denial may be sabotaging your chances for happiness.
Seeking help for this elusive problem may be the only way you
can stop the divorce cycle in your own life.

One of the major benefits I have experienced as a Christian has been in the area of handling my own denial. Through the years, my faith in God has, I believe, helped me be more honest with myself and to confront the unpleasant aspects of my life more directly. This has happened because I know I can trust God to help me face and cope with my negative experiences. And hiding from my pain only robs me of this wonderful resource. Being fully in touch with my life—even its painful aspects—helps me to trust God for grace and courage. And the more I turn to God for grace, the easier it becomes not to retreat into denial.

Though the years, then, I have come to see the wisdom of Proverbs 3:5-6:

Trust in the Lord with all your heart
And lean not on your own understanding;
In all your ways acknowledge him,
And he will make your paths straight.

CHAPTER **11**

Success Strategies for a Life of Recovery

Throughout this book, I have tried to help you understand just what being an adult child of divorce means in your life. In the process, I have learned more than I ever expected about what being an ACOD means to me. My background research into the psychological costs of divorce to children has opened my eyes to many issues even I had not thought about. I think I am a better person for having written this book. I hope you are better off for having read it.

I especially hope you have come to the end of these chapters with a strong sense that you *can* overcome the damage of your past. If you've read this far and you still hold a cynical view of marriage, a fatalistic resignation to your childhood pain, I will have failed in my purpose. For my message is not one of defeat, but of hope. It is not an invitation to despair, but a call to take control of your life now and implement changes that will make you a happier person.

I sincerely believe that, while divorce is a tragedy for children, they can turn it into a triumph, with the right kind of help. But you don't just outgrow the impact of divorce in your life. You must take control and implement changes. If you make these changes, your pain can become your portal to effective personal growth. Your hurts and humiliation can be healed to produce stronger character and more determined resiliency.

Resiliency, the ability to "bounce back" from life's unfair blows, is not just an inherited trait. It is true that some people seem to have a special gift for coming through troubles unscathed. But it is also a form of learned behavior—the sum total of our healthy choices. When a child is guided through the valley of divorce with sensitivity, honesty, love, and courage, he or she develops this resiliency naturally. But even when a child grows to adulthood without this guidance, the damage can still be repaired.

You don't just outgrow the impact of divorce in your life.
You must take control and implement changes.

This is the heart of my message. I can commend it to you with integrity because I am an adult child of divorce. I have worked hard to counterbalance the detrimental effects of my parents' marital problems. And I believe I have been moderately successful in achieving a happy life.

TAKING CHARGE OF YOUR FUTURE

There is nothing you can do with the past except understand and learn from it. Too many ACODs feel trapped by their pasts, immobilized by the fears they developed in childhood and by faulty beliefs about being inferior, inadequate, and incomplete. Like prisoners in a rock quarry, they are burdened with ball and chain. They can't run. They can't fly. They have a hard time even walking normally. But it doesn't have to be that way.

You as an ACOD cannot change what happened to you as a child. In a sense, you were truly a victim of circumstance. Things happened to you that you couldn't control, and your little mind and body would not grow up fast enough for you to be strong. You may have floundered when forced to be mature and staggered when caught in the emotional crossfire of angry parents. You probably learned faulty, counterproductive ways of handling stress, managing relationships, taking care of yourself.

But now you are grown up. The past is past. And you do have the freedom to change if you so choose. You can release yourself from the past to enjoy freedom in your present.

And you can also have a future. So much lies ahead that is yours to determine. You make choices all the time that form and shape your future direction. You have control over where you will go, what you will do, whom you will do it with, and when you will quit doing it. The sky is the limit. And if God is in your sky, it is vast indeed.

Some of you may remember the beautiful musical called *Yentl*.[1] It is the story of a nineteenth-century Jewish girl, the daughter of a rabbi, who desperately wants to follow in her father's footsteps. In her part of Europe, Jewish tradition forbids women from studying to be rabbis. So she masquerades as a man, infiltrates the rabbinic seminary, and gets herself into a flurry of messes because of her hidden identity.

There is one song in *Yentl* that has affected me deeply. It is called "A Piece of Sky," and Yentl sings it after she has finally stopped the masquerade and revealed her femininity to Avigdor, a fellow student with whom she is deeply in love. He, though, is in love with the person Yentl has supposedly married in the masquerade. He is shocked. He never suspected she was a woman, and he is disturbed that he has been spending his time so intimately with a female. He is also enraged because she has violated the Talmud and all Jewish traditions.

But Yentl is far more than a mere female; she is a woman ahead of her time. Avigdor is a prisoner to his. She makes plans to leave and go to the United States, where she hears things are different.

And here is really the theme of the entire musical. Yentl has refused to allow the circumstances of her past to determine her life. And her song, carried through her new beginning as she sails toward an unknown world, is a summary of what she has done in her life. She sings of how her life began to change the day she noticed a piece of sky through her window. It seemed so small, so finite. But when she stepped outside and looked around, it was vastly wider and higher than she had dreamed.

Suddenly, in the midst of her song, Yentl realizes she is free. She had been held down by circumstances—being the wrong sex in the wrong place at the wrong time. Now, even though it once felt safer to stay on the ground, she is ready to try her wings.

I am always deeply moved by her song. It resonates with my deep feelings as a child who also felt tied down by unhappy circumstances. I think that for too many years I settled for the safety of terra firma. My experiences forced me to play things safe, to give in to fear, to avoid risks. "Don't go beyond your self-imposed limits. Don't trust your feelings. Life really doesn't have much to offer you." These were the feelings of my childhood and adolescent years, and they traveled with me into my adulthood.

Then one day I stepped outside myself and saw my sky. I looked up and found it was so wide. My time had come to try my wings. And even though it seemed that I might come crashing down, I took charge of my life and learned to "fly" despite my past.

Yes, tomorrow is yours to do with as you please. To make the most of your future, you must choose to take charge of it. But "taking charge" is not the same thing as "going it alone." In fact, if you try to fly by just flapping your own arms, chances are you won't get off the ground. You can improvise, adjust, invent, devise, or do any other human thing imaginable and still not make any difference to the way you will live your future.

So, once you have chosen to fly, what do you need in order to soar into tomorrow?

You need help.

You may need the help of other people—friends, support groups, perhaps even therapists—who can love you, support you, encourage you when you lose heart, and help you see yourself more clearly.

But "taking charge" is not the same thing as "going it alone." In fact, if you try to fly by just flapping your arms, chances are you won't get off the ground.

But even more important, you need spiritual help. With God as the "wind beneath your wings," your resolve to take charge of your future can become a reality.

I can't imagine what my world would be like without God. And I don't know how I could have come to know him without my experience of Christ. I came to know him at a very personal level at the end of my teens, just as I was finishing high school. With the help of friends, I stepped into the reality of life with God, and I shudder to think that I could have moved into adulthood without his help. I truly believe there would have been no healing, no reason for tenderness, no forgiving of the past, no replenishment of hope, no need to change, and no one to help me change. The very thought sends a shudder down my spine.

With God as the "wind beneath your wings," your resolve to take charge of your future can become a reality.

As you take inventory of your own life and reflect on how the things you do and the feelings you feel have been shaped by your childhood divorce, I hope you will also allow God to be a part of your future. Without spiritual resources, you will have little incentive to carry out the crucial healing task of forgiving your hurts. And most important of all, you'll be without a teacher to gently guide you through this frightening world.

STRATEGIES FOR SURVIVAL—AND SUCCESS

As I reflect on what I have not said thus far and what should be said before I close this book, it seems that I can gather some suggestions together under the general heading of "success strategies." (If you are really struggling, it may be more helpful to think of them as "survival strategies.") If asked, "What general advice could I give for someone trying to break free from negative childhood influences?" here is what I would recommend:

1. Never drop out of the game. The reason so many adults who have been hurt by childhood divorce live unhappily until they die is that they have given up the effort to overcome their past. They hope they will outgrow their misery without consciously having to work at overcoming it. But life just doesn't work that way.

Several years back I was fascinated by the movie *War Games,* which concerns a United States government computer that is accidentally programmed by some juvenile "hackers" to start a global nuclear war—as if it were some kind of great computer game. All attempts to alter the computer program are futile, and it seems that the "brain machine" is going to destroy the world. But then, at the last second, the computer comes to a halt and flashes this message on the screen:

"Interesting game. The only way to win is not to play!"

This may be true for nuclear war. It may even be true for those who dabble in drugs, crime, and other aberrations of human existence. But it is not true for life in general. We *must play* if we are going to win. When we give up hope and stop endeavoring to overcome our childhood influences—we have lost!

The reason so many adults live unhappily until they die is that they have given up the effort to overcome their past.

---

2. Don't try to replace your missing childhood. Many ACODs spend a lot of precious time and energy in the futile effort to make up for their unhappy childhood. They may do this in several ways:

- They may marry a person who serves as a "surrogate" mother or father.
- They may seek experiences that recreate their childhoods—becoming hung up on "adult" toys or engaging in childlike activities.
- They may regress, when under pressure, to a childish way of dealing with problems. For example, they might cry a lot or have temper tantrums.
- They may become excessive in their quest for nurture and love—"clinging," becoming jealous, surrendering their rights.
- They may fantasize that somehow their parents, even in old age, will finally come around to giving them love and validating them for who they are.

It is quite common for an ACOD with deficient parental love to develop a "transference" to his or her therapist. Some transference is normal in therapy, and some therapies even capitalize on it. In this situation, however, the ACOD goes beyond normal therapeutic transference and makes the therapist into a substitute parent, giving him or her the feelings that belong to the natural parent. The ACOD then becomes excessively dependent and even jealous of the therapist's other patients or family members and has great difficulty pulling this transference back at a later stage.

The fact that you were robbed of your childhood may be heartbreaking. Your memories of loss may cause you anguish and misery. But if you want to move forward into health, you must stop searching for and trying to replace your missing childhood. It is gone forever. You cannot restore it or relive it. Grieve this loss, if necessary. Cry as many tears as you want to. But resist the tendency to "fix" your childhood or to manipulate others into being parent substitutes.

Your memories of loss may cause you anguish and misery. But if you want to move forward into health, you must stop searching for and trying to replace your missing childhood.

---

3. Release your parents from your resentment. Consciously or unconsciously, most ACODs carry a heavy load of resentment. It comes out in dreams and fantasy. It hovers like a dark cloud over their lives. Some suppress this resentment by hiding behind their religious activity. ("Good Christian people aren't supposed to be unforgiving.") Others deny it ("They are my parents, I can't hate them!") or try to ignore it ("I've got better things to do with my life than bother with my folks"), but it is there nevertheless.

Before you can be free to get on with your life, you must release this resentment. This is a theme I have sounded again and again, but I want to repeat it because it is so crucial: Let your parents go free. Keeping them imprisoned by your resentment keeps you in prison as well.

One of the steps in releasing your resentment is to make a conscious decision to let your parents be who they are. Usually parents are the ones who try to mold their children, but the reverse can also be true. I often hear divorced parents complain that even though they are quite successful and functioning very well, their children try to make them into something they are not.

For instance, a gentleman in his late fifties once told me: "I am a very successful businessman. I have made my fortune. But my daughter doesn't respect me for it—or for anything else that I do well. She's still angry at me for divorcing her mother, and she never fails to remind me of her disappointment every time I see her. I just don't know what she wants me to be."

For whatever reason, your parents are who they are.
They have made their own decisions, and you can't change
them. If you feel ashamed of your parents,
then this is now your problem.

For whatever reason, your parents are who they are. They have made their own decisions, and you can't change them. If you feel ashamed of your parents, then this is now *your* problem. If they embarrass you, your pride—not their behavior—is probably the real issue, and that is your problem as well. Your efforts to turn them into "perfect parents" whom you can feel proud of just robs you of the energy you need to build your own life and family. If you wait for them to change before getting on with your own life, you may wait forever!

4. Build a support system around you. Human beings were never meant to function in a void. We *all* need a small group of close acquaintances with whom we can share, cry, and talk at an intimate level. It is when this support is lacking that we run the risk of developing emotional disease.

If you are a Christian, you may be accustomed to thinking of Christ as the "burden bearer." You may quote verses like Isaiah 53:4: "Surely he has borne our griefs and carried our sorrows." And you are right. Christ is the great burden bearer, the ultimate source of our comfort. But God often provides the support and caring we need by means of *other people*. Turning to God for direct support through prayer and meditation can be vital. But we also must to be open to both receiving help from and giving help to one another, thus putting hands and feet on Christ's burden bearing or God's comfort: "We then that are strong ought to bear with the scruples of the weak, and not to please ourselves "(Romans 15:1). "Bear one another's burdens, and so fulfill the law of Christ" (Galatians 6:2).

In this age of increasing isolation and loneliness, we need support systems more than at any other time in human history. Sadly, there are many in our world who do not have such support. Every day, in every city across this nation—and even in many churches—scores of people feel lonely, isolated, and cut off from human support. Some even die of loneliness. Deprived of companionship, they give up hope and waste away.

Shopping centers have evolved into much more than retail outlets. They are places where lonely people can bump, feel, touch, smile, and even smell another human being. For many people, this is the only human contact in their lives.

Even married people can be lonely. In many homes, there is no intimacy, no companionship, no sharing, and not even any touching. The TV set or romance novels become a vicarious source of love and tenderness. Pets become the object of affection and attention. But these cannot meet one of our most basic needs—the urge to share feelings and hurts with another human being and to satisfy our craving for closeness and comfort.

I once experienced such profound loneliness that it burned an indelible mark on my memory. I had been invited to speak at a conference of missionaries in Holland, but my wife couldn't accompany me. Since I love visiting England and Europe, I decided to go ten days ahead and do some travel.

I arrived in London, slept off my jet lag, and took in a few sights. The first few days were okay, but then I discovered I had an urge to talk to someone. A few conversations with strangers helped a little, but an aching void began forming inside me. I longed to talk to my wife or a friend—someone who wasn't a stranger. I moved on to Europe, catching the train to Dover and the jet-boat to Oostende. I stopped in Brussels for a few days and found I couldn't even talk to strangers because few spoke English. For three days, I was virtually speechless. I went on to Amsterdam and headed for the conference on the southern coast of the Netherlands. By this time, my loneliness was beginning to drive me crazy. So much to see—no one to share it with. My thinking became distorted. I even began to feel paranoid. Everyone seemed to be looking at me.

Support systems are not optional; they are lifelines.

A long bus ride brought me to within two miles of the conference center where I was to speak. My heart was racing with anticipation. At last, after ten days, I would see, feel, touch and be able to talk to someone I knew. I have never valued friendships so much before.

As I stepped off the bus, it was raining softly. Someone pointed me in the direction of the center. No, there was no taxi; I would have to wait or walk. I couldn't wait. Through the soft rain I trudged, carrying my travel bags. It was the longest walk I have ever taken. As dusk fell I saw the lights—and the beautiful faces. Sopping wet, I hugged everyone I knew. I realized, with an intensity I had never felt before, that people are precious. Support systems are not optional; they are lifelines.

There are several ways that you can build a stronger support system into your life:

- Give relationships a high priority in your life. You get out of friendships what you put into them. Sow nothing, and chances are you will reap nothing!
- Take the initiative in building a support system. Offer to be a support to one, two, or three others, and ask if they will reciprocate. Don't wait for friends to call you; call them first.
- If someone doesn't want to be a support for you, move on to someone else. Don't waste time with people who don't value or respect you. Choose friends who are helpful, and avoid those who are spiteful.
- Be specific in your sharing. Don't waste your friendships on vague generalities. Be honest and open. This may drive some

people away—but such people don't make a very good support system, anyway. True friends will respect your honesty, and they won't take advantage of it.

- Try putting together a formal support group. Make sure you commit yourself to each member in the group. Meet as often as you would like. Some groups find it helpful to gather every day. They share, pray, laugh, and cry together. Others find that once a week or even once a month is enough. Once a year is definitely too little. You need more time than that to enable relationships to grow.

- Ask a pastor or counselor to guide you as you develop your support system. They can give you lots of good advice on what to do and what to avoid. And they may be a great source of possible group members.

Most of the time, the key to feeling better about yourself is reaching out to others.

---

5. Develop your self-identity. At several points throughout this book I have touched on issues of personal identity and self-esteem. The destruction that childhood divorce causes at the core of the self is, for me, a very serious concern.

Your healing as an ACOD will unavoidably revolve around the healing of your self and the restoration of a sense of self-value. The prevalence of self-hatred in our culture is frightening. Since children of divorce are especially vulnerable in this area, you need to be extra solicitous about repairing your sense of self-identity.

How do you improve your self-esteem? I have already mentioned several ideas, but here I want to focus on an especially important principle. Most of the time, *the key to feeling better about yourself is reaching out to others.*

So often a patient will say to me, "I feel terrible. I feel so useless and worthless that I don't want to live." I respond by asking whether the patient is doing anything to make *someone else* feel valuable and loved. The answer is usually "not really." I then urge the patient to try attending to how they treat others. Amazingly, as they change their focus from themselves to others, they really do begin to feel better.

Self-hate is a close relative of self-preoccupation. Healthy self-love comes not from intensified self-interest, but from a loss of self-absorption. Unfortunately, the pain of your childhood divorce may have forced you to focus inwardly, distorting your self-identity by too much self-preoccupation. You can reverse this process by moving your focus outside yourself. This will help you define who you are and heal your identity crises.

6. Give yourself the gift of reality. As I have mentioned several times, ACODs are apt to respond to the pain in their childhood by becoming adept escape artists. Many go to great lengths to avoid reality, and this habit carries over into adult life.

Denial is one of the most common ways of escaping reality. ACODs often learn in childhood to cope with problems by blotting out conscious awareness of them. As I indicated in an earlier chapter, this defense mechanism may become entrenched in the personality and require professional help to overcome.

A close relative of denial is *avoidance*. This is not an unconscious defense, but it functions in somewhat the same way. Whenever you

---

The greatest gift you can give yourself is the gift of reality—and the courage to face it head on.

---

are faced with an unpleasant responsibility, you procrastinate. You use delaying tactics, allowing yourself to be sidetracked to less threatening activities. For example, a student who is studying for exams may suddenly discover that the tires on his car are getting smooth and that they need urgent attention. So he spends the day at the local tire store, observing the technician as he changes, balances, and fits new tires. If he continues avoiding his books in this way, he may set himself up to fail his exams.

Because childhood divorce often forces children into a "hiding" mode, ACODs are especially prone to avoidance tactics. You may have learned in childhood to avoid anxiety by sidestepping important decisions, quibbling over petty problems, eluding friends, shirking worrisome responsibilities, or shying away from vexations. And the consequences may be similar to those of full-blown denial: your troubles multiply through neglect and eventually bowl you over.

The greatest gift you can give yourself is the gift of reality—and the courage to face it head on. So often I find myself hiding from a problem I don't want to face or a feeling that is gnawing at me. I procrastinate. I put off decisions. I postpone confrontations. And the longer I wait, the more frightened I become.

I wrote a book once about "reality thinking," which I defined as "a way of ensuring that all we believe is tied as closely as possible to the world *as it really is* and to God...."[2] I contrasted this approach with the popular idea of "positive thinking" and tried to show that staying in touch with reality is always positive in its outcome.

Most of us—ACODs, especially—are highly influenced by unreality. Novels, movies, and even some preaching would have us believe that we can escape from the hard facts of life. But the very opposite is true. Thomas Merton writes in the opening remarks of his book, *Thoughts in Solitude,*[3] "There is no greater disaster in the spiritual life than to be immersed in unreality." And I would apply that statement to *all* of life, not just spirituality.

I urge you, therefore, to summon the courage to tackle your life head on—problems and all. Dare to face reality without flinching. Don't turn away from hard choices. Face every shadow of despair. When you do this, I predict you will find that the shadow vanishes. Fear thrives on avoidance, and attempts to run away from threats merely increase the fear.

Now, I don't mean you must try to solve all your problems at once or take on responsibility for the whole world. Most difficulties are best handled one step at a time, and you may need to put some problems "on hold" in your mind to avoid becoming paralyzed by them. Nevertheless, you need a *basic determination* to remain reality-oriented as you continue down the road to healing.

7. Keep on forgiving. You will never stop needing to forgive; the world is just too imperfect to allow this. You will experience new hurts that you must handle with forgiveness. And you may need to continue exploring your past to uncover hidden hurts that also need forgiving.

This is important because *forgiveness must be specific.* After all, you can only forgive the hurt you understand. "Fill-in-the-blank forgiveness" just doesn't work; it is meaningless to pray, "Lord, I forgive and I want you to forgive my parent for the contributions he/she has made to my emotional problems—whatever they are." Forgiveness *has* to be specific. We can forget blanket hurts (in that they no longer have the power to offend us), but we cannot forgive them all at once.

You will never stop needing to forgive.

I believe this is one reason so many people struggle with forgiveness. To them, the effort to understand the why, how, when, where of their hurts is just too much work. And they may also unconsciously fear that if they did stop and reflect on specific hurts, they might discover that they, too, need forgiveness.

Sometimes we need to forgive ourselves as well as those who have hurt us. If you can evaluate and judge yourself (and we're all capable of this), then you must be willing to forgive yourself as well. In effect, this means you stop punishing yourself—and leave God to do the judging.

Do we need to forgive God? Some Christian therapists say yes. I have some problems with this idea, although I understand where it comes from. What many well-meaning advocates of "God forgiving" have in mind is that the accumulation of undeserved and unfortunate life hurts may cause us to become resentful toward God. "God is bigger than us," they say. "He understands why we need to forgive him."

I disagree with this basic approach because I think it fosters a faulty understanding of God. If you believe that God is out to get you and make life as miserable as possible (and there are some who believe this), then perhaps you do need to forgive God. But what you need even more desperately is a more accurate concept of who God is!

After all, if you believe:

- that God desires only the very best for us,
- that much or even all suffering is either self-inflicted or brought on by other people,
- that God knows what we need much better than we ourselves, and
- that God is with us in the midst of our problems, hurting along with us

then why would you need to forgive God?

As a child, I was very angry that God didn't fix my parents' marriage. Although I prayed fervently, things got worse, not better. But was my situation God's fault? No. God is God. If he chooses not to change things, I have no right to feel resentful about it.

Now, this doesn't mean I can't express my honest feelings to God in prayer. After all, he knows what I am feeling better than I do. Being dishonest with God about our negative feelings—even resentment—can stunt our relationships with him. But there's a big difference between sharing our honest feelings and assuming a stance of blame or forgiveness.

While I don't believe we need to forgive God, I do think we need a new understanding—and healing for our unbelief. Like Job, who suffered some terrible and unexplainable experiences in his life, we need to reach the point when we can pray:

For I know that my Redeemer lives, and he shall stand at last on the earth; and after my skin is destroyed, this I know, that in my flesh I shall see God. Job 19:25-26

This is faith. This is maturity. And this is the way to healing. If you struggle with this, perhaps you need spiritual healing at a more fundamental level. Perhaps you need to know Christ or to open your life more fully to him. If so, I recommend that you go back to the section on spiritual healing in chapter 6. And by all means seek out someone for whom Christ seems to be an important reality. Ask questions, and observe how God operates in that person's life. Your spiritual quest may take some time, but it will not disappoint you.

It takes a lot of courage to be willing to expose your innermost being to another—and to yourself.

---

8. Be willing to talk about your hurts. Exposing the hurts of your childhood is essential to your healing. You need to talk about them, relive them if necessary, and develop a new perspective on them. You may need therapy to help you uncover "unfinished business," or you may just need some reassurance that you are on the right track. But chances are that you do need to talk to *somebody*.

To turn to another person for help, especially if that person has had some training in understanding the affairs of the mind, is not a sign of weakness. It takes a lot of courage to be willing to expose your innermost being to another—and to yourself.

I never view a troubled person coming to me for professional help as in any way inferior. If anything, I respect him or her all the more for determination to get better. They defy stereotypes and thumb their noses at stoics who pride themselves on being able to solve all their own problems. Far from being weak and cowardly, they have the guts to get to the bottom of their problems.

How can you tell if you need professional help? Perhaps you're wondering whether you really have a problem or not, or whether you can justify the expense. Isn't it sufficient to just talk to some friends or let off steam? Perhaps! But you might want to seek professional help if:

- you feel your problems are continuing to get worse rather than stabilizing or improving,
- you feel you cannot cope any longer and you don't have sufficient personal resources to make any changes in your life,
- you have no one else to turn to for help,
- your problems are getting you into trouble either with the law, in your job, or in your close relationships,

- you are experiencing a deep depression or debilitating anxiety,
- you want to gain a better insight and understanding into the nature of your problem,
- there is any danger that you might harm yourself or someone else,
- you need an objective outsider to help you understand your problems,
- you want to stop wasting time and speed up your recovery.

If in doubt, you might try having at least one counseling session just to explore your options. And please remember that getting professional help does not have to cost a lot. Many churches now have counseling centers that offer free or low-cost services, and many community centers offer help on a sliding scale. (You pay what you can afford.) Call your pastor or, if you don't belong to a church, call the church nearest to you. I'm sure they will be able to point you to a source of help. Community mental-health organizations can also be a valuable resource.

9. Give yourself to personal and spiritual growth. Recently, a woman was sharing with me her frustration about her husband. Both had grown up in divorced homes, and both had been married before. So they had known divorce both as children and as adults. She told of her deep longing to make her present marriage work.

"What's stopping you?" I asked. She had made tremendous progress in therapy and was becoming a very healthy person.

"I'm afraid I will outgrow my husband," she replied. "He'll get upset and leave me."

Myra's husband is a dyed-in-the-wool stoic. He is self-controlled, impassive, unresponsive, unfeeling, made of granite and just as cold. He doesn't seem to need anyone. He lives his life as he pleases, and he cares little about how he hurts others. Unfortunately, this personality type is not at all unusual in men. In my mail and in my seminars, I often hear it described. As yet we don't have a diagnostic category for this type—but we're getting closer!

I looked at this dear woman and told her: "You passed him by a long time ago; there is no going back now. If your psychological and spiritual growth is truly healthy, it will never offend a reasonable person. And furthermore," I told her, "You cannot hold yourself back just because your husband has a problem."

My client's fear was not unusual. Many people are afraid that something will happen to them in the course of their growth that makes them less acceptable to the significant people in their lives. And it is very possible that your growth may take you beyond your spouse—even to the extent that you have little in common. This is sad, but you won't help your relationship by refusing to grow. And your new maturity may well make it easier for you to handle the problems in your relationship.

It's true that sometimes the wrong sort of growth releases anger, resentment, and rebellion in such a way that it alienates others and divides and destroys marriages. It doesn't invite the spouses to grow; it causes a rift. But this isn't emotional health; it is emotional rebellion. There is a type of therapy that teaches acrimony and ill-humor and calls it mental health. Assertiveness becomes aggression; self-esteem turns to self-aggrandizement and selfishness.

---

*You must expect to fall, rise, and fall again.
Each time you fall, remember that there is only one positive
response: get up again!*

Have nothing to do with this type of therapy. Seek out a therapist who is balanced and healthy—and don't hesitate to find another therapist if you feel uncomfortable with a particular therapist's approach. If therapy doesn't make you more Christlike, it is not worth anything. It should help you to develop a gentle spirit and to be more considerate as well as less self-demeaning. Good therapy helps you become more self-defined, but it doesn't teach you to trample on others in the process. No one is offended by such health; if anything, they are attracted to it.

One more point to remember about personal and spiritual growth: it is never linear. You never progress in a straight upward line from beginning to end. Instead, the line usually goes up, down, sideways, backward, forward—and then possibly turns you inside out. You must expect to fall, rise, and fall again. Each time you fall, remember that there is only one positive response: *get up again!* Failure is the *modus operandi* for growing. Losers are people who quit trying.

I pray you will discover that loving people are all around you and that God is beside you, ready to comfort and empower you in your quest for wholeness.

"HIDE ME IN THE SHADOW OF YOUR WINGS"

There are some children who, even though they were exposed to severe traumatic experiences through their parents' divorce, come into adulthood with no apparent deficits. They are healthy, happy, and hopeful about their futures. But unfortunately, they are in the minority. Most adult children of divorce have to work hard to overcome the detrimental effects of their unfortunate and unhappy childhoods.

My hope is that this book has helped you to chart a new life for yourself. Whatever other help you may also seek, I want more than anything else to point you to the healing you can receive through spiritual counseling, prayer, and the exercise of faith. I pray you will discover that loving people are all around you and that God is beside you, ready to comfort and empower you in your quest for wholeness.

I would like to commend to you a beautiful psalm—a prayer that King David of Israel probably spoke at a time of great personal need. I will use the Living Bible translation because it expresses the prayer so beautifully.

It begins with a plea for God to listen:

I am pleading for your help, O Lord; for I have been honest and have done what is right, and you must listen to my earnest cry!... Why am I praying like this? Because I know you will answer me, O God! Yes, listen as I pray.

Then comes this heartfelt cry:

> Protect me as you would the pupil of your eye; hide me in the shadow of your wings as you hover over me. **Psalm 17:1, 6, 8**

There are two vivid metaphors in this line. First, God's protection is compared to the eyelid, which quickly moves to protect the pupil, that delicate part of the eye, from any unexpected flying object. Second, it is compared to the "shadow" of a wing. The shadow was a conventional Hebrew metaphor used to describe how one can be protected against oppression. Shade was crucial for protection from the oppressive heat of the hot desert sun, and kings were also spoken of as "shade" because they provided protection to their followers.

"Hide me in the shadow of your wings." What a beautiful prayer for every adult child of divorce. God, who loves us far better and more dependably than even the best human parent could, hovers over us, comforting us and protecting us from harm. He longs to gather us under those wings, "as a hen gathers her chicks" (Matthew 23:37). Again and again, as I have struggled to cope with the aftermath of my own childhood divorce, I have been helped and uplifted by the knowledge that the wings of God are there to protect me from the heat of painful noonday. Will you join me there?

Notes

INTRODUCTION
The ACOD Syndrome

1. Reported in *Psychology Today*, November 1989, 10.
2. *Journal of Divorce*, 12 (nos. 2/3, 1988/89):5.
3. Judith Wallerstein and Sandra Blakeslee, *Second Chances* (New York: Ticknor and Fields, 1989).
4. Diane Medved, *The Case against Divorce* (New York: Donald I. Fine, 1989).
5. Archibald D. Hart, *Children and Divorce* (Waco, Tex.: Word, 1982).
6. Joanne Pedro-Carroll, address to the 1990 Convention of the American Psychological Association, reported in *The Monitor*, October 1990, 22.
7. *Journal of Divorce*, 12 (nos. 2/3, 1988/89).
8. *Journal of Divorce*, 12.
9. Reported in *Psychology Today*, January 1980, 74.
10. *Journal of Divorce*, 12:1.
11. Marcia and Thomas Lasswell, *Marriage and the Family* (Lexington, Mass.: D.C. Heath, 1982).

ONE
Growing Up in a Divorced Family

1. Archibald D. Hart, *Healing Life's Hidden Addictions* (Ann Arbor, Mich.: Servant Publications, 1990).

TWO
Assessing the Divorce Damage in Your Life

1. Hart, *Children and Divorce*.
2. Judith Wallerstein and Joan Kelly, "California's Children of Divorce," *Psychology Today*, January 1980, 67.
3. Wallerstein and Kelly, "California's Children," 67.

4. Wallerstein and Kelly, "California's Children," 67.
5. *Parade*, 7 June 1987, 4.
6. Lasswell, *Marriage and the Family*, 409.

FOUR
Facing Your Unfinished Business

1. N. Kalter, B. Reimer, A. Brickman, J.W. Chen, "Implications of Parental Divorce for Female Development," *Journal of the American Academy of Child Psychiatry* 24 (1985):438-544.
2. Kalter, Reimer, Brickman, Chen, "Implications of Parental Divorce," 438-544.
3. Archibald D. Hart, *Unlocking the Mystery of Your Emotions* (Irving, Tex.: Word, 1990), chapter 7.

SIX
Taking Care of Your ACOD Self

1. J.B. Phillips, *Your God Is Too Small* (New York: Macmillan, 1961).
2. Philip Yancey, *Disappointment with God* (Grand Rapids, Mich.: Zondervan, 1988).

SEVEN
Rewriting Your Life-Script

1. Claude Steiner, *Scripts People Live* (New York: Bantam, 1974), 92.
2. Steiner, *Scripts People Live*, 218.
3. Steiner, *Scripts People Live*, 181.
4. Claude Steiner, *Games Alcoholics Play: The Analysis of Life Scripts* (New York: Grove, 1971), 25.

EIGHT
Getting On with Your Life

1. Harold S. Kushner, *When Bad Things Happen to Good People* (New York: Avon, 1981), 142.
2. Wallerstein and Blakeslee, *Second Chances*, 64.
3. Thomas Oden, *Game Free: The Meaning of Intimacy* (New York: Harper & Row, 1976), 34.
4. Richard A. Gardner, *The Parent's Book about Divorce* (New York: Bantam, 1977), 210.

NINE
Building Your Own Happy Family

1. Michael Nichols, *Family Therapy: Concepts and Methods* (New York: Gardner Press, 1984), 163.
2. Herbert A. Otto, "What is a Strong Family?," *Marriage and Family Living*, February 1962.
3. Gardner, *Parent's Book about Divorce*, 604.
4. Hart, *Unlocking the Mystery of Your Emotions*, 146.
5. Margery Williams, *The Velveteen Rabbit* (Philadelphia: Running Press/ Courage Books, 1984), 6-7.
6. Lewis B. Smedes, *Caring and Commitment* (San Francisco: Harper & Row, 1988), 1.
7. Nick Stinnett, Greg Sanders, and John DeFrain, "Strong Families: A National Study," in *Family Strengths: Roots of Wellbeing*, (Lincoln, Neb.: Univ. of Nebraska Press, 1981), 33-41.
8. "Divorce Begins in the Nursery," *Daily News*, London Bureau, 15 February 1971.
9. Joseph Oppawsky, "Family Dysfunctional Patterns During Divorce: From the View of Children," *Journal of Divorce*, 12 (nos. 2/3, 1988/89): 145.

TEN
Breaking the Divorce Cycle

1. Susan Forward, *Toxic Parents* (New York: Bantam, 1989), 166.
2. Joseph Guttmann, "Intimacy in Young Adult Males' Relationships as a Function of Divorced and Non-divorced Family of Origin Structure," *Journal of Divorce*, 12 (nos. 2/3, 1988/89): 255.
3. J. Landis, "The Patterns of Divorce in Three Generations," *Social Forces*, 34 (March 1956):213-216.
4. C. Mueller and H. Pope, "Marital Instability: The Study of Transmission Between Generations," *Journal of Marriage and Family*, 39 (February 1977).
5. Wallerstein and Blakeslee, *Second Chances*, 170.
6. Gardner, *Parent's Book about Divorce*, 414.
7. Gardner, *Parent's Book about Divorce*, 414.
8. J. Dominian, *Marital Breakdown* (New York: Penguin Books, 1969), 123.
9. L.J. Weitzman, *The Divorce Revolution* (New York: Free Press, 1985), 353-354.
10. Claire Berman, "A 'Good-Enough' Marriage," *Family Circle*, 8 January 1991, 120.

11. Carol Tavris, *Anger: The Misunderstood Emotion* (New York: Simon & Schuster, 1982), 45.
12. Hart, *Unlocking the Mystery of Your Emotions,* chapters 4 and 5.

ELEVEN
Success Strategies for a Life of Recovery

1. *Yentl,* lyrics by Alan and Marilyn Bergman, music by Michel LeGrang, Emanuel Music, 1983.
2. Hart, *The Success Factor* (Old Tappan, NJ: Power Books/Fleming H. Revell, 1984), 38.
3. Thomas Merton, *Thoughts in Solitude* (New York: Image Books, 1958), 19.